The American Threat

THE
AMERICAN THREAT

The Fear of War as an
Instrument of Foreign Policy

JAMES L. PAYNE

MARKHAM PUBLISHING COMPANY • CHICAGO

MARKHAM POLITICAL SCIENCE SERIES
Aaron Wildavsky, Editor

Selections from *The Penkovskiy Papers*, by Oleg Penkovskiy, translated and with an Introduction and Commentary by Frank Gibney, reprinted by permission of Doubleday & Company, Inc.

We have, from our own side, the problem of assuring that the pledged word of the United States means something to the opposition. Again, it is not easy, in public session, to underline that in all its seriousness but, when Chairman Khrushchev presented President Eisenhower with an ultimatum on Berlin in the late 1950's, and when Chairman Khrushchev said to President Kennedy what he said in June 1961 about Berlin, and about the consequences if President Kennedy did not yield, I cannot tell you how important it was to the peace of the world that the President of the United States, whether it was President Eisenhower or President Kennedy, or now President Johnson, be believed when they say to the other side: "Gentlemen, this you must not do." Because, if we ever get to a point where that simple statement is not believed, then I don't know where the future and the safety of this country is, or that the possibilities of general peace would exist.

Secretary of State Dean Rusk in testimony before the Senate Foreign Relations Committee, February 18, 1966.

CONTENTS

Credible Threat More Than
The Citizen Does
Sacrifices or Risks?
The Past and the Future

INTRODUCTION

In any trade or profession a tension arises between the practitioner and the layman. The professional has developed, from experience with his subject, certain attitudes and perspectives which the outsider, who lacks this experience, little understands. When he pauses to evaluate the behavior of the practitioner, therefore, the outsider is often critical—but usually for the wrong reasons. The layman can seldom fairly criticize the lawyer, the labor leader, or the policeman because he does not understand the reality within which these men must act.

Once the reality faced by the practitioner is understood, many of the usual attacks and criticisms will appear misguided or unwarranted. An illustration is the changing attitude of political scientists toward the U.S. Congress and congressmen. Until recently, many venerable practices were roundly and almost universally condemned: the dispersion of authority in many committees and subcommittees, the control of the agenda by the House Rules Committee, the seniority system, the Senate filibuster, and weak party discipline. These practices survived, it was often supposed, because congressmen were intellectually or even morally deficient individuals. The research on Congress which has taken place in the last few decades has steadily undermined these criticisms. Scholars have discovered that once the nature and role of Congress are understood the above practices are reasonable, even necessary adjustments. The congressman, formerly viewed with scorn and impatience, now deserves, in the eyes of many political scientists, a certain appreciation.

Of all the occupations in our 20th century world, perhaps the one most subject to scrutiny and criticism is that of statesman: the profession of managing the nation's foreign relations. We need not look far to discover why this occupation receives so much attention. The statesman is responsible for the vitally important matter of war and peace. Naturally he is highly visible and readily judged. Yet rarely do we understand the problems and perspectives of these men whom we so easily criticize. Statesmanship is a profession as much as medicine or engineering. It has a distinctive orientation toward its subject and its own traditions and techniques. Unless we make a special effort to understand the statesman's reality, we are not likely to appreciate these traditions and practices.

Central to the statesman's distinctive perspective is his appreciation of the enormous importance of the threat of war in world affairs. His thoughts, his words, his deeds are shaped by this appreciation. As the carpenter uses wood, and the pharmacist, drugs, the statesman, year in and year out works with the threat of war. To be sure, his occupation involves much more besides. He arranges and adjusts dozens of matters not involving the threat of force, from the tourist traffic to the international monetary system. Between some nations the possibility of war is so remote that threats of hostile military action virtually disappear from their relationship. But between other states, which we may call "hostile" states, conflicts are so profound that war and the threat of war become instruments of competition. Because a great nation is rarely, if ever, without hostile opponents, the application of the threat of war becomes an indispensable part of statecraft.

The observation that the threat of war is central in regulating the relationships between hostile powers is certainly not new. Ever since there have been human groups capable of making war, their leaders have concerned themselves with threats. The great preoccupation of statesmen throughout history has been threats of war: making them, maintaining them, and interpreting them. Nevertheless, the citizen often fails to realize their critical role. Speeches, documents, conferences, treaties: the real meaning of these matters is often lost upon him because he does not see the threat of war behind them. A diplomatic note quietly sent to a foreign power voicing "concern" may contain a grave threat of war, but the citizen would never know it. We can observe the actual use of force in international relations but we are curiously insensitive to the threat of force. We know that war is possible and the thought of war frightens us. But we do not realize that nations manipulate this fear day after day as an instrument of policy.

It is to some extent understandable that differences arise between the perspectives of the statesman and those of the layman. War, force and violence are not pleasant to contemplate. Nor is the possibility of war readily taken seriously when we are surrounded by a comfortable and tranquil daily routine. In addition, many of us have emotional or philosophical biases against admitting the importance of force and violence in human affairs.

Statesmen themselves have generally been of little assistance in making us understand the primacy of threats in their affairs. Often, the reality of threat is so obvious to them that they suppose everyone else sees it too. Many times the statesman cannot candidly talk about threats he makes because to do so would change the nature of the threats. Also, to a large extent, the statesman's understanding of threats and their implications takes the form of intuition or rules of thumb: he knows what to do—and he is right—but he cannot advance a general theory or analysis to explain his position to others. Certainly Winston Churchill had a profound understanding of threats in world affairs. His works of diplomatic history, such as *The Gathering Storm,* display an unmatched mastery of the issues involved in specific international episodes. Yet he gives us very little general analysis. He perceptively describes why Munich was a disaster, but when he briefly attempts to give general rules about Munich-type situations, he offers only ambiguous and contradictory platitudes.

Ask almost any U.S. diplomat if we should give up Quemoy and Matsu to Red China and he will side against it. Yet when pressed to give an explanation for this position, he cannot present a convincing analytical argument. He may say "one doesn't give things away for nothing"; yet, under certain circumstances—e.g. the Philippines in 1946—one does. Therefore that rule is not helpful. In his inclination to hold on to Quemoy and Matsu the diplomat is, as I shall argue, taking the correct position. Traditional rules of behavior and long experience guide him to the result which the layman can achieve only through tedious analysis.

Finally, statesmen, at least in a democratic society, are reluctant to explain the importance of the threat of war because most citizens do not wish to be reminded that we live on the brink of war. The layman would be startled and dismayed to be made fully aware of the many times we have approached war, of the scores of circumstances under which we might go to war next week or next year. But if he is going to criticize the management of foreign policy then he ought to be made aware of these constant and unavoidable dangers. Only if he understands the pervasive importance of the threat of war and its ramifications can the layman sympathetically criticize the statesman.

Until quite recently, academics have done surprisingly little to explore and explain the perspectives of the statesman. One can plow through a pile of current college textbooks on international relations without finding more than a passing reference to the threat of war, to the enormous and complicated problems which arise in making, maintaining and interpreting threats. Somehow the subject is avoided or taken for granted. Recently, a few scholars have begun to fill this void with specific discussions of the role of threat in international relations. But judging from the ease with which academics, senators and clergymen have succumbed to fallacies and misconceptions about world politics in connection with the Vietnam war, the efforts of these scholars have not been assimilated. Perhaps they are too abstract; probably their emphasis on nuclear diplomacy has weakened their impact. Indeed, when today one speaks of "deterrence," most people think of nuclear weapons, anti-missiles, and fallout shelters. But nuclear strategy forms only a part of deterrence, and perhaps the most academic part. The statesman is more acutely concerned with the scores of day-to-day middle range threats, and deterrence problems of limited military dimensions.

This study attempts to broaden understanding of international affairs by offering an analysis of the threat of war as an instrument of foreign policy. This is not a work advancing specific policy recommendations. Nor is it a review of our foreign policy or our defense policy. Rather, it is an attempt to delineate some basic problems and perspectives of the statesman, particularly of the American statesman in the Cold War era. It is a primer containing observations which, I hope, will be useful to those who might wish to review policy or make recommendations.

Chapter 1

THREATS AND THE APPEASEMENT
THEORY OF WAR

Who is responsible for aggression and war?

On June 25, 1950, the North Koreans launched a surprise attack on South Korea. The invasion force of 90,000 men and 150 T-34 tanks swept over the lightly held South Korean positions and drove southward in an attempt to capture the entire peninsula. The invasion had been planned long in advance with Soviet cooperation and Soviet approval. The North Koreans were heavily dependent upon the Russians for military equipment, military advisors, and vital resources, such as oil and gasoline. Clearly, the Soviets sponsored the invasion. The responsibility for this aggression and the ensuing war, therefore, lay with the North Koreans and the Russians. They were to blame.

If a man discovers someone else's automobile with the doors unlocked and the motor running and drives it away he, too, would be to blame. A court of law would find him guilty of theft. But someone interested in preventing crime would look deeper. He would start by accepting the fact that there are people who are inclined to steal automobiles. He would then explore ways to thwart or weaken this inclination. In his analysis, not only the thief but those who fail to discourage theft would be responsible.

In the years prior to the Korean war, American strength and American commitments in the Pacific were steadily cut back. An economy-minded Congress whittled down an already low defense budget. Standing forces in the United States in 1950 were only one and one-third divisions. Military men spoke of the foolishness of fighting a land war in Asia. We announced that Formosa and South Korea were outside our defense perimeters. And we withdrew our troops from South Korea, the last units leaving on June 29, 1949. We had told our opponents in many voices and in many ways that we were unable and unwilling to defend South Korea. We left the door open and the motor running.

Who is responsible for aggression and war?

While it might be morally satisfying to blame the side immediately responsible, the practical statesman cannot adopt this attitude. Aggression and the wars which result from aggression are too dangerous and too costly simply to condemn. The statesman must seek to prevent them. Whatever the fault of his opponent may be, the statesman must act to keep that fault from having unfortunate consequences for everyone. And, insofar as it is within his power, he must act to correct the fault. He must be his brother's keeper. It is too dangerous not to be.

The United States is not the first country ever to discover this fact. It has, to varying degrees, been the guiding principle of statesmen for centuries. Facing hostile or potentially hostile states, that is, nations which are or might become aggressive, statesmen have sought by *their actions* to restrain or subdue the aggressive inclinations of such nations. The statesman of a great power believes it is in his power to reduce the probability of aggression and war.

This belief seems to contradict the many social, economic and ideological explanations for war. But these themes account more properly for hostility and the potential for aggression. Social systems, religious or ideological doctrines, economic necessities, historical memories and antipathies, racial differences, and national feelings: international conflicts surely have their roots in such phenomena. Yet hostility is not war. Between the two lies the process of diplomacy, the actions and reactions of the statesman. His is a science—or art—of its own. He takes as given the fact of hostility, regardless of its roots, and works to reduce the likelihood of war. Or, if war there must be, he seeks to reduce its destructiveness. The seeds of war may be strewn about the world irrevocably, yet the statesman may keep these seeds from germinating or, if they have sprouted, he may cause the plants to wither.

The diplomat's task of managing hostility is sometimes thought to involve merely the amicable and far-sighted adjustment of disputes through negotiation and compromise. Hostile nations discover their outstanding conflicts and then sit down together to work out an arrangement which reduces friction on both sides. Tension is lowered, statesmanship has triumphed. This description greatly underrates the statesman's role. Once the desire to compromise is manifest and peaceful compromise proves feasible, the hardest part is over.

What if compromise is not possible and the other side insists on settling the matter? What if the opponent will not respect your rights? What if he uses force or the threat of force to take what he seeks? Then what does the statesman do? It is very nice to bargain peaceably at a conference table with each side renouncing the use of force and respecting the rights of the other. But there is no automatic law of human nature which ensures this state of affairs. Indeed, if an opponent can have what he wants at low cost through the application of force, why should he bother to respect rights and make compromises? Here, then, is the difficult task: compelling a hostile power to refrain from aggression, compelling it to respect the standing compromise of rights and territories.

The statesman's major instrument for inhibiting aggression of hostile powers and bringing about peaceful settlement of international conflicts is the threat of war. It is not that he chooses this instrument in preference to others. If the basic relationship between hostile states could be regulated by other means, the statesman would gladly adopt them. But the conflicts underlying aggression are too profound to be adjusted by anything less than the threat of war. Persuasion, debate, social intercourse, cultural exchanges, international law, appeals to morality: these have their place but they are not adequate weapons for countering aggression. Aggression, that is, the use of force or the threat of force against other states' rights, is the supreme issue in international relationships. As such, it demands the supreme instrument in response: force or, much more frequently, the threat of force.

The application of a few simple axioms suffices to explain why the threat of war plays such a critical role in world affairs. National leaders can, at least to some degree, see ahead into the future. They can speculate upon the nature, costs, and outcome of a war that is likely to result if they act in a certain manner. If they believe that adopting one alternative probably will provoke war, they are less inclined to choose it. National leaders may, of course, decide to accept war as worth the objectives of their policy. But it is still true that the larger and more dangerous the threatened war appears to them, the less attractive the alternative that leads to it, and the more likely they are to forego or compromise their objectives to avoid it. On the basis of threats of war, hostile nations continually adjust—or stabilize—their relationships.

Hitler's gains in Austria and Czechoslovakia in 1938 and 1939, for example, were achieved by threats and not by the use of force. Against Austria, Hitler used his threat of war to coerce Chancellor Schuschnigg to cease building defensive works on the German frontier, appoint a Nazi as Austrian Minister of Security, free all Austrian Nazis under detention, postpone a plebiscite designed to strengthen the Austrian government and, finally, permit, unopposed, the German occupation of Austria on March 11, 1938. Czechoslovakia gave Hitler the Sude'enland portions of the country in October, 1938, under threat of war. The threat of war caused France and England to approv ather than resist this acquisition. Then, on March 15, 1939, he Czechs peaceably acceded to Hitler's conquest of the rest oi heir country, again frightened by the prospect of fighting a bloody, losing war if they resisted.

The history of international relations is replete with illustrations of this kind, often less dramatic, of course, but nonetheless real. It would not seem correct, therefore, to say that the use of force governs relations between hostile powers. Instead, it is the threat of force. For every conflict decided through war, there are dozens "decided" on the basis of the expected costs and outcome of a war never fought.

When we use the word "threat" we normally place a narrow, literal construction on the word. A threat is an explicit statement of the form "If you do (or don't do) this, I will do that." This understanding of threat will serve us poorly in the study of relations between hostile states. We need a broader definition: *the creation of expectations about one's likely punitive action in response to the future action (or inaction) of another.*

In this conception, explicit verbal st ements of intent are not the only, or even the most important, way to threaten. Without saying a word, the large, muscular man walking down the street threatens a stranger with physical violence if he calls him dirty names. The trade union official who walks into the manager's office saying, "Hey, Bill, the men are annoyed about this problem . . . " is projecting the threat of a strike. In cases like these, the threat, the expectation of likely punitive action, is created not by words but flows from our broader understanding of the context: our knowledge of the actors and their capabilities, the values they represent, what they have done in the past, and what our knowledge of their psychology—and human psychology in general—suggests they might do in this particular case.

Among hostile powers, the making and manipulation of the threat of war is confined largely to the implicit creation of expectations. Rarely will we see a nation explicitly announce, literally, a threat of war. At best we see phrases like "grave concern" or "unforseeable consequences" in diplomatic communications. And even these words constitute the lesser part of the implicit threat of war. The central components of a nation's threat are its capabilities and its values (including the value it places on avoiding war) which are communicated mainly through its actions.

The layman often fails to appreciate the importance of threats in international relations because he is unaware of his own nation's threat. A good way to illustrate this dimension is to consider the threats of opposing nations which we have less difficulty perceiving. If, for example, one proposes in a purely hypothetical way that the United States should have invaded North Vietnam early in the Vietnam war, one of the first considerations raised against this proposal would be the possibility of Red China's entering the war. Discouraging us from adopting this alternative, then, would be our expectation of the Chinese reaction, that is, the Chinese threat.

Pursuing the matter further, we might ask: What gives us an idea that China might have intervened in those circumstances? One of our first pieces of eviden would be: look at what they did in Korea. This quite natural and obvious reaction illustrates a point we shall examine at length later: the immense importance of prior *actions* in defining and supporting a nation's threat. The Chinese soldiers who died on Pork Chop Hill in Korea almost twenty years ago died not only—or even primarily—for victory in that battle; they died in support of their nation's threat. Many years later, their sacrifice live , on as an element of Chinese power, affecting the decisions opposing nations might make to challenge China's interests. In a similar fashion, the United States has, through its past actions, also projected a threat to defend its values in the world.

The United States faces today two hostile powers, the Soviet Union and China, and their allies. It is not even necessary to argue whether either of these nations is contemplating aggression now. It is sufficient to accept the proposition that given the opportunity these nations and their allies could forcibly challenge our interests. There is considerable ground for hostility between us: serious ideological, political, and cultural dissimilarities, a record of confrontations in the recent past, no less than four divided nations (Germany, Korea, Vietnam, and China), and dangerous trouble spots almost too numerous to mention. Any American president who ignored the communist powers and their allies in the hope that no aggression would take place would be seriously negligent. He must recognize that the potential for aggression exists and act to keep that potential from being realized.

The primary instrument we have employed for over 20 years to block or inhibit the aggressive tendencies of our opponents and their allies is the threat of war. Gradually, often from painful experiences such as Korea, we have erected a structure of deterrent threats so elaborate and so delicate that forcible communist expansion almost anywhere in the free world will probably lead to some form of American military involvement. This policy of deterrent threats has been wise and necessary; it is the safest course through a dangerous era. Unraveling this paradox—that through the threat of war, one reduces the incidence of war—is the purpose of this book.

The Appeasement Theory of War

Why should we be concerned about aggression of the communist powers and their allies? Why should we care if they take this or that piece of distant real estate? Certainly, we shall fight for our own independence and that of a few close friends, but why are we making threats that go far beyond this?

Two answers are customarily given to these questions. First, it is argued, a communist dictatorship is an unjust, often brutal and thoroughly undesirable form of government. Therefore, we oppose the establishment of such regimes for humanitarian reasons. Furthermore, whether we consider communist dictatorships good or bad, establishing them by outside force is destructive of human values: people are killed and left homeless in the attacks our opponents make upon other countries. And that we oppose.

While true in a general and fundamental way, this argument is often inadequate in specific instances. In some places, such as the island of Quemoy, off the Chinese coast, it would be possible to evacuate everyone peacefully. In response to a Chinese demand for that bit of territory, not one soul need be killed or condemned to live under a communist regime. A similar argument might apply to West Berlin.

In other cases where we have confronted actual or potential aggression, it can be argued that we might do more damage to the people by trying to defend them than the communists would do if allowed to conquer the country without opposition. Also, it may not be clear to some Americans, at least, that a communist regime would represent a markedly worse form of government for a particular people than the one it already has or is likely to have in the future. When such considerations are weighed against the American lives and resources which would have to be expended to defend a particular territory, the resulting judgment could easily be that an American military effort is unjustified. It does not appear, then, that the entire network of American deterrent threats can or should be defended on the grounds that, in each and every case, the moral and humanitarian values we are protecting would justify the risks and sacrifices involved.

The second argument often supposed to justify our policy is a doctrine which in a later chapter is called the "strategic value theory." This view recognizes that communist regimes—whatever their internal practices—are almost invariably hostile to us and identified with our major opponents. Consequently, when a communist regime is established, we allow human and economic resources to fall into the hands of our opponents. As a result, they would have a greater potential for bringing economic pressure to bear upon us or for winning a future war against us. That is, the balance of human, economic and military potential shifts in their favor. Again, while perhaps true in a fundamental or ultimate sense, this argument is deficient because it fails to recognize that the amount of military or economic power which the communists might have won from the West in recent confrontations is infinitesimal compared to the vast forces and resources at the disposal of the superpowers. It is difficult to believe that the Laotian army would be of significance to either side in a global confrontation; it is equally hard to believe that the sugar production of Taiwan is vital to our economy.

One could modify this strategic value argument with reference to local aggression. By bringing our opponents into geographical contact with other countries, the acquisition of one country makes further aggression easier. This argument would apply in Vietnam, but not in many other places where we have resisted encroachments: Korea, Berlin, Quemoy. It apparently is not military-strategic considerations, then, that determine our actions.

Nor, I might add, did such considerations determine the action of nations in the past. Many of the most dangerous crises between nations have taken place over bits of territory or fragments of privilege which scarcely altered the balance of military potential between the powers. The Agadir crisis of 1911 between Germany and France, for example, involved a German demand for protection of her actual and potential commercial interests in Morocco. This demand, whether granted or not, could not have materially affected Germany's war-making potential. Nevertheless, the conflict propelled the European powers toward general war. The same can be said of the Algeciras crisis (1905-6), and the Austrian ultimatum to Serbia which provoked the war in 1914. These disputes, as we shall see, involved vital matters; but their importance lay not in a supposed change in the distribution of war-making potential.

Why, then, should we so widely oppose the aggression of our opponents? The answer is bound up in this observation: we do have interests—idealistic and practical—abroad and on many occasions we *would* be willing to employ force to defend them against the only nations likely to seriously challenge these interests: Russia, China, and their allies. There exists, therefore, the danger of war, particularly the danger of large and violent war. And the scope and frequency of war is something we greatly desire to reduce.

It is difficult—and at this point unnecessary—to specify all our national values and describe how our opponents would have to challenge them to provoke us into war. But we do have such values and they apply to much beyond our own survival narrowly defined. One would suppose, for example, that if we found a friendly country under attack by a communist state using brutal tactics to establish a brutal regime in that country, we might feel emotionally constrained to come to its defense. This view has not generally prevailed concerning South Vietnam, but it could in another situation. Indeed, it would be a shocking condemnation of our society and its ideals to argue that we would *always* be indifferent to such an event.

The point at which the combination of emotional tides, perceptions, ideals, and economic self-interest would, in the natural course of events, bring us to war is uncertain in its determination. Therein lies much of the danger of war. The issue is not whether we shall go to war in defense of our values abroad: on occasion we would. The problem is to make our use of military force *predictable* so that our opponents can understand *and avoid* the dangers they run in their conflict with us.

To be predictable is to defend values consistently. In practice, consistency is achieved by resisting the aggression of one's opponents even when, *in the particular case,* the practical and idealistic values at issue may not justify the risks and sacrifices of resistance. The alternative policy of ignoring aggression unless the entire nation is emotionally aroused and anxious to resist (e.g., Pearl Harbor) is inconsistent. It is the road to more war and major war. Several psychological and political processes operate to make this so.

Hostile powers are constantly bargaining with each other. They are giving and taking or refraining from giving and taking on the many disputes that arise between them. What makes the bargaining between hostile states so special is that the primary weapon each is using to coerce the other is the threat of war. Not strikes, not court trials, not fines, not election defeats: war is the threatened punishment.

In bargaining with each other with their threats, hostile powers demand and yield on the basis of their fears of war. The side which greatly fears war will give up more to preserve peace than the side which is less troubled by the prospect of war. If, for example, one nation has greater military power than the other, it will probably fear war less than its opponent, since it will win if war takes place. Hence, it will demand, and probably receive, more of the objects it disputes with the weaker side.

Relative military potential, however, is only one variable which determines each country's fear of war. The other is courage or will. Any war, whether won or lost, involves sacrifices. Some countries may be unwilling to suffer the costs of fighting even a winning war. When they bargain with weaker but more courageous nations, they will give up a great deal to avoid war. Britain, for example, dramatically and idealistically led the League of Nations into a resounding condemnation of Italy's aggression against Ethiopia in 1935. Yet, although Britain's naval forces were vastly superior to Mussolini's, she was unwilling to pay the price of war to oppose him. And so Italy, the militarily weaker power, succeeded in its conquest.

A year later, Hitler, in flagrant violation of the Versailles Treaty, remilitarized the Rhineland. France and Britain naturally objected to this move and at the time could easily have defeated Germany in war. Nevertheless, they feared war too much to act. Hitler, militarily weaker but with greater determination, won the dispute.

How can nations learn about each other's courage? They can compute relative military potentials in missiles, tanks, men, and airplanes, but what indicators exist to reveal how much a nation fears war? Mr. Khrushchev wants Berlin and says he is willing to go to war for it. Mr. Kennedy says he may not have Berlin and he will go to war to keep it. These words alone reveal little about each man's determination to face war. They might be completely true or half-true or empty bluff. It is all very easy for a leader to say he will risk war, but when the terrible choice is before him who knows how big a risk he will take? Does he know himself? Knowing the opponent's courage is vitally important because it enables a nation to predict what he will let it take and what he will fight (or risk) a war over.

Since words alone are not valid indicators of a nation's fear of war, the level of each nation's determination must be estimated indirectly, particularly from its actions. By observing what risks and sacrifices a nation accepts (or fails to accept) to defend its interests in particular disputes, other nations gain an idea about its relative courage. It is in this context that aggression plays a critical role as an information-gathering device. One nation forcibly attempts to settle a dispute in its favor. If the dispute is over a piece of territory, for example, it invades. Since only war, or a process that threatens to lead to war, will constitute a meaningful response to this use of force, the defensive nation is confronted with an opportunity to demonstrate, in a practical and meaningful way, just how much it fears war.

If the defensive power does not respond several pieces of information are communicated. First, it fears war too much to prevent its enemy from taking the item in dispute. That is self-evident. More importantly, the aggressor properly draws the conclusion that the defensive power will probably not respond to the capture of other items of similar apparent value to the defender, and might not respond to encroachments on issues of somewhat greater importance.

It is possible, of course, that our hypothetical issue is the only outstanding conflict between the two hostile powers. In this case, the aggression would be of little consequence. The aggressor concludes that the defender will not fight a war to protect the issue, but since there are no other outstanding issues of conflict this information has no further consequences.

But hostile states with only one outstanding issue of conflict are imaginary. Typically there are dozens of outstanding issues and the potential conflicts number in the hundreds. A vast number of actual and potential disputes characterized the hostility between the Triple Alliance and the Triple Entente prior to World War I, between the Axis and Allies prior to World War II and, of course, exist between East and West in our day. With so many outstanding issues, an opponent's belief that the defensive power will not risk war to protect a certain interest has profound and dangerous consequences.

There are bound to be many other issues of apparently similar value to the defensive power. Thus far, the aggressor may have refrained from forcibly settling them in his favor because he fears war. Now he has evidence that on one of these similar issues the defensive power was not willing to risk war. He reasonably concludes, therefore, that he runs little risk in forcibly settling some of these other issues. For this reason a power which permits its opponent to commit aggression is likely to experience more aggression.

One of the best-known illustrations of this pattern of increasing aggression is Hitler's steady encroachments in the late 1930s. His belief that Britain and France feared to act against him was reinforced by their failure to respond to his remilitarization of the Rhineland in 1936. In March 1938, he confidently annexed Austria without fear of an Allied response. Since there was none, this fact confirmed his belief that the Allies would not act if he invaded Czechoslovakia. Although France had pledged, by treaty, to protect Czechoslovakia, Hitler believed that the fear of war would cause France to renege on its obligation—even though the balance of military power still favored the Allies. He was right. On the eve of a threatened invasion of Czechoslovakia, the Allies yielded to Hitler.

If a nation has more than one opponent, the dangers of appeasement are multiplied, for each opponent is drawing conclusions from the retreat in question. When Hitler moved into the Rhineland on March 7, 1936, he already had good reason to suspect that Britain and France were mightily afraid of war. Against Mussolini's invasion of Ethiopia in October 1935, neither power had acted. France made an agreement with Italy; Britain stood holding the mandate of the League of Nations against Italy yet failed to act. Appeasement of one aggressor, by demonstrating that the defensive power fears war more than previously suspected, communicates important information to other potential aggressors. These countries may have abstained from aggression in the fear of a response from their opponent. When this opponent tolerates aggression elsewhere it displays its fear of war. Potential aggressors find that aggression which seemed too dangerous before is now worth trying. Therefore, tolerating aggression not only increases the probability of more aggression from the same power, but stimulates other, formerly quiescent enemies to undertake aggression.

The power which tolerates the use of force by its enemies to change the status quo in their favor suffers a decline in the coerciveness of its threat of war. This threat is what has induced opponents to compromise disputed issues and to respect the standing compromise as it exists. Allow this threat to weaken and enemies will expect and demand a bigger share of the disputed issues. In relations between hostile states these increased demands take the form of aggression.

It is for this reason that nations often go to the brink of war— or to war—over such apparently small issues. Many people, noticing the grave crises which tiny conflicts often provoke between nations—Bosnia, Agadir, Quemoy—conclude that statesmen must have a grossly distorted sense of value to risk war over such insignificant things. But the statesman is contesting small issues because he realizes that his bargaining power, the coerciveness of his threat, is being established in such crises. This threat will be useful day after day for years to come in forestalling war and making his opponent compromise with him on a wide range of vital issues.

Frederick the Great, in describing the foreign policy of his father, gave a perceptive illustration of this proposition:

> In the year 1727, there were some differences between him and Hanover, concerning trifles, which ended in

reconciliation. Shortly after he had other disputes, equally unimportant, with the Dutch; and which were in like manner accommodated. From these two examples of moderation, his neighbours and those who envied him concluded he might be insulted with impunity; that, instead of real, his was but apparent strength; that his officers were not men of understanding, but fencing-masters; and his brave soldiers mercenaries, who had little affection for the state; and that, with respect to himself, he continually threatened but never struck.

* * *

An insignificant bishop of Liege prided himself on the mortifications which he gave the king. Some subjects of the lordship of Herstall, appertaining to Prussia, had revolted, and the bishop granted them his protection. The late king sent colonel Kreutz to Liege, with a credential letter to accommodate the matter. And who should think proper to refuse suffering him to come into his presence? Why truly my lord the bishop; who, three successive days, saw the attendants of this envoy in the court of his palace, and as often refused him admission.

This event, and many others, the omission of which brevity occasions, taught the king [the writer] that a monarch ought to make himself, and particularly his nation, respected; that moderation is a virtue which statesmen ought not too rigorously to practice; because of the corruption of the age; and that, at the commencement of a reign, it was better to give marks of determination than of mildness. 1

Another illustration of this point is found in an observation David Hartley, British Commissioner for negotiating peace with America, made in a letter to Benjamin Franklin in May, 1782. The British had been moving slowly on the arrangements for a peace conference to settle the American Revolutionary war, contesting apparently small issues such as the location of the conference and the status of the various delegations. To Franklin, such an interest in national honor seemed sterile. But Britain, with interests from Gibraltar to Canada and many potential opponents to challenge those interests, had a reputation to protect, as Hartley pointed out:

I agree with you, that the equitable and the philosophical principles of politics can alone form a solid foundation of permanent peace; and the contraries to them, though highly patronized by nations themselves, and their ministers, are no better than vulgar errors; but

nations are slow to convictions from the personal arguments of individuals. They are "jealous in honor, seeking
the *bubble reputation* even in the cannon's mouth." But
until a confirmed millennium, founded upon wiser principles, shall be generally established, the *reputation* of nations is not merely a *bubble*. It forms their real security. 2

How does a policy of appeasement affect the general probability of war? Clearly, in order to resist aggression a nation must
go to war or at least give a sufficiently convincing impression that
it will. Confronting aggression, therefore, involves some risk of
war. Hence, one might argue, the risk of war remains the same
whether one confronts a hostile power at the first aggression or the
fifth. Certainly one has lost some things of value in the meantime,
but the danger of war is still the same. This argument misses some
important points. First, since tolerating aggression causes a pro-
gressive decline in the defender's threat, aggression is likely to
occur more frequently, and by more hostile nations and over issues
of increasing importance. Hence there will be more opportunities
for confrontations, any of which could lead to war.

Even without assuming that confrontations will increase in
frequency and scope, it still seems true that confronting aggression
in its earlier stages is safer than trying later. When the first en-
croachment takes place, the aggressor is uncertain about his
opponent's reaction. He has no solid basis in experience to predict
the response. He has hunches, of course, but his opponent's courage
is, as yet, a largely unknown quantity. In this state of mind the
aggressor is most responsive to warnings issued by his opponent:
a strong diplomatic note, an ultimatum or a military alert.

When the aggressor finds that no reaction to his first move is
forthcoming, his uncertainty is considerably reduced. He now has
evidence that his opponent will not fight to stop him from taking
objectives such as the one he just took. Therefore, on later attempts at aggression he is less likely to heed the preliminary warnings of war issued by the other side. He *knows* that his opponent
yielded on a similar issue, and he is therefore more inclined to
view the warning as a bluff. If, however, the defender had decided to
halt aggression this time, his warning is not a bluff and the war,
unintended by the aggressor, will take place. As a general rule, the
toleration of aggression leads the aggressor to discount the signals
which the defensive power would use to communicate a threat of

war, leaving war itself as the only workable means of halting aggression.

This process of discounting, for example, constituted one of the important links in the chain of events leading to World War I: the Austrian ultimatum to Serbia on July 23, 1914. Because the demand was deliberately framed to be rejected, it amounted to a declaration of war against Serbia. If the Austrians and their German allies had believed that Russia would come to the aid of Serbia and mobilize for war, it seems they would not have taken this drastic step against Serbia. But although they realized a Russian response was a possibility, they obviously thought it unlikely. From his discussion with German Kaiser William II, on July 5, 1914— over two weeks before the Austrian ultimatum was sent—the Austrian ambassador, Szogyeny, reported:

> Russia, furthermore, he [the Kaiser] thought, as things stand today, was in no way ready for war and would certainly ponder very seriously before appealing to arms.[3]

Indeed, the Austrians delayed issuing their ultimatum to Serbia while the French President Poincaré was visiting St. Petersburg in the fear that the French President would urge the Russians to respond more forcefully than they otherwise would.[4]

The Austrian and German belief in the probable inaction of Russia was not without foundation. In 1908-9, Austria had annexed Bosnia and Herzegovina over the vigorous objections of Serbia. Although Russia was displeased, she made no vigorous effort to oppose the annexation.[5] In October, 1913, Serbia was again forced to back down before Austria without assistance from her Russian protector. Austria issued an ultimatum to Serbia to withdraw her troops from Albania within eight days. Serbia, under threat of invasion by Austria, complied:

> . . . Austria had acted quickly and energetically on her own account, by sending a peremptory ultimatum, Serbia had heeded her demands immediately, Russia had not interfered, and the Vienna Foreign Office had accomplished its immediate purpose.[6]

Less than a year later, on July 18, 1914 (a week before Austria issued her ultimatum) the Russian foreign minister Sazonov tried to warn the Austrians that the Russians would go to war to protect Serbia. "Russia," he told the Austrian Ambassador, "would not be indifferent to any effort to humiliate Serbia. Russia could not permit Austria to use menacing language or military measures against Serbia."7   Normally such stern words would probably communicate a threat of war. But only nine months before, Austria *had* humiliated Serbia and *had* used menacing language *and the Russians had done nothing.* The Austrians could reasonably conclude that these words, so incongruous with past Russian behavior, were a bluff. But they were not.

Perhaps the most incisive statement of the relationship between appeasement and the danger of more aggression and war was given by Niccolo Machiavelli in his Discourse entitled, "Men often deceive themselves in believing that by humility they can overcome insolence:"

> . . . no prince should ever forego his rank, nor should he ever voluntarily give up anything (wishing to do so honorably) unless he is able or believes himself able to hold it. For it is almost always better (matters having come to the point that he cannot give it up in the above manner) to allow it to be taken from him by force, rather than by the apprehension of force. For if he yields it from fear, it is for the purpose of avoiding war, and he will rarely escape from that; for he to whom he has from cowardice conceded the one thing will not be satisfied, but will want to take other things from him, and his arrogance will increase as his esteem for the prince is lessened. And, on the other hand, the zeal of the prince's friends will be chilled on seeing him appear feeble or cowardly. But if, so soon as he discerns his adversary's intention, he prepares his forces, even though they be inferior, the enemy will begin to respect him, and the other neighboring princes will appreciate him the more; and seeing him armed for defence, those even will come to his aid who, seeing him give up himself, would never have assisted him.8

This same point was made by Oleg Penkovskiy in a modern frame of reference. Penkovskiy was a colonel in the Russian military intelligence (GRU) who, reacting against the Khrushchev regime, became a double agent for the West. He remained in his post (until he was apprehended and executed) and wrote down observations, later smuggled to the West, about the policy of Khrushchev and what should be done about it. Writing in mid-1962 he advised:

> Kennedy must carry out a firm and consistent policy in regard to Khrushchev. There is nothing to fear. Khrushchev is not ready for war. He has to be slapped down again and again every time he gets ready to set off on one of his adventures.
>
> Kennedy has just as much right to help the patriots of Cuba [at the Bay of Pigs] as we had when we "helped" the Hungarians.
>
> This is not just my opinion. Everyone at the General Staff said this. It was said in Varentsov's home, even on the streetcars in Moscow. If the West does not maintain a firm policy, then Khrushchev's position will become stronger, he will think even more about his might and right, and in this case he might strike.
>
> Everyone should know this. Once other countries begin to believe in his strength, Khrushchev will begin to dictate anything he wants.[9]

The proposition that tolerating aggression greatly increases the chances of more aggression and war follows from the preceding analysis of the learning processes and behavior of rational statesmen. It is not necessary to assume that these men are unreasonable or subject to domestic pressures. As we look beyond the purely rational processes which shape the patterns of aggression and war, we discover several important emotional and institutional phenomena which reinforce the conclusion that appeasement increases the danger of war. Perhaps the most important is the "exhilaration effect."

Victory, whether achieved through brief wars or merely threats, has an exhilarating effect. The discovery that one's enemies are inferior—in their courage or capabilities—frequently tends to make one bolder and more demanding. Since we observe this phenomenon in many human and animal relationships, it may perhaps be an instinctive, natural reaction requiring no explanation. When the enemy shows courage and great capability, we maintain our distance and carefully fence with him. When he shows fear or weakness, we grow more confident and are inclined to press our advantage.

Even American foreign policy has suffered the pernicious results of the exhilaration effect. In Korea, for example, our inability to stop when we were winning led to much unnecessary sacrifice. After the successful Inchon landing on September 15, 1950, and the reconquest of Seoul, South Korea, we had achieved an adequate victory. We had reinforced the American deterrent threat to oppose communist aggression; we had vindicated the United Nations as a viable peace-keeping body; we had reconquered all of South Korea and had destroyed the invading North Korean army. At the same time the threat of Soviet or Chinese intervention cast a shadow of danger upon an attempt to reconquer all of Korea. In retrospect it is clear that stopping at the 38th parallel (or a suitable defensive line above it) would have been a wise policy.

In June, 1950, shortly after the attack on South Korea, we had apparently felt that the US-UN action was intended "solely for the purpose of restoring the Republic of Korea to its status prior to the invasion from the north."[10] But in the flush of the September victory, this view shifted. We had dramatically routed the North Koreans. Our confidence in our capabilities soared. We did not listen thoughtfully to what the Chinese were saying. Their threat to enter the Korean War seemed to be empty bluster of a basically cautious power. As we saw the scene at the time, it would have been foolish, even immoral, not to press our apparent advantage. So we marched north, the Chinese crossed the Yalu, and we reaped two years of war. Thus the United States, a mature and pragmatic nation, fell victim to a miscalculation under the exhilaration of victory.

This simple emotional exhilaration in victory has important institutional consequences in a nation-state. If war and the threat of war prove successful, ideologies glorifying war and emphasizing its utility and necessity are likely to emerge to sustain the aggressive orientation of the state. Moreover, in the wake of successful aggression those leadership factions opposing foreign conquest are weakened by the obvious accomplishments of the pro-war leaders. Thus, moderates are defeated and militant leaders more likely to prevail.

The firm American position of worldwide defense has, to a large extent, made the aggression of our opponents risky and unprofitable. It has, therefore, fostered world peace through its effects on communist attitudes, ideologies, and patterns of leadership selection. The removal of the "hare-brained" (as he was denounced by later Soviet leaders) Khrushchev seems to illustrate the importance of American firmness in deflecting Soviet leadership away from aggressive inclinations. What made Khrushchev "hare-brained" instead of "farsighted" was that he failed. And he failed because the United States was firm on the Cuban missile issue. Had we permitted him to succeed, the more moderate opposition which over-threw him might have lacked the necessary support.

Among many Eastern European communists, Ho Chi Minh is reportedly considered a "romantic." Again, what is it that produces this evaluation? If South Vietnam had fallen to the communists neatly and at low cost in the early 1960's, it would have had to be considered a master stroke of communist strategy. Instead, the effort provoked a dangerous and destructive American counteraction. Because of the United States resistance Ho is a "romantic," not to be emulated, rather than a "tower of tactical brilliance" deserving applause and imitation throughout the communist world.

In most discussions of aggression, we neglect to mention the consequences of appeasement for the defensive power. We assume that its foreign policy orientation will be constant throughout the process of retreat. But this is often a false assumption. Each retreat may stimulate cries of "cowardice," "dishonor," and "shame." As more appeasement takes place, those clamoring for a forceful reaction grow stronger and may come to influence or even control the government. Thus, the process of retreat may cause the defending nation to change its policy from timidity to belligerence.

We can see this phenomenon in the changing British attitude toward Hitler prior to World War II. The British were timid, peaceable, and appeasing on German rearmament, German occupation of the Rhineland, German annexation of Austria, and the German annexation of the Sudetenland. Then, when Hitler, ignoring his promise to Chamberlain, completed his conquest of Czechoslovakia in March, 1939, British opinion abruptly reversed. Prime Minister Chamberlain was indignant, the House of Commons urged firm action, and "public opinion," which just a few months earlier had been strongly pacifist, rallied to the cause of war. The British then announced their intention to make war on Germany if Hitler invaded Poland. How could the Germans, however, take this warning seriously when it so obviously contradicted their past experience with Britain? Yet the British certainly meant it.

A similar reversal is possible in the United States during the Cold War. Americans are, for the most part, satisfied with the international stalemate. We have more or less held our own; no important drift against us can be discerned. Consequently, there is little support for a belligerent, adventurous foreign policy. It could be otherwise. Imagine what would have been the outcome of the 1964 Johnson-Goldwater presidential election if: 1) we had given Khrushchev Berlin following his threat of war in 1961; 2) we had permitted missiles to remain in Cuba; 3) we had allowed the communists to capture Laos and South Vietnam. Surely, such retreats would have strengthened the domestic position of the more "hawkish" Goldwater. It is useful to remember, in this connection, how the belligerent anti-communism led by Senator Joseph R. McCarthy fed upon the communist victory in China.

Ultimately, a policy of appeasement is dangerous because we could not sustain it. At some point, and fairly early in the process of retreat, we would feel impelled to stand firm. Goaded by shame of a previous, seemingly cowardly retreat, such as the desertion of a friendly nation in need or by outrage at the apparent brutality, injustice or immorality of a particular aggression, a policy of appeasement would be cast aside. It should not be forgotten that there are serious value conflicts underlying the Cold War. Most Americans profoundly dislike seeing communist regimes forcibly imposed upon other peoples. We might, in certain places and under certain circumstances, be disinclined to resist a communist advance. But there are many, many points at which this nation would want to, indeed, would insist upon, forcible resistance.

This, then, is the fatal shortcoming of an appeasement policy: we simply would not pursue it consistently. Even those who advocate, explicitly or implicitly, a policy of ignoring the aggression of an opponent in a particular case would not support ignoring *all* aggression. On the abstract rational level, there is little support for a policy of allowing our opponents and their allies to do as they pleased with the rest of the world without interference from us. Emotionally, in practice, a policy of continued, consistent appeasement would command even less support.

Tolerating aggression by a hostile power, then, has these effects: a decline in the coerciveness of the defensive power's threat; an increased level of aggression by opponents; a discounting of warning signals that might be given to the enemy; a sense of exhilaration and over-confidence of the enemy; and, eventually, a mood of reaction in the defensive camp. These are the processes associated with appeasement that set the scene for major war. The aggressor, buoyed by past successes, believes he faces a frightened and retreating enemy. But he collides with a bitter opponent who now believes that the aggressor already has more than he may be permitted to hold.

War is always possible. There seems to be no practical method for abolishing it. But the surest way to increase the danger of war is to allow our threat to lose its deterrent value by tolerating the aggression of our opponents. This threat protects us from increasing aggression and from larger wars. Therefore, our threat of war is a vitally important national asset and must be assiduously sustained. Its maintenance should be a prime object of our policies.

This injunction is substantially different from the one which urges us to *oppose* aggression. Opposing aggression is not the objective; it is only an implication or necessary consequence of a policy of maintaining our threat. We do not want to kill communist soldiers when they invade; we want our enemies to believe that we *will* kill their soldiers if they invade. In Korea, in effect, we followed a policy of merely opposing aggression when it happened. We let our enemies believe we would not fight if they invaded, and then we fought when they did invade. But how wasteful it was! Far more efficient would have been a convincing demonstration of our intention to fight. Our acts, our bloodshed, our wars must be in support of a policy of threatening to oppose the aggression of our opponents.

Some practical consequences of the difference between a policy of *opposing* and *threatening to oppose* may be illustrated briefly. In 1965-68, the United States was bombing North Vietnam. If our policy was merely to oppose the North Vietnamese attack on South Vietnam, the bombing should have been evaluated on the basis of whether and how much it helped us end this particular attack. But if we focus on the American threat, an additional dimension must be added: What did our bombing of North Vietnam say to other potential aggressors—or to North Vietnam for future reference? Or, what might our failure to bomb communicate? That aggression is a low-risk alternative because, even if the United States intervenes, the worst it would do is repel the aggression in the territory of the defender. By bombing North Vietnam, we pointed up an additional cost to other potential aggressors.

It is often observed that the German bombing of Great Britain during World War II did not weaken the British will to fight but probably strengthened it. But bombing is one thing, the threat of bombing quite another. It is almost always forgotten that prior to the war, when Chamberlain was bargaining with Hitler over matters such as Czechoslovakia, the *fear* of air raids on British cities was important in stimulating Chamberlain to make concessions to Hitler.[11]

The evaluation of the Vietnam war itself can be made in two different ways, depending on the strategy one supposes we are following. A policy of merely opposing our adversary's aggression leads to an evaluation based only upon the specific dispute. One attempts to assess the value of keeping this number of people and their territory and economic resources out of our opponents' hands, and matches this against the costs in lives, money and the moral agony of doing it. This perspective has led many to conclude that Vietnam is not "worth it."

A policy of threatening to oppose aggression places the Vietnam involvement in a different context. The American threat, or reputation for action, is working for us around the world in discouraging the aggression of our opponents. If we maintain that threat, it will continue to work for us time and again to obviate the actual use of force. The war in Vietnam challenged us with an opportunity to uphold our reputation for defending our interests. Thus, ten years from now, if the United States Secretary of State privately warns an opponent that we view "with grave concern" its course of action, the memory of Vietnam would give these words a force they otherwise would not have.

The costs of the Vietnam war, then, must be distributed against all the "victories" we have won and shall win through our threat alone; the sacrifices must be matched to all the wars our enemies never start and attacks they never make because they fear our reaction. Threats, after all, cannot be made without cost. It would be foolish to imagine we could bend determined opponents by mere speeches and position papers. To establish and maintain a credible threat we must convince our opponents (and our allies) that we really are willing to make sacrifices to protect our values abroad. Ultimately, the only way to demonstrate that you will make sacrifices is to make them when your threat is challenged.

The analysis of that realm of American foreign policy which involves the maintenance and application of the threat of war, therefore, requires that American action be assessed, not in terms of each specific episode, but in relation to its impact on present and future expectations about American action around the world.

Chapter 2

THE APPLICATION OF THREAT: THREE CASES

Do threats really work? Although the theory appears sound, one might reasonably doubt that it has extensive practical application. Somehow a threat seems too flimsy a weapon to obtain important results. To dispel this impression, I have chosen to discuss three specific applications of the American threat: the Russian withdrawal from Iran in 1946, the "neutralization" of Laos in 1961-62, and the Cuban missile crisis of 1962. In each we obtained, through the use of a threat, important concessions from the communists. These three episodes illustrate only a tiny fraction of the instances where we have achieved our ends by threat, but they provide an interesting cross-section of the many possibilities.

Russian Troops in Iran

During the Second World War, Russia and Great Britain found it desirable, for strategic purposes, to station troops in Iran. To normalize the presence of these troops, an Anglo-Soviet-Iranian treaty was signed on January 29, 1942, which stipulated the withdrawal of all foreign troops six months after the end of the war, that is, March 2, 1946. Great Britain and the United States (which later subscribed to the treaty) complied, withdrawing their troops by that date. The Russians did not. Indeed, in the early days of March, 1946, they increased their contingent in the Iranian region of Azerbaijan from about 30,000 to 60,000 men.

The Russian refusal to remove troops had ominous implications. With Soviet assistance, a movement for autonomy had been created in Azerbaijan. In November, 1945, a revolt had occurred, and an Iranian detachment of 1,500 troops sent to quell it was refused entry into Azerbaijan by Soviet troops. Iran protested to Russia and to the United Nations Security Council in January, with no apparent results. During February, 1946, the premier of Iran, Ahmed Ghavam went to Moscow to negotiate the removal of Russian troops. It later came out that Russian demands in these negotiations included 1) Iranian recognition of the autonomy of Azerbaijan and 2) Iranian acceptance of Russian troops on parts of Iranian territory for an indefinite length of time.

Given the overwhelming strength of the Red army compared to that of Iran and the presence of Russian troops in Iran, Ghavam was clearly in a poor bargaining position. In Iran, the anticommunist parliament, although harassed by the pro-communist Tudeh party, approved a measure invalidating any agreement Ghavam might make with the Russians. Ghavam had made no concessions when he left Moscow on March 7, 1946. Obviously, in the absence of any countervailing threat against the Russians from Great Britain and the United States, neither Ghavam nor the Iranian parliament would have been able to withstand the Russian demands.

In the early days of March, when the Soviet Union was supposed to withdraw its troops, the crisis broadened. The rebels in Azerbaijan, with Russian assistance, expanded their control to new areas including the town of Karganrud. The Soviet Union voiced a territorial demand upon Turkey, insisting that the regions of Kars and Ardahan be ceded by Turkey to Russia. The Russians sent additional troops and tanks into Iran and began ambiguous but provocative armored advances across Iranian territory toward the capital, Teheran, and toward Turkey.

The Iranians, informed by Stalin that a protest to the United Nations would be considered an "unfriendly act," were not intimidated and protested on March 19, 1946. On March 27, the Security Council met and voted, over the Soviet objection, to consider the complaint of Iran. Gromyko, the Soviet delegate, walked out of the session in protest. The complaint of the Iranian ambassador was heard and the Security Council agreed, on March 29, to adjourn until April 3, when it would inspect the progress of the current Soviet-Iranian negotiations. The Soviet Union had steadily relaxed its position, first announcing on March 24 that it would withdraw from Iran in five to six weeks if nothing "unforeseen" happened; and later dropped the reservation about the "unforeseen." By April 3, the Iranian ambassador could announce that the Russians had unconditionally agreed to withdraw their troops. This withdrawal was begun early in April and concluded in May. Later, in December, 1946, Iranian troops entered Azerbaijan and the revolt, which earlier had seemed so formidable under Soviet tutelage, quickly collapsed.

And so, Russian aims, backed by force and the threat of force, were defeated. The Red army left Iran, Azerbaijan was kept out of communist hands and neither Iran nor Turkey made any territorial concessions to Russia. There were no hostilities, no use of force on our part, only speeches, notes, and debates. How was this victory accomplished? What made the Russians change their minds?

First, we might suppose that the Russians had intended to withdraw anyway and that their delay was merely a matter of administrative incompetence or forgetfulness. The record shows that this cannot have been so. If the Soviets had no designs upon Iran they could have withdrawn much earlier. At the Potsdam Conference, on July 23, 1945, Truman, Churchill and Stalin discussed Iran. After the victory in Europe, there was no further need for the allies to maintain troops in Iran. Truman announced that the United States was withdrawing troops already. Churchill urged that troops be withdrawn at the earliest date. Stalin declined to agree.[1]

At the Moscow conference of December, 1945, the United States Secretary of State, James F. Byrnes again reminded Stalin that he had no excuse for keeping troops in Iran—and certainly no right to interfere as he had in Iranian politics. Stalin brushed the matter off with a vague promise, "we will do nothing that will make you blush."[2] Had the Russians been without territorial interests in Iran, their troops could have been withdrawn many months before March, 1946. The other parties, Great Britain, the United States, Iran, were quite willing. The clear rejection of the March 2 deadline, the troop reinforcements, the armored columns, the demands made upon Turkey and upon Ghavam: this was aggression planned many months in advance.

Did the Russians withdraw in response to "world opinion," that is in deference to the attitudes of other countries? It would be extraordinarily difficult to argue such a case. Of all the world

leaders at the time, Stalin had the most notorious record of disregard for the sensitivities of the West: the trials, purges and
massacres of the 1930s; the pact with Hitler; the partition of Poland in 1939; the attack on Finland; the arrest and imprisonment
in March, 1945, of leaders of the pro-democratic Polish under-
ground who had travelled to Moscow for discussions with a written
guarantee of their personal safety. Stalin was clearly not one who
felt a need for world approval.

Did the Russians withdraw because they believed in the intrinsic value of the United Nations and its peace-keeping ideals?
No, for they denied the UN had a right to consider the Iranian
matter; they threatened the Iranians over going to the Security
Council; they walked out when the Security Council ignored their
protest and heard the Iranians.

The explanation which best fits the facts is that the Russians
withdrew from Iran because the United States and Great Britain
had acted in a manner that threatened to end in war if Russia did
not yield. The Russians decided that their objectives in Iran were
not worth risking the threatened war.

We sent the Russians many warning signals. As far back as
December, 1945, Secretary of State Byrnes told Stalin, at the
Moscow conference, that he was "seriously disturbed" about the
Iranian matter.[3] On February 28, 1946, the Secretary of State
gave a speech before the Overseas Press Club in which he declared:

> . . . we cannot overlook a unilateral gnawing away at
> the status quo. The [UN] Charter forbids aggression
> and we cannot allow aggression to be accomplished by
> coercion or pressure or by subterfuges such as political
> infiltration.

Perhaps even more startling was the American attitude toward
the Soviet UN veto:

> . . . the mere legal veto by one of the permanent members
> of the Council does not in fact relieve any state, large or
> small, of its moral obligation to act in accordance with
> the purposes and principles of the Charter.[4]

These words were intended, as Byrnes himself later noted, for the
Kremlin on the eve of the Iranian crisis.[5]

Following the Russian refusal to withdraw on March 2, 1946,
the United States sent a firm note to Russia on March 7 announc-

ing that the Soviet Union "had created a situation with regard to which the Government of the United States . . . cannot remain indifferent." The British government sent a similar note. On March 16, Byrnes made a speech before the Society of the Friendly Sons of St. Patrick which made the American intention more explicit:

> The United States is committed to the support of the charter of the United Nations. Should the occasion arise, our military strength will be used to support the purposes and principles of that charter.6

The most dramatic allied communication was, however, the famous "Iron Curtain" speech of Winston Churchill in Fulton, Missouri, on March 5, three days after the Soviet violation of the Iranian treaty. Although Churchill was speaking as a private citizen, he was closely identified with the British Government in the Russian view. Moreover, as Churchill pointedly noted, President Truman had "travelled a thousand miles to dignify and magnify our meeting here today." Churchill denounced the "expansive and proselytizing tendencies" of the Soviet Union and called for an Anglo-American alliance to oppose the Russians with strength because "there is nothing they admire so much as strength."7

In addition to these and other public communications, it seems likely that some forceful private messages had also been sent to the Russians. Our reason for suspecting this rests upon Truman's attitude toward Russian aggression. As early as December, 1945, Truman had concluded that the Russians were aggressive and must be opposed firmly. He wrote a private letter to Secretary of State Byrnes which he read aloud to the Secretary on January 5, 1946. Reviewing Russian moves in the Near and Far East, he voiced the opinion that "There isn't a doubt in my mind that Russia intends an invasion of Turkey and the seizure of the Black Sea Straits to the Mediterranean. Unless Russia is faced with an iron fist and strong language another war is in the making. Only one language do they understand—'how many divisions have you?'" Truman considered the specific case of aggression against Iran "another outrage" and felt "we should let our position on Iran be known in no uncertain terms . . . I do not think we should play compromise any longer"8

If Truman considered Russian activities in Iran in November-December, 1945, an "outrage," he must have been infuriated after

March 2, 1946, when the Russian design became more clearly aggressive. Instead of showing concern however, Truman was publically serene and confident.

His press conference remarks reveal surprising poise:

(Press conference of March 8, 1946)
Q. Mr. President, do you have any plans, if Russia declines to withdraw from Iran?
The President. That is a matter that will be handled when it comes up.
Q. If Russia refuses to withdraw, Mr. President, do you think that that means that the United Nations Organization is likely to collapse?
The President. No, I do not. The United Nations Organization is not going to collapse. We are not going to let it collapse.
Q. Do you mean, sir, then, that you favor the other nations going ahead with it, even if Russia insists or persists going down a one-way street on these matters?
The President. I don't think Russia is going to go down a one-way street.

(Press conference of March 14, 1946)
Q. Specifically, Mr. President, could you say whether you think the situation is as fraught with danger as a great many people think it is?
The President. I do not think it is.
* * *
Q. Well, are you optimistic that we will work out of this?
The President. I am sure we will work out of it.

How can we account for the President's confident attitude when practically everyone else believed we were in a major crisis? Harry Truman prided himself in making decisions and then sticking to them. For him a crisis was resolved when his decision was made—even though the most dangerous moments lay ahead. We know that Truman had long pondered the Iranian question, that many months in advance he could envisage the nature of the crisis, and that he had resolved to oppose the Russians firmly. The available public evidence suggests that Truman's decision was something like the following plan.

The Iranian complaint would be taken to the United Nations Security Council (on March 14, 1946 the U. S. announced its intention to take the Iranian case before the Council even if Iran—

having been intimidated—did not). The United States with the assistance of Britain and other friendly nations, would then see that the matter was considered, ignoring any Soviet veto (as it was ignored) against putting the matter on the agenda. The council would make a finding of aggression by majority vote—again ignoring the protests of the Soviet Union and any other country (Poland). Then the Security Council, that is, the United States and Great Britain, would implement the UN decision ("We are not going to let it collapse").

The allies would probably land troops in Iran and proceed to confront the Russians. If they did not withdraw, combat might eventually begin. Of course, the Soviets would have a comfortable superiority in ground forces, but the United States had the atomic bomb. The bomb had been used twice less than a year previously; there was no tradition against its use. The Soviet Union could expect, therefore, that if a ground battle went poorly for the Americans, the A-bomb might soon be used against it. Once the United States was engaged in a war with the Soviet Union, we might be expected to force a Russian retreat everywhere. Poland, East Germany, Austria, Bulgaria, Romania, Korea . . . Indeed, Stalin might have believed that the Western "capitalists" would want to obliterate communism in Russia.

Did the Russians perceive this threat voiced through public, and we suppose, private channels? There are many indications that they did. The reaction to Churchill's speech began in a low key, with *Pravda* making the perfunctory announcement of the speech and noting that it was unkind to the Soviet Union. But after a few days passed and the Soviet hierarchy had had time to assimilate the speech, the response grew fierce. On March 11, *Pravda* ran a long editorial (which appeared throughout Russia and was broadcast four times in Russian and four times in English) scoring Churchill's speech: Churchill "urges a new war and a war against the Soviet Union." [9]

On March 13, Stalin himself gave a long public interview attacking Churchill:

> In substance, Mr. Churchill now stands in the position of a firebrand of war. And Mr. Churchill is not alone here. He has friends not only in England but also in the United States of America.
>
> In this respect, one is reminded remarkably of Hitler and his friends.

As suggested above, the Russians did fear a "capitalist" attempt to destroy "socialism." Stalin recalled the post-World War I Allied action in Russia and insisted "they will be beaten, just as they were beaten twenty-six years ago."[10]

Although American public officials never mentioned the atomic bomb, the communists apparently believed we might use it. Writing in *Izvestia* on March 12, Soviet columnist Eugene Tarle said that Churchill was threatening Russia "with the latest forms of military weapons."[11]

The communist party line soon included "atomic diplomacy" as a standard phrase. On March 30, 1946, after the U. S. had ignored Gromyko's protests in the UN against hearing the Iranian case, the New York *Daily Worker* called the American posture "an exhibition of American atom bomb diplomacy."[12] Alexander Leontiev, Soviet lecturer, in a speech later published in *Pravda* said that "certain quarters in the United States were still attempting to employ 'atomic diplomacy' to bend the world to American will." Leontiev complained that "a war of nerves was being directed against the Soviet Union."[13]

And indeed it was!

Since the United States was using United Nations machinery to create a popular rationale for intervention in Iran, the Soviet Union became quite anxious to influence that body. Truman had a steamroller going against the Russians; they desperately tried to deflect it. They attempted to keep Iran from protesting; they attempted to veto the discussion of the case; they let it be known that even though Gromyko had walked out of the session of March 27, they were still very much in the United Nations. Obviously, it would have played into Truman's hands to retire from the UN. The Security Council's finding of aggression would be made that much more easily. The Russian's only chance was to remain in the UN and hope that its veto might be respected—or at least that it could delay or confuse the issue. In a move designed to keep them squarely in the United Nations, the Soviet Union paid, on March 31, 1946 (three days after the Gromyko walkout), its entire UN quota of $1,723,000. No other nation, including the United States, had yet made its full contribution.[14]

Truman kept the pressure on, however, refusing to yield to a Soviet request to postpone the Security Council deliberations from April 3 to April 10 and refusing to respect the Soviet veto. The

Russian position crumbled. To forestall a possible adverse Security Council decision on April 3, the Russians announced that they were willing to withdraw. Reports that they were withdrawing were received on April 1. When the Security Council met on April 3, the Russians were completely routed, and the matter was set aside to see if the Russians would follow through.

Some newspapers hailed the Russian withdrawal as a victory for the United Nations, but only in a limited sense was this so. The UN provided a means of slowly tightening the screws on the Russians, enabling them to see clearly the course of events if they did not yield. Without the Security Council deliberations—leading clearly to a dangerous conclusion for the Russians—the United States would have had to take sudden, direct action to convince the Russians we meant business. Also, the UN provided a better basis for eventual American action—and hence, a more plausible threat. Domestically, it would have been difficult to jump directly into action against the Russians; "saving the United Nations" would be a much more popular rationale.

But the backbone of this victory was the American and British willingness to press the matter through the United Nations and their apparent willingness to mobilize force against Russia when the Security Council made its eventual finding of aggression. Without this determination, without this veiled threat to use force, the activities of the Security Council would have been fruitless and the UN would have been a sham.

Ironically, many of the same Westerners who criticized Churchill's "Iron Curtain" speech as provocative and warlike, hailed the withdrawal of Russian troops from Iran as a wonderful UN victory. One writer, who charges Churchill with fostering the Cold War, saw the Iranian episode as "A real victory for the position of small nations in the United nations . . . "[15] But it was Churchill's speech, perhaps more than any other communication, that assisted us in frightening the Russians out of Iran. It contained a threat of war; and naturally the Russians were displeased and upset. That is why it was effective.

Apparently, many individuals were ready to embrace the victory but unwilling or unable to recognize how that victory was accomplished. The Iranian episode was explained by empty phrases which hid the reality: "victory for the United Nations. . . . ," "diplomatic pressures," "pressure of world opinion" and " . . .

moral power prevailed." Such confusion is unhealthy for a democratic people who must sustain an intelligent foreign policy. The
Russians withdrew from Iran because they thought there was a
chance that they would become embroiled in a war with us if they
did not, and they did not want to fight—not for Iran, anyway. Azerbaijan and Iran itself are not in communist hands today because
Harry Truman threatened the Russians with a process leading
toward a war. The war did not take place because the Russians
believed the threat.

Laotian Neutrality

To those Americans who know what and where it is, the little
Southeast Asian kingdom of Laos is improbable. That this backward, landlocked nation should exist at all is itself surprising.
The sprawling mountainous territory, the lack of communication
and transportation, the many isolated tribal villages: Laos, surrounded by six other countries, seems more of a residue than a nation. Its warring, shifting political factions perplex the distant
observer; the survival of its monarchy provokes amazement. Most
improbable of all, however, is that in 1969 Laos was not in communist hands. Few Americans would have dared predict such an
outcome in the dark days of 1961.

The immediate communist threat to Laos came from the Pathet
Lao guerrillas who had regrouped in the northeastern region of
the country following the 1954 Geneva Accords. In late 1960,
after several years of quiescence, the Pathet Lao, (perhaps
encouraged by the turbulent Laotian political scene) began a movement of conquest. By early 1961, they had overrun about two-thirds
of the territory of Laos, although they had not captured the royal
city of Luang Prabang or the capital, Vientiane. The Pathet Lao
received arms, supplies, and men from North Vietnam and assistance from the Russians—who, between December, 1960 and
March, 1961, made about 1,000 flights airlifting supplies to the
Pathet Lao. The Royal Lao army proved itself singularly unable
to halt the communist advance.

By March, 1961, President Kennedy faced, therefore, the real
possibility that the communists would be victorious in the then
SEATO-protected Laos unless we did something to stop them.

Having concluded that he could not allow our threat to defend Laos to be freely and dramatically flouted, Kennedy had a choice: to intervene with American troops or to threaten to intervene. He chose the latter.

In one respect, Kennedy's policy toward Laos was a special one. He did not feel the American threat to defend Laos was a wise one, and he did not believe that keeping Laos out of communist hands was worth an American war. As I shall point out in the next chapter, Kennedy sought to retreat from Laos. But he realized that he could not permit an immediate, full-scale communist victory; it would damage too severely the credibility of American threats.

Kennedy threatened the communists with American intervention if they attempted an immediate victory; he induced them to postpone an immediate attempt for a later attempt which would probably incur much lower risks of American involvement. It is important to recognize this point because had Kennedy merely threatened American intervention without implicitly suggesting that the United States would not prevent a later, less dramatic victory, it is improbable that the communists would have ceased fighting. They could reasonably believe that even if we came in we would eventually withdraw, finding ourselves greatly frustrated in an anti-guerrilla campaign waged under such unfavorable conditions.

The Laotian arrangement, then, embodied this bargain: the United States would implicitly recognize the gains already made by the Pathet Lao, if they would refrain from an immediate victory. This bargain was confirmed in our willingness to sign the neutralization agreement while the communists continued to hold their newly-won territory and by our abrogation of the SEATO commitment to Laos. The rest of the neutralization agreement was largely diplomatic static: the tri-partite Laotian government, the "withdrawal of foreign troops," the non-use of Laos as a supply route, and the International Control Commission. As expected, all these other arrangements broke down almost immediately after the agreement was signed in July, 1962.

In order to make the communists forego attempting an immediate victory, however, they had to believe that the United States would intervene to prevent it. They had to believe that Kennedy *was* willing to fight a massive anti-guerrilla war in Southeast

Asia. In his press conference of March 15, 1961, Kennedy cautiously voiced his intentions:

> We are determined to support the government and the people of Laos in resisting this attempt [by the communists to capture the country].

At first, the communists were uninterested in Kennedy's call for a cease-fire and a conference. On March 18, U. S. Secretary of State, Dean Rusk, met with Soviet Foreign Minister Gromyko to urge the Russians to support a cease-fire—with no apparent success. In Laos, the fighting continued with the communists making more gains. In his press conference of March 23, 1961, Kennedy expressed the American intention more firmly in a formal statement. He classified Laos as a "grave problem"; he pointed to our SEATO treaty commitment and argued that the safety of Laos "runs with the safety of us all." "No one should doubt our resolutions on this point," he said. Prior to the press conference, Kennedy had ordered the Seventh Fleet into the South China Sea and put certain Marine units on alert. These movements were leaked and a reporter publicly noted them at the conference.

On March 26, Kennedy met with British Prime Minister Macmillan in Bermuda to garner a pledge of British military support if the U.S. had to intervene to stop the communist advance in Laos. Their joint statement noted:

> They agree that the situation in Laos cannot be allowed to deteriorate.

A meeting of SEATO was called for March 27-29, 1961, to consider the communist thrust in Laos. The communique issued on March 30 was somewhat vague since some SEATO nations, particularly France, were unwilling to make any contribution to the defense of Laos:

> If [the present efforts for a cessation of hostilities] . . . fail, however, and there continues to be an active military attempt to obtain control of Laos, members of SEATO are prepared, within the terms of the treaty, to take whatever action may be appropriate in the circumstances.

The American interpretation of this statement was, given the context, quite firm. "Read the resolution over thoughtfully," Secretary of State Rusk told a reporter, "and you'll find that it contains all that is necessary."[16]

The Russians began to react favorably as the threat of American intervention became real. On March 24, a communication came from Gromyko through Stevenson that Moscow was interested in a cease-fire.[17] On April 1, the Russians sent a note to the British, who had been pressing them for an agreement to a cease-fire conference, announcing that they were "positively disposed to the proposal that the two chairmen of the Geneva Conference [the UK and USSR] appeal for a cease-fire in Laos."

But the fighting in Laos continued, and the Russians delayed actually appealing for a cease-fire. On April 20, Kennedy converted the military advisors in Laos into a formal Military Assistance and Advisory Group, wearing uniforms, thus suggesting a first phase of a U.S. military presence.[18] On April 24, the Russians finally issued, with the British, a joint appeal for a cease-fire in Laos. In Laos itself, a cease-fire was arranged early in May.

The truce was an uneasy one, occasionally broken by minor Pathet Lao advances. But additional American verbal warnings and suggestive military alerts managed to discourage major campaigns. Finally, at Geneva on July 23, 1962, the 17-nation agreement on Laotian neutrality was signed. The formal agreement altered the basic facts of the situation very little. The United States, although exempting Laos from SEATO, still cast a threat. Obviously we could not allow the "neutrality" of Laos, which we had so industriously negotiated and assured, to collapse immediately. So the uneasy stand-off continued. One writer summarized the situation at the end of 1963:

> Any time the Pathet Lao and their Viet Minh backers want to pick up the remnant bits and pieces of the country, they can be on the Mekong River in a week or less. They are deterred not by Phoumi's 50,000-man anti-Communist army, or by the no-longer neutral forces led by General Kong Le, but by fear of what Washington's reaction would be if they were to put the knife to the remaining and sadly frayed threads of pretense and policy still holding the Geneva Agreement and Laos together.[19]

What, then, did we achieve in Laos? A temporary halt in the communist drive to capture the country. There can be little doubt

about how we achieved this end. Observers agree that the Pathet
Lao and North Vietnamese forces could have taken the country in
those critical years, 1961-62, and would have except for the threat
of American intervention.[20]

There is often wisdom, however, in delaying an enemy even
when you may be prepared to concede his eventual victory. Circumstances may change. Although the cease-fire and neutralization arrangements seemed to provide only a temporary check upon
the communist advance in Laos, the stalemate has been considerably prolonged.

The most important alteration in the context was the massive
American involvement in Vietnam. Aside from causing North Vietnam to direct her resources away from the Pathet Lao, our whole-
hearted intervention gave the American threat a new reality in the
entire area. We were obviously ready, willing, and able to fight a
guerrilla war in Southeast Asia. The Pathet Lao and the North
Vietnamese probably feared that we could be provoked into including Laos and its bothersome Ho Chi Minh trail into our campaign.

At the same time, the Pathet Lao suffered a certain decline in
numbers and morale. Laotian government forces, on the other
hand, grew stronger. After the communists withdrew from the
Laotian government coalition, the "rightists" and "leftists" drifted
together into a general anti-communist position. The United States
has given substantial aid to the government and its armed forces, as
well as to the Meo tribesmen who, having been deprived of their
land by the Pathet Lao, harass the communists with some vigor.

The eventual outcome in Laos is, of course, still in doubt. It
appears that the Pathet Lao alone would be unable to conquer the
country in the near future. But if they get substantial assistance
from North Vietnam, which has long expressed an interest in a
communist victory, they could present a substantial danger.

Whether North Vietnam supports the conquest of Laos will depend, of course, on many considerations. Important among these
will be North Vietnamese expectations about the reaction of the
United States and U.S.-supported allies to such a move. Hope-
fully, the allied action in South Vietnam has made North Vietnam
sufficiently cautious about pushing for the conquest of its neighbors
to inhibit an all-out attack on Laos.

At least it can be said that had the United States withdrawn in
defeat from South Vietnam, Laos would have had scarcely a prayer,

for there would have been nothing for the North Vietnamese to be cautious about.

The Cuban Missile Crisis

There exists perhaps no clearer illustration of an international threat at work than the Cuban missile crisis of October, 1962. In contrast to the Iranian and Laotian episodes where the threat of force was hidden behind a great facade of diplomatic interaction, the missile crisis was unvarnished and uncomplicated. The man in the street could grasp what had happened: the Soviet Union sought to place missiles in Cuba; the United States threatened the Russians with a small war which might have grown hotter; they were sufficiently frightened to dismantle the bases and ship the missiles back to Russia.

Events in the missile crisis unfolded rapidly. The United States had considered the possibility that Russia might introduce missiles into Cuba to complement its massive military assistance program. To inhibit the Russians from taking such a step, President Kennedy explicitly warned the Russians in a public statement issued on September 4, 1962, that if offensive ground-to-ground missiles were placed in Cuba, "the gravest issues would arise." In his press conference of September 13, 1962, the President made his point again:

> . . . if Cuba should ever . . . become an offensive military base of significant capacity for the Soviet Union, then this country will do whatever must be done to protect its own security and that of its allies.

The Russians had certainly heard our position, for they insisted many times that they had not and would not place missiles in Cuba.[21]

On October 15, 1962, we learned the Russians *had* begun to station medium range missiles in Cuba. They had disregarded our threat. The missile crisis was on.

There was general agreement in the administration that the missiles must be removed. Without attempting to document why policy-makers came to this conclusion, I might mention several reasons which made it the correct policy. Of overwhelming importance was the issue of American determination. If we failed to respond to this thrust, both the communists and our allies might come to doubt our lack of determination to a dangerous degree. Under Kennedy, as I will attempt to show later, the American reputation for action had already suffered a dangerous decline. Not to respond to this new Russian thrust in Cuba might convince the Russians that we were too frightened or too complacent to meet future challenges. To leave our enemies with this belief would measurably increase the dangers of aggression around the world.

There were also direct practical reasons for insisting upon the removal of missiles from Cuba. They would give the Soviet Union a substantial increment in first-strike nuclear capability which would otherwise have cost them billions of dollars. The presence of missiles in Cuba would have a dangerously unsettling effect upon American policy-makers and the American electorate. The missiles were in the hands of the Russians, but who could guarantee that Castro might not suddenly seize, or be given, them and use them recklessly?

The missiles would greatly complicate hemispheric defense problems. Without missiles Castro would move cautiously in his designs on neighboring countries. He would live under the threat that the United States would defeat any invasion he launched against a Carribbean nation and possibly invade Cuba. But defended by atomic missiles, Castro would have no fear of invasion and might even threaten to use the missiles if we interfered with his aggressive designs.

Finally, the missiles would make it nearly impossible for Cuba to slip out of communist hands. While the United States would accept the communist regime in Cuba, we did not consider Cuba within the Russian defense orbit. We wanted to protect an Hungarian-type revolution from Russian suppression. With missiles present in Cuba, the United States would be reluctant to lift a finger to protect an anti-communist revolution. And in a few days the Russians could fly in enough troops to crush it.

To remove the missiles by force, the United States would have had to take costly, and possibly dangerous actions. At a minimum, we would have had to bomb all the missile sites, including the Russians at the sites. If we failed to knock out all the missiles, retaliation might follow. Or, even if we succeeded, the Russians or the Cubans might react in anger in a way which would require further response from us.

To threaten the Russians, however, was more difficult than otherwise might have been the case. We had already employed verbal communications which the Russians had disregarded. It was reasonable to suppose that further messages expressing "alarm" or "grave concern" would be equally ineffective. Probably even a threatened deadline would have been inadequate to convince the Russians we meant business. The credibility of our verbal messages had sunk too low.

Our threat, then, had to be communicated by more than words. To bolster our demand for the removal of the missiles, President Kennedy adopted display-of-force communications: the naval quarantine of Cuba and the mobilization of U.S. troops and air forces in the Southeastern United States. We were prepared for an invasion of Cuba.

The quarantine was not, in itself, a way to remove the missiles —or even prevent their further introduction. Additional parts of warheads could have been flown to Cuba by plane or transported by submarine. Instead, the blockade was a signal of our willingness to confront the Soviets with force. It displayed determination. It startled the Russians into taking Kennedy's verbal message of October 22, 1962, seriously and, combined with the mobilization of troops, convinced the Russians that they had only a few days to re-move the missiles before we would act. In a television interview on December 17, 1962, Kennedy explained the nature of the threat:

> . . . we were starting in a sense at a minimum place.
> Then if that were unsuccessful, we could have gradually
> stepped it up until we had gone into a much more massive
> action, which might have become necessary if the first step
> had been unsuccessful.

As we remember so clearly, the Russians caved in under this threat, tore up the bases and shipped the missiles back to Russia. Although a certain facade of give-and-take bargaining was main-tained, the Russians, in fact, obtained nothing. The pledge never to invade Cuba they had requested was not given; we declared that we had not obtained the inspection guarantees we demanded. In-deed, in a statement on November 20, 1962, winding up the crisis, Kennedy reaffirmed "our purpose and hope that the Cuban people shall some day be truly free."

An interesting sidelight of the missile crisis involved the removal of the 42 IL-28 bombers which the Russians had given Castro. Compared to the coercive value of missiles, the symbolic and strategic value of these weapons to Cuba was slight. In his television declaration of October 22 announcing the missile crisis, Kennedy mentioned the bombers only once, in passing. The entire presentation centered on the missiles: the word "missile" appears 16 times in the text.

It seems probable that had the dispute been negotiated in a package deal at the moment of the crisis, Kennedy would have settled for removal of the missiles and allowed Castro to keep his IL-28's. In those first days, Kennedy was probably as frightened as Khrushchev about the consequences of a confrontation. No such package deal was possible, however. Under imminent threat of an American attack on Cuba, Khrushchev announced the withdrawal of missiles six days after Kennedy's October 22 statement.

Then negotiations on the removal of the bombers began. The quarantine was maintained, the U.S. Armed Forces remained on the alert. Finally, on November 20, Khrushchev and Castro gave in, agreeing to remove the bombers. It seems quite likely that, at this point, Kennedy was only bluffing. Did he intend to bomb or invade Cuba for the IL-28's? They were not worth it. Had Khrushchev delayed several more weeks, Kennedy, feigning preparations for an invasion but never carrying out his threat, would have begun to look foolish and weak.

Kennedy's view of things was apparently different. Although he had clearly been most wary of the Soviets during the preceding two years, he now had new insight: he could intimidate *them*. On October 26, Khrushchev had sent Kennedy a rambling letter containing overtones of fright and panic, and he had hastily destroyed the missile sites several days later. Perhaps surprised at the efficacy of his threat in intimidating the Russians, Kennedy apparently decided to press harder than he had originally intended. Certainly in threatening war over the bombers, it seems he was pressing harder than was prudent.

We have, therefore, a limited illustration of the exhilaration effect noted earlier: when an enemy shows fear or incapacity, one grows more confident and more demanding. Kennedy, who had already achieved a satisfactory settlement from the American point of view, risked the future credibility of American threats, or possible hostilities, for a little more.

The Cuban missile crisis, while it illustrates the efficacy of a threat, demonstrates even more dramatically the terrible dangers which result from unheeded threats. The missile crisis brought us closer to nuclear war than we had been for a decade. And it came about because the Russians *did not believe that we would act* if they placed missiles in Cuba. They miscalculated; when they learned we *would* act, they retreated. Obviously, then, if they had believed us from the first, no missile crisis would ever have taken place.

Fortunately, in this particular case, it was possible to teach the Russians they had mistaken our intentions without waging a war. Next time we may not be so lucky.

The Unseen Effects of Threat

These three examples, diverse as they are, illustrate only one application of American threats in influencing the behavior of hostile nations. Our opponents had made a more or less public decision and then changed their minds in response to our threat. Much more frequent, although less dramatic and often impossible to identify, are the decisions which our opponents never take because they fear our reaction. There are simply dozens of techniques for aggression and our opponents would probably wish to try them out on scores of countries: nuclear blackmail of Japan by China; a sea invasion of the Dominican Republic by Cuba; a coastal blockade of South Korea by China and the North Koreans; a land and air blockade of Berlin by the Russians; and, of course, familiar invasion, infiltration and subversion techniques.

If the United States should suddenly sink into the sea, there is little doubt that many communist countries would get around to testing these techniques on their neighbors. Perhaps not immediately, but eventually. But the United States exists and is powerful and makes threats. These threats cause communist decision-makers to shelve aggressive plans as "dangerous and absurd." In this way, we are preventing aggression and avoiding wars in many places around the world without the general public ever realizing it.

If, as time goes on, we continue to sustain our threats with firmness and clarity, we may reach the point when at least some aggressive actions will be so preposterously dangerous as to pass from the scope of realistic calculations. If every Russian learns, from his high school days, that aggression in Europe is impos-

sibly risky and therefore unthinkable, then perhaps some real possibilities for enduring peace in that area would exist.

Another unseen effect of our threats concerns the decisions of
our allies and neutral countries. Our threat to oppose communist
aggression encourages them to divert their resources away from
the military sphere and into productive activities. Instead of each
country, from Ecuador to Italy, attempting to maintain a military
establishment large enough to meaningfully deter the communists,
they trust us (often without realizing it) to keep the world safe for
them. If we betray this trust, one of the first things that is likely to
happen is the spread of nuclear weapons. Nations, realizing that
they live in a ruthless and disordered world, will each seek the
means to defend themselves.

Chapter 3

HOW A THREAT FAILS

To threaten is to cause your adversary to believe that under certain circumstances you will act against him. It is therefore misleading to call the verbal announcement of one's intentions a threat.

When one first encounters the threat principle in international relations, there is a temptation to apply it in a simple and straightforward manner. Let us send letters, one might advise, to Mao and the rest, telling them exactly what they can have and what they cannot have, what we will fight a war over and what we will not fight a war over. Once these letters are duly posted, the Cold War will have been settled in a peaceable and business-like way.

As with almost all simple solutions to difficult problems, it has been tried and found wanting. We have done more than send letters. We have devised lengthy documents on weighty vellum, plastered with seals and ribbons and signed with golden pens by important government officials. And yet attempts at aggression continue. The UN charter threatens action against aggression, still the North Koreans did not believe it in 1950. SEATO threatened American action in Laos but the communists doubted it in 1961. SEATO threatened U.S. action in South Vietnam but the communists did not heed it. NATO promises a war over West Berlin, yet the Russians have nibbled and thrust there.

One need not look far to understand why words alone are inadequate to establish credible threats among nations. Words are cheap; the actions they threaten are enormously expensive. When actually faced with the possibility of war, nations are so inclined to reinterpret, slither out of, or forget their earlier pronouncements, that words alone cannot coerce. Notice, for example, the many

proofs and briefs that have been offered to demonstrate that neither
SEATO nor the UN charter required our presence in Vietnam.
Had we lacked the determination to stay there, we could easily
have reinterpreted the letter of our pledge to fight.

Words, then, are not threats. A threat is the enemy's *belief*
that you have the will and capability to fight a war with him in
designated circumstances. Making an enemy believe this is a task
demanding considerable insight, skill and courage.

Capability and will: these are requisites for any threat. The
antagonist must believe you are able to act and have the determination to act. It is immediately apparent that capability is, in large
part, a function of will. The more desperate a nation is, the more
money and men it will allocate to war. Nations which have very
little resources may, under certain conditions, have greater capabilities than far richer nations because they are more willing to
sustain sacrifices. Wealthy nations may have great potential capabilities but, lacking determination, they may mobilize only a small
fraction of their resources for war. For this reason, many of the
extensive calculations made by planners about the size and strength
of military forces and the costs of different kinds of engagements
tell us little about who will fight which war and who will win it.
They do not include the vitally important dimension of determination.

Capabilities are important, however, because they affect what
a nation with a given level of willpower can do. Having a high
capability makes it possible to fight (and therefore credibly
threaten) a war even when one's level of determination is low. But,
as the Vietnam involvement so clearly demonstrates, the American
willingness to fight the wars it has threatened is always an uncertain quantity. We have the capability to fight Vietnam-type
wars anywhere on earth with comparatively modest sacrifices. Indeed, we could fight two or three more such wars at the same time
and still not make the sacrifices we sustained in World War II.
But are we willing to make even small sacrifices to carry out our
threats? Will we make any sacrifices? We can go all the way. We
can run any risks and accept any costs. But what risks and what
costs will we, in fact, accept?

Everyone can see that, at one extreme, we are firmly determined to protect United States territory. At the other extreme, it is
clear that we are not willing to land American troops in Laos to

defend one isolated village from the Pathet Lao. But when will we land troops? If two villages are threatened? Ten or one hundred villages? All around the world our threats are subject to this scrutiny: what risks and sacrifices will we accept to prevent how much aggression and where? How determined are we?

Obviously, we would like our enemies and allies to believe we are implacably determined. How can we show our determination?

The formal pronouncements of the administration and treaties are one way to demonstrate our intentions. If the United States has a reputation for carrying out its announced intentions in almost every case, then a public statement of intention will have considerable force. The mobilization of troops also displays a willingness to act. And so does stationing these troops in areas likely to be attacked. The opinions of Congressmen and newspapers can reflect our willingness to carry out threats. Public opinion polls and electoral results are also relevant because, after all, it is the American electorate which will sustain or reject a war.

Although all these things affect the coerciveness of our threats abroad, none has the decisive impact given by our past sacrifices—or our failure to make sacrifices. Nations have broken defense treaties; indeed, we abrogated our SEATO commitment to Laos rather than face war in 1961-62. Executive pronouncements have been forgotten. And, in any case, they are numerous and laden with stock cliché's and ambiguities; the enemy discounts them heavily. Stationing troops does not necessarily indicate sticking power; they may be withdrawn prior to hostilities. So many politicians and newspapers saying so. many different things puzzle an enemy. Public opinion is diffuse and volatile; it is often difficult to know precisely how it will react to a future war and what effect this reaction would have on policy.

The communist decision-makers interpret our statements, our troop movements, our politicians, and our public opinion through their ideological lenses and from a position of considerable distance. It seems almost certain that they have found themselves mistaken so often in their predictions of future American policy based upon domestic political data (as in our wholly unexpected response in Korea) that they are hesitant to rely too heavily on their analyses. Consequently, our past and present actions constitute their primary guide to the meaning of our treaties, our statements and our public opinion.

Unfortunately the past is continually renewing itself. Obviously, our opponents want to know what *this* American president will do *this* year about *these* particular confrontations. They will look to the immediate past record of the administration for indications. Although sacrifices we have made in the past will contribute to the coerciveness of our threats, our opponents realize as well as we do that one president can be determined, another less so. At one time, our nation may be robustly confident, at another, confused and uncertain. For this reason the American reputation is always being tested, and we must make constant efforts to protect it. Our reputation ebbs and flows depending on the sacrifices we have recently made—or failed to make—in support of our threats.

Why We Had a Missile Crisis

The dynamic nature of threat coerciveness can be illustrated in a study of the events which led to the Cuban missile crisis. It is generally conceded that Kennedy handled the missile crisis well. But why did we have a missile crisis at all? There is a tendency to blame the whole thing on Khrushchev, as a reckless, scheming communist leader. Perhaps he was from our point of view—as Mao, Ho Chi Minh, and Castro are reckless in our eyes. But Khrushchev was typical of the antagonists we have confronted and will confront again: men willing to take risks to advance the international position of their state and their doctrine. We must learn from confrontations with such leaders; we ought not to regard these men as simply abnormal.

The pertinent fact of the Cuban missile crisis was this: Khrushchev and his advisors did not believe our threat to act if they placed missiles in Cuba. The Russians had certainly heard us say we would not permit them to station missiles. There can be no doubt about that. And, by their subsequent retreat under an American threat of invasion, they showed that they did not seek a U.S. invasion of Cuba or a world war over placing missiles in Cuba. The Russians stationed missiles in Cuba because they thought they might be permitted to do so; they thought that Kennedy might not respond. *They did not believe our threat.* Since this fact could have had such deadly consequences, it is important that we seek an explanation for it.

An inspection of the events in the 18 months preceding the

missile crisis reveals how the Soviet Union may have come to doubt our word. On a number of occasions when our explicit or implicit threats were tested, our responses could be interpreted as displaying a lack of determination, a marked reluctance to accept the risks and sacrifices our threats entailed. The Russians did not miscalculate in Cuba; they drew a reasonable conclusion from our behavior.

1. On April 17, 1961, a group of about 1,200 Cuban exiles, picked, trained, and supplied by the United States government made the Bay of Pigs landing on Cuba. The attempt to overthrow Castro was unsuccessful; the invaders met with Castro's superior forces and, while the United States stood by refusing to use its own forces to support the invasion, the rebels were killed or captured.

The Bay of Pigs episode was unfortunate, not so much as an example of poor planning nor for its "interventionist" overtones. The misfortune of the Bay of Pigs was its damaging impact on the American reputation. Through its admitted complicity in planning the invasion, the United States demonstrated its strong desire to remove Castro. But by failing to support the invasion, Kennedy exhibited an unwillingness to accept the risks and sacrifices consistent with that objective.

Although this conclusion may have been unclear for most Americans, the Russians could hardly fail to reach it. When Hungary, in the Soviet orbit, went "free," Khrushchev sent Soviet forces to crush the revolution. Why, Khrushchev may have asked himself, did not the Americans do the same in Cuba? The U.S. role in the invasion indicated a clear desire to remove Castro, yet we allowed these "fighters for freedom" to die unsupported on the beaches. Why did the United States hesitate? When people manifestly *want* and they do not *take,* Khrushchev could have reasoned, they must fear something. Was the United States frightened of Castro? Hardly.

But we could have been frightened by the threat of a Soviet response. Earlier, Khrushchev had ambiguously threatened a response in defense of Cuba. On July 9, 1960, he said, ". . . we shall do everything to support Cuba and her courageous people in their struggle . . . " and "Figuratively speaking, if need be, Soviet artillerymen can support the Cuban people with their rocket fire, should the aggressive forces in the Pentagon dare to start intervention against Cuba."[1] The Russians, then, could reasonably conclude that we failed to support the invasion of Cuba partially because we feared a response from them.

But Cuba was not within the Soviet protective sphere, as was Hungary. Therefore, what appeared to be an implicit American recognition of a Soviet role as defender of Cuba represented a dramatic alteration of the status quo in favor of the Russians. Although we had not in fact recognized such an alteration (as the missile crisis later demonstrated), the Bay of Pigs suggested that we had.

The conclusion is not that Kennedy failed to support the invasion because *he* was afraid of the Russian reaction. It seems likely that he had other reasons for not acting, particularly his desire to avoid a nasty, Hungarian-type struggle to topple Castro. Nor can we say that he should have intervened despite this terrible cost. The point is simply that, in failing to act, Kennedy paid a heavy price. Perhaps avoiding a war in Cuba was worth it, but we should clearly understand what this price was: he left the Russians with the impression that if they threatened war, he would allow them to alter the status quo in their favor. And that is an extremely dangerous impression to leave with an enemy.

2. In the Bay of Pigs episode we demonstrated a lack of determination somewhat by accident; in Laos we really did lack determination. In the preceding chapter, I discussed the brave side of our Laotian involvement: Kennedy threatened war if the communists took everything, so they were deterred from trying to take everything. But there was a weak aspect to our policy in Laos which the communists did not fail to notice. Early in 1961 the communists made, as noted earlier, substantial advances in Laos —advances which Kennedy publicly recognized in his press conference of March 23, 1961. In 1954 Laos was included as a protocol state under the protective threat of SEATO. In 1961 the United States was still pledged to protect it. Yet Kennedy publicly noted the great gains the externally-supported Pathet Lao were making and did nothing to throw them back. Indeed, in his call for a conference and neutralization, he implicitly agreed to recognize the communist gains and withdraw SEATO protection from Laos. These concessions were imbedded in the Geneva agreement signed on July 23, 1962: the Pathet Lao kept what they had, and the United States struck Laos out of SEATO.

How credible, then, were our threats after the Laotian episode? We allowed the communists to capture half of the country and then did our best to slip out of the obligation "gracefully." The spirit of the SEATO treaty said that we would fight a war to defend Laos. But when called upon to make large sacrifices to back up our words, we retreated from our obligation. It does not necessarily follow that we should have fought a war to drive back the Pathet Lao-North Vietnamese forces. That issue cannot be decided here. There were obviously great risks. Indeed, the Vietnam war has brought home to us the full gravity of such risks. All I am attempting to show is that the costs of not acting were much larger than many people would at first suppose. These costs were not primarily the loss of Laotian territory, but rather a lower estimation in the eyes of both opponents and allies, of our determination to defend the American position. Since this lower estimation of our will would increase the probability of future enemy thrusts, confrontations and wars, it was a serious cost indeed.

In Laos, Kennedy demonstrated that American threats were uncertain, that the United States might compromise and, consequently, give things up rather than fight the war which its promises —even its most emphatic promises—implied. In his conversation with Khrushchev in Vienna (June, 1961), Kennedy unwisely revealed his true feelings about Laos to the Soviet leader:

> America wanted to reduce its involvement in Laos, Kennedy said, and he hoped the Soviet Union would wish to do the same.

* * *

> Kennedy responded that the commitments had been made before he became President; why they were undertaken was not an issue here. Whatever had happened in the past, the issue now was to decrease commitments on both sides and get a neutral and independent Laos. Krushchev doubted whether these commitments were altogether a legacy; after all, Kennedy had put the American military advisors into uniform and had ordered a landing of Marines.

* * *

> Kennedy said that he had been reluctant to send in the Marines.[2]

What may have seemed so reasonable and peace-like to Kennedy, however, could actually have been read as evidence of his lack of determination. How is an enemy to interpret your expressed desire to "reduce a commitment" to a nation under his gun? When the enemy has conquered two-thirds of this nation you have sworn to protect, when you publicly acknowledge this conquest and brand it as "aggression" but do nothing about it, and then announce a desire to reduce your involvement, what can it mean?

It is simply inaccurate, of course, to suggest that Kennedy was not familiar with the general idea of deterrence. It seems, however, that he had not fully grasped the implications of threats and what was demanded of him to make them credible. To some extent, he may have labored under the mechanical view of threats I noted previously. He imagined that he could remove this or that threat and have opponents believe that the others were still firm. It is possible, in certain cases, to cancel treaty commitments without such action being interpreted as a lack of determination. But when the countries involved are actually threatened, it is all but impossible to escape this interpretation. Kennedy was not breaching our commitments to Portugal, to Ecuador or to New Zealand. He was cancelling the U.S. commitment where we were being challenged to fight a war to honor it.

The communists could certainly interpret Laos as an American retreat:

> . . . the Laotian people, by persisting in struggle, frustrated U.S. aggression and intervention again and again.[3]
>
> The quenching of the flames of war in Laos, the formation of the Laotian Government of National Union and the re-establishment of the neutral status of Laos signify a big defeat for U.S. plots of aggression in Southeast Asia and a major setback for its policies of aggression and war.[4]

Although Kennedy may have believed that he was merely making a "sensible" readjustment of commitments, it is clear that this meant he was backing away from war.

> The President himself was reluctant to order a limited troop movement into the Mekong. He knew how weak the conventional strength of the United States was, and, with Cuba in the wings, troubles in Vietnam and the Congo and the ever-present problem of Berlin, he did not want to tie up armed force indefinitely in Laos.[5]

This comment also suggests that Kennedy (or perhaps only

the advisor who alleges it) had succumbed to the overcommitment fallacy. In essence, this fallacy arises from the failure to realize that power, that is, the coerciveness of one's threats, is a function of both military capabilities and the opponent's perception of your determination. By actually carrying out a threat in one place, one strengthens the integrity of other threats so that enemies hesitate to nibble. To fail to carry out a threat encourages more voracious bites elsewhere as opponents come to believe you have not the will to defend your position. Naturally, this argument assumes that one has military resources beyond those required for the action at hand. But certainly we had such resources in 1961 when one includes our standing reserves, the draft, our naval and air forces and, of course, our atomic arsenal.

It also seems that Kennedy had loosely accepted what I call in Chapter 5 the "strategic value theory" of American defense strategy. He was apparently inclined to evaluate the wisdom of a specific war on the basis of whether the country to be defended justified the American sacrifice. At first, this line of reasoning seems eminently practical: why fight a bloody, costly war to keep Laos, which has no significant military or economic potential, out of communist hands? The answer is that by retreating you show weakness. You give your enemies reason to believe that you will tolerate marginal advances rather than confront them. So naturally they are encouraged to make more and larger marginal advances.*

Kennedy's remark to Khrushchev at Vienna that he was not necessarily sympathetic to commitments made by the former ad-

---

*In his October 22, 1962 address on the missile crisis, Kennedy alluded to another principle which may have contributed to his overly tolerant attitude toward the advances of his opponents:

Our policy has been one of patience and restraint, as befits a peaceful and powerful nation, which leads a worldwide alliance. We have been determined not to be diverted from our central concerns by mere irritants and fanatics.

Unfortunately, a "fanatic" can undermine a threat as well as anyone else. Indeed, the first challenges to any deterrence system usually come from the more reckless actors. Once they demonstrate what it is possible to get away with, then the more "rational" actors follow. The first men to highjack planes to Cuba in the early 1960's may have been fanatics, but they demonstrated the feasibility of an act on which a veritable industry is now based.

Therefore, in deterrence matters, it becomes important to pay attention to and ensure the failure of those one considers "fanatics," to demonstrate that they are indeed fanatics with a profoundly mistaken view of what is acceptable and successful behavior.

ministration was unwise. The basic logic of deterrence requires that
threats be firm. To announce that every administration will disregard prior pledges at will plunges a deterrence strategy into
chaos. Enemies are tempted to start aggression all over again;
allies who have made sacrifices and taken risks to help you in the
expectation of future protection in return are thrown into confusion.

In the context, Kennedy's remark was particularly unwise
insofar as the example of Laos suggested the basis on which Kennedy would abrogate former commitments: whenever the commitments could be honored only at the cost of a war. Accordingly,
the Russians could conclude that the way to get the U.S. to retreat
from other commitments was to threaten war there, too.

Without realizing it, Kennedy had presented the Russians with
reason to believe that they could gain something from a thrust in
Berlin.

3. And they acted on this belief.

The best-known feature of the Soviet pressure on Berlin was
Khrushchev's threat to sign a separate peace treaty with East Germany and thus give the East Germans the handling of allied access
rights to Berlin. Khrushchev repeated this threat at the Vienna
conference, giving the allies until the end of 1961 to negotiate their
way out of Berlin. After such a treaty was signed, East Germany
would be in charge of the Berlin problem. It was assumed that East
Germany might then block allied access to West Berlin or even
invade it.

In fact, of course, the East Germans would face the same
problem as the Russians in trying to block access or invade: war
with the allies. Nevertheless, the Russian threat to sign a separate
peace treaty was, in view of East German Chancellor Ulbrict's
statements about dealing harshly with West Berlin when he was
given control, a veiled threat to allow war to be provoked over
Berlin. Khrushchev was threatening Kennedy with a risk of war
if the allies did not withdraw from Berlin.

The broad outlines of the episode in Berlin indicate a victory
for the United States. Our threat to face up to war over Berlin
was sufficiently credible to dissuade Khrushchev from taking any
drastic aggressive moves. On October 17, 1961, Khrushchev modified his threat to sign a separate peace treaty with the East Germans by the end of the year.

But Khrushchev's October 17 speech could scarcely be called an allied victory. Khrushchev repeated his demand that "A German peace treaty must and will be signed, with or without the Western powers." His relaxing of the deadline did not indicate a cessation of Russian pressures on Berlin, but a temporizing step designed to give the allies more time to find a way out of Berlin:

> The question of a time limit for the signing of a German peace treaty will not be so important if the Western powers show a readiness to settle the German problem.

In his policy toward Berlin, Khrushchev was attempting to corral the four Western allies into a withdrawal. But disagreements on how to "ease" the Berlin crisis among these allies—the U.S., U.K., France, and Germany—apparently prevented them from adopting a concerted position for retreat. Khrushchev still believed that the potential for retreat was there; he simply needed more time, more pulling and pushing to get the cattle into the stockade. Why did he hold this belief?

Behind the broad outlines of the Berlin crisis many events reflected poorly on the American determination to stay in Berlin under a threat of war. West Berlin is vulnerable to communist encroachments in dozens of ways. The arrangements for land access, air corridors and interzonal movement offer almost endless possibilities for marginal aggression by the communists. No particular thrust would seem to merit an allied response which could lead to war, but each time a thrust is left unanswered, established Soviet "rights" get larger. In declining to meet these aggressive moves, the United States would indicate its lack of determination, its unwillingness to risk war to prevent marginal alterations in the status quo.

During the Berlin crisis of 1961-62, the Soviet Union made a seemingly endless number of aggressive but marginal thrusts. Often we failed to react with necessary firmness.

One of the first indications of allied timidity concerned the proposed annual meeting of the West German Senate in West Berlin on June 16, 1961. The purpose of this meeting was of course, symbolic: to demonstrate a West German interest in Berlin. Such meetings had taken place annually since 1955, with the exception of 1960. But on June 8, 1961, shortly after the Kennedy-Khrushchev

Vienna conference, the Soviets protested this proposed meeting in a note given to the West Germans:

> The Soviet Government would like to stress that it cannot be indifferent to the new international provocation prepared by the Federal Republic of Germany in West Berlin.

The United States induced the West Germans to call off this meeting—which they did on June 11.[6]

This episode illustrates the pattern of American diplomacy in these years. At first it seems reasonable to relinquish such an insignificant privilege to avoid "provoking" the Russians. They were already rattling their sabres; there was no need to provide them with additional excuses for aggression. This plausible defense crumbles when stripped to essentials: we gave up something in return for nothing because we feared war. To provoke an enemy by taking away something that belongs to him is one thing. But if an enemy says he will be angry if you do not give him something that is yours, then he must be challenged. Otherwise, he learns that by huffing and puffing and threatening war you can be made to yield. So he may continue to huff and puff over bigger things.

If a nation's reputation is secure for other reasons, then certain minor concessions to an enemy may be permissible and desirable, if only to demonstrate that you will not be the aggressor. But in June, 1961, the international belief in the American determination to defend its interests had already been badly undermined by the Bay of Pigs, Laos, and our failure to respond adequately in Vietnam. In Berlin itself, we had just been confronted with a flagrantly aggressive ultimatum. If he wanted to head off increased Russian pressures on Berlin, Kennedy needed to show that he was determined, that he feared war no more than Khrushchev. He had to show that we would risk war to prevent marginal communist aggression. He should have strongly encouraged the West Germans to hold their Bundesrat meeting.

We recognized the closing of the East Berlin border and construction of the wall in August, 1961, as "a flagrant, and particularly serious, violation of the quadripartite status of Berlin" (U.S. note of August 17, 1961), but we continued our pleading for negotiations. A military response was not appropriate, for reasons given in the next chapter, but surely an emphatic end to all Western pleas for "negotiations" on Berlin was in order.

Following our failure to react to the wall, the Russians made more thrusts. On August 22 the East Germans closed many East-West checkpoints, tried to establish a prohibited zone 100 meters from the East-West boundary, and interfered greatly with American military access to East Berlin. On August 23, the Soviet Union demanded participation in the control of air corridors leading into West Berlin—a flagrantly aggressive demand.

These various demands and alterations in the status quo were not particularly significant in themselves; what was significant was the failure of the United States and its allies to respond with the necessary courage and indignation. Panic-stricken by the possibility of war over Berlin, they were apparently willing to suffer any indignity to preserve the possibility of "negotiations." The Soviet Union had behaved in a most aggressive, irresponsible and unscrupulous way. Yet we still sought "to ascertain if there exists a reasonable basis for negotiations with the Soviet Union" (Four-power communique, September 16, 1961).

In September, 1961, Kennedy sent General Lucius Clay as his personal ambassador to Berlin. Clay, highly respected by Berliners for his bold attitude toward communist encroachments during the 1948 Berlin crisis, was expected to react firmly to communist threats. With this appointment, then, Kennedy could signal our determination to stay in Berlin at all costs. But because Kennedy was not willing to take the risks which were necessary to demonstrate that determination, Clay's efforts were often undermined. One observer summed up the situation in April, 1962:

> The American government's determination to negotiate while deliberately avoiding a test of wills has paralyzed the defense of Berlin because it prevents the local command from countering each single threat quickly enough and adequately—if at all.

* * *

> This was the sense of what has been called Clay's "brinkmanship." He attempted to bring the full weight of allied political and strategic considerations to bear directly on Berlin and thus offset the natural tactical advantage of the Soviets and the political use they make of it. The attempt failed insofar as the allies themselves—including the Americans—became alarmed by General Clay's moves in Berlin and fell into anxious indecisiveness. [7]

The aggressive Soviet thrusts at Berlin continued to the end of 1961 and during most of 1962: buzzing of air corridors; dropping anti-radar chaff to confuse air guidance in the corridors; the elimination of several rail entry points into West Berlin. Our responses continued to be uneven: occasionally firm (and successful), but usually indecisive and weak. On August 22, 1962, at about the time the Soviet Union began its shipment of missiles to Cuba, the Russians closed their office of Commandant of East Berlin and turned his duties over to the East Germans. This move marked another attempt to shift responsibility for Berlin to the inflamatory East German Chancellor Ulbricht. Naturally we protested this provocative, unilateral alteration of existing practices; but we repeated our "proposal for a quadripartite meeting" with the Russians (U.S. note of August 24, 1962).

Oleg Penkovskiy gave the view of one, inside the Kremlin, sympathetic to the West:

> I always wonder: Why does the West trust Khrushchev? It is difficult to understand. We in the GRU [Soviet military intelligence] sit around, talk, and laugh: What fools, they believed us again! Of course, the West must talk with Khrushchev, but it must maintain a firm policy. Do not retreat a single step from a firm policy, let Khrushchev know that the time of listening to his military psychosis has come to an end. Under no circumstances give any concessions to Khrushchev. He only gains time and by this prolongs his existence. If the West again [referring to the Berlin Wall?] makes even the smallest concession to Khrushchev, he will scream loudly about his power and will proclaim to the entire world: "See how powerful I am," etc.[8]

One wonders what flagrantly aggressive and unreasonable acts would have convinced us that negotiations with the Russians were absurd, that they simply wanted to take what was ours by threatening war. Apparently we did not realize that our persistent plea for negotiations while under the Russian gun only communicated how frightened we were.

Can we blame DeGaulle, who was against negotiations in these circumstances, for wanting a nuclear force of his own after witnessing the American reluctance to meet firmly the threat of war which our European commitments entailed?

4. The challenge posed in South Vietnam resembled that of

Laos: local communist guerrillas with outside aid were becoming increasingly successful in their attempt to conquer the country. As in Laos, the United States had "threatened" to defend the country. South Vietnam was included as a protocol state in SEATO, we had given much economic and military assistance to the country, and U.S. advisors were there. Did these signals constitute a credible threat to defend South Vietnam? Not after Laos. In Laos, we had demonstrated that we were not willing to fight a big war for a small Southeast Asian country. We had indicated that SEATO, our solemn word, was expendable under pressure. We demonstrated that American aid did not signal a firm U.S. involvement; we showed that uniformed MAAG advisors could be withdrawn when the going got difficult.

How could the United States show that it really would honor its commitment to defend South Vietnam? How could we hope to convince opponents that we would not retreat under pressure again? By sending a large contingent of ground combat troops. It might not have worked, but it would at least have given us bargaining power for delaying or diverting the communist campaign. Our failure to send troops would indicate that Laos would be repeated, that the United States would eventually withdraw when the pressure mounted.

But Kennedy studiously refused to put in ground troops. In April-May, 1961, a task force and the Joint Chiefs of Staff recommended putting ground troops in South Vietnam. Kennedy rejected it. In October-November, 1961, with the guerrillas making steady progress, Kennedy again vetoed proposals for placing combat troops in Vietnam: "He was unwilling to commit American troops to fighting Asians on the Asian mainland for speculative psychological reasons."9

Kennedy's failure to respond forcefully enough in Vietnam at an early date, had several adverse consequences. It permitted the communists to make substantial headway so that when American troops became absolutely necessary to save South Vietnam, the job had become longer and bloodier. It encouraged the communists to conclude that their "people's war" tactic was really as invincible as Mao declared and, hence, could and should be practiced elsewhere.

Finally, it confirmed the impression Kennedy had given his enemies of an irresolute leader, of a leader unwilling to risk or fight wars to protect the position of the free world. In South Vietnam, the communists were making headway in a country the United States had pledged to defend; yet we took only half-hearted and inadequate measures to defend it. Could the communists fail to believe we would give up South Vietnam in the end?

5. During the period 1960-62, communist weapons had been shipped into Cuba. At first the build-up began cautiously as the Soviets tested our reaction. Experiencing none, the trickle of arms became a torrent by mid-1962. Somewhat alarmed, Kennedy issued a statement on September 4, 1962, noting that if Cuba should gain "significant offensive capability" then "the gravest issues would arise." Kennedy added:

> The Cuban question must be considered as a part of the world-wide challenge posed by Communist threats to the peace. It must be dealt with as a part of that larger issue as well as in the context of the special relationships which have long characterized the inter-American system.

In handling the arms build-up in Cuba, it seems that Kennedy allowed his words grossly to exceed his intentions. The above statement, for example, identifies Cuba as a serious challenge which must be "dealt with." But did Kennedy intend to do anything about it? At all events, he did nothing about it. Why, then, should he use such strong language?

The "significant offensive capability" phrase is perplexing. If Kennedy intended to act only if IRBM's were placed in Cuba (as apparently was his intention), then why not mention these and these alone? Perhaps Kennedy hoped that he could frighten the Russians out of sending any *more* SAM's, MIG's, or missile-carrying patrol boats. If this was what Kennedy had in mind, then he failed to perceive the low Russian opinion of his determination. Why, after Kennedy had shied away from war so many times, should the Russians read serious threats into his words? Words have coercive value only if similar words in the past have been followed by action. And Kennedy's reputation for action was not high. The Russians could trust him to under-react. And again they had confirmation for their belief. Cuba was armed to the teeth, as Kennedy admitted in his September 4 statement, and we had done nothing.

Kennedy also unwisely accepted the false distinction between offensive and defensive weapons. Any weapon can be used for either offense or defense, depending on the circumstances; therefore a distinction between them on this basis is untenable. To take an extreme example, Hitler's fortification of Germany's western frontier after 1936 was, at that time, an offensive move because it protected him against France while he carried out aggression against Czechoslovakia and Poland. No weapon, then, no matter how passive it may appear, can be categorically labeled "defensive."

What, then, were the Russians to conclude when they stuffed all sorts of potentially offensive weapons into Cuba—MIG jets, motor torpedo boats with ship-to-ship guided missiles, mortars, automatic weapons—which the United States doggedly insisted were not offensive weapons? That we did not care enough to take action and were excusing ourselves with the face-saving verbal device of "offensive and defensive weapons."

Follow Kennedy's announcement of American intentions given at a press conference on September 13, 1962:

> But let me make this clear once again: If at any time the Communist buildup in Cuba were to endanger or inter-fere with our security in any way, including our base at Guantanamo, our passage to the Panama canal, our missile and space activities at Cape Canaveral, or the lives of American citizens in this country, or if Cuba should ever attempt to export its aggressive purposes by force or the threat of force against any nation in this hemisphere, or become an offensive military base of significant capacity for the Soviet Union, then this coun-try will do whatever must be done to protect its own security and that of its allies.

But did not tanks and mortars given to Cuba endanger the security of Guantanamo? Did not the missile-carrying patrol boats endanger our passage to the Panama Canal? In his February 2, 1962 address to the nation about the Punta del Este conference, Secretary of State Dean Rusk declared that the Castro regime "used its embassies in Latin America as centers of espionage and subversion . . . " that it "sought to intimidate, subvert, and harass free governments and nations . . . " But six months later, Kennedy declared that "if Cuba should ever attempt to export its aggressive purposes . . . we will do whatever must be done . . . "

Cuba and the Russians had done just about everything Ken-nedy warned them not to do and we had not reacted. Once again, the American reputation suffered. We had made a threat, a sweeping and flamboyant threat, and failed to carry it out.

Again, let us not suppose that there was a simple response to this problem. Attacking Cuba in reaction to the arms build-up would have been a costly and distasteful step. And, on the other hand, Kennedy had to make some protest against the arming of Cuba or the Russians might conclude that we had no interest whatever in the matter. One can, of course, make suggestions: perhaps Kennedy should not have been so embarassingly frank and verbose in protesting the armaments; perhaps he could have engaged in a parallel American build-up in Guantanamo to demonstrate our concern. Our purpose is not to argue what could or should have been done, but simply to illustrate how, as events unfolded, our threat was impaired and to show the perilous consequences of this impairment.

It was, therefore, quite reasonable and natural that the Russians should have disregarded our threat to act if they placed missiles in Cuba. We had given them a two-year lesson: our words did not reflect our true intentions; we lacked the determination to oppose with force alterations in the status quo.

Charles Burton Marshall summed up our situation at the time of the missile crisis:

> We had bespoken determination over Laos, only to settle for the troika there. We had flinched on following through at the Bay of Pigs. The pattern of the call-up of reserves in mid-1961 had prefigured an addition of five or six divisions to our Army. After words of rage privately conveyed from Khrushchev, the plan had petered out. We had huffed and dawdled as a wall rose in Berlin.
> Admittedly, the problem of discoursing both to give pause to adversaries and to humor the timorous and uncommitted is not easy, but we had long overdone the latter aspect with maxims about no alternative to negotiation and about willingness ever to traverse another last mile in parleying—this last an invitation to adversaries to go on setting up mileposts along an interminable course.[10]

If anything was surprising about the missile crisis it was the Russian willingness to back down in the face of our second, blockade-mobilization threat. They had ample reason to believe that the American president was too irresolute to carry out his threat to invade Cuba. But, I believe we would have invaded and become involved in a bloody war.

This account of the prelude to the Cuban missile crisis illustrates the dynamic nature of threat credibility I discussed earlier. The American threat to oppose the aggression of its adversaries is not credible simply because we have signed it into a treaty. It is credible only if they are shown, by our recent sacrifices, that we have the determination to carry out our words.

What, we might ask, could Kennedy have done to maintain the American threat? The answer is simple but deeply unsettling: make sacrifices, take more risks. This is not to say Kennedy had to take the strongest response in every case. But he had to mix strong responses with the weak ones to avoid establishing a pattern of weakness. After the Bay of Pigs, he should have looked for an opportunity to reverse the image of American timidity. After the Bay of Pigs *and* Laos, he definitely needed a strong response. It is a great mistake to examine each confrontation as an isolated case. The statesman must see what kind of pattern he is projecting to his opponents. If he has shown a lack of determination earlier, then he must make a stronger response at the next opportunity.

Chapter 4

THE EXCITATION THEORY OF WAR AND THE STATUS QUO

Parents know how difficult it often is to determine blame between quarreling children. The original provocation seems lost in an apparently infinite regression of accusations. Each child claims, in turn, that he only reacted to the injury done by the other. The harassed parent probably concludes that both children are equally at fault, that the quarrel was mutually provoked. He threatens to deprive both of TV privileges if they fight again. They are sternly told that "It takes two to quarrel."

It is often thought that wars between nations take place in a fashion resembling the disputes of children. Neither belligerent is at fault; they drift into war through a process of mutual excitation. An original hostility over some ideological, racial, geographic or economic issue causes each nation to fear the other and suspect its every move. Stereotypes and irrational prejudices cause leaders on each side to "perceive" hostility where none exists and to exaggerate the evil intentions of the other. As each nation reacts to what it feels is a hostile act of the other, it, in turn, exacerbates the tension and mutual suspicion.

A verbal insult provokes a counter insult which causes the detention of an ambassador which leads to the shooting down of an airplane which provokes the rupture of diplomatic relations. The upward spiral of hostility continues toward war as each country reacts, perhaps for reasons of pride, perhaps to maintain its reputation for firmness and the credibility of its threats, to the successive affronts of the other. Newspapers inflame animosity on both sides. Public officials of each nation insist they will not supinely tolerate the provocations of their enemy. Each side suspects the other of making military preparations and begins mobilizing for war. Then, perhaps some careless soldier fires across a border, and war breaks out.

Briefly described, this is the "excitation" theory of war. Neither hostile nation may desire war, yet war may come about as each reacts to the apparent provocation of the other. Neither side specifically chooses war; it just happens. It is the cumulative result of successive misunderstandings.

Inspection of the rhetoric of world politics today—or at other times for that matter—lends support to the excitation theory. American leaders say they seek peace; the communist leaders equate "socialist" with "peace-loving." We accuse the communists of aggression in Vietnam; they accuse us of "imperialist aggression against the Vietnamese people." We say we are bombing North Vietnam in retaliation for Northern aggression in the South; the Russians send MIG fighters in retaliation for our bombing; we respond by bombing North Vietnamese airfields. Each side accuses the other of provoking wider conflict. If both sides are correct, then we are equally at fault. We are all caught in a semi-automatic process of mutual excitation.

If valid, the excitation theory of war would have profound implications for the management of foreign policy. The theory suggests that war is caused by the failure of one side to break the upward spiral of conflict. Therefore one side—that is, the United States—should allow apparent provocations to go unanswered. In this way, a reverse process of lowering tension will take place. If we do not provoke our enemies, they will relax their suspicions of us and will cease, in turn, to make such provocative moves toward us. The excitation theory advises us to *turn the other cheek* rather than respond firmly.

Communist China, for example, appears to be war-like and dangerous. The excitation theory suggests that the Chinese are belligerent because they are suspicious of *us*. They feel encircled and threatened. By signing collective defense treaties with neighboring nations, stationing the 7th fleet off China's shores, fighting in Vietnam, and opposing Red China's entrance into the United Nations, the United States is exciting the Chinese. We are confirming their suspicions of our hostile intentions. To reduce Chinese hostility, therefore, we should abrogate collective defense treaties, withdraw from Vietnam, bring China into the United Nations and the 7th fleet home.

Somehow this plan seems defective and unlikely to succeed. For something is missing in the excitation theory. Perhaps an extreme illustration will show what it is. Suppose the communist Chinese claim they are encircled because we have bases on Hawaii. They insist we are planning to launch an attack on them from Hawaii, that we are using the islands as a center for subversion and espionage. Red guards surge through Peking demanding the cessation of American imperialist aggression in Hawaii. They demand a withdrawal of all U.S. troops.

Are we exciting the Chinese? Should we withdraw and thereby put their minds at rest? Such advice clashes with common sense. The Chinese demand is flagrantly aggressive.

This illustration reveals what it is that the excitation theory ignores: between hostile nations there is a *mutually perceptible* distribution of rights over which war may be provoked. There is a conception of "ours" and "theirs," of "not ours" and "not theirs" which both sides can recognize. The excitation theory overlooks this fact. It assumes that hostile nations can see no lines, no boundaries separating what is theirs from what belongs to the opponent. Consequently, neither side ever really knows when it is provoking war. But such lines do exist and they make it almost impossible to drift inadvertently into war. Each side can see that attempting to take what belongs to the other would provoke or risk war.

When, in our illustration, China demands Hawaii, we know that they know Hawaii is *ours*. They are trying to take something away from us by the threat of force. If they attempt to invade Hawaii, they know they are risking war with us. They know that this invasion would be entirely different from calling us names and prophesying our destruction, or imprisoning an American newsman, or sending rice to Cuba. They know the former action risks war and the latter actions do not.

As an explanation for war, the excitation theory has a serious defect: *it cannot explain peace.* The world has always been copiously supplied with pairs of hostile nations, nations arming against each other, even hating each other. But most of these nations, for long periods of time, avoid war. France and Germany were profoundly hostile following the 1871 Franco-Prussian war. Yet they coexisted without war for 43 years. The United States had serious border disputes with Canada and her British protectors at several points in the last century (1837-40, 1844-46), but never was there a war. The Arab-Israeli conflict reflects an extremely hostile relationship. Nevertheless, periods of peace have separated the wars in that area: eight years (1948-56) and eleven years (1956-67). Other hostile relationships characterized by the absence of war for long periods of time include, in 1969: North and South Korea (16 years); Nationalist and Red China (20 years); the United States and Russia (25 years); the United States and Red China (16 years).

Those who point out that opposing nations view each other with suspicion and hold distorted images of each other prior to and during wars, are not, therefore, providing us with a useful theory of war. Such antipathy is evident during long periods of peace too. The significant issue is this: given hostility and the mutual antipathies, exaggerations, and prejudices which normally accompany it, how do states manage their relationships to avoid war for long periods of time? It is not, to employ an analogy, of interest to learn that greed is associated with theft. That we already knew, almost by definition. Of interest is, given the recurrent and unavoidable presence of greed in human affairs, how theft is often discouraged and prevented.

Hostile states are not propelled inexorably and perpetually into war. Somehow they find a point in their rivalry at which to stop. This is the central fact of international life that the excitation theory overlooks.

Even in the simplest conflicts, thresholds will often exist which enable hostile groups to avoid an unintended clash. Two armed groups are advancing toward each other across a large open field. The groups are hostile and suspicious of each other, yet they would rather avoid fighting. If the field is unbroken by any landmarks, it is possible that a process of excitation will take place. A step forward by one side, even if made by a soldier only moving into the shade of a tree, may be interpreted as an advance and provoke an advance on the other side.

But what if there is a stone wall or a creek running approximately through the middle of the field? Both sides will immediately perceive that this landmark separates the field into two territories, into "ours" and "theirs." Both will realize that crossing the wall or stream will be a battle-provoking act. It would indicate a conscious decision of the other side to provoke a fight. Both sides also realize that merely walking forward, whether to a shady tree or elsewhere is not a *casus belli*. Each group recognizes the right of the other to walk anywhere it wants on its side of the line.

Because there is a mutually recognized demarcation line, therefore, the excitation theory will not apply. Both sides know how to avoid fighting: do not cross the line.

The term given to the demarcation lines which exist between hostile nations is the "status quo." Status quo refers to the recognition we make that some things are "ours," and others are not, that some things belong to the opponent and others do not. Put more carefully, the status quo is the *mutually perceptible* distribution of rights over which war may be provoked between hostile nations (or alliances of nations).

The status quo is perhaps the most fundamental concept in international relations. Without it, our vocabulary loses its meaning. Without it, the statesman turns in aimless circles.

The words "aggression," "defense" and "appeasement," for example, have meaning only in terms of the status quo. Unless we have a conception of what belongs to whom, we cannot speak of "taking" (aggression) or preventing someone from "taking" (defense) or allowing someone to "take" (appeasement). Appeasement cannot mean giving in to an opponent under any conceivable circumstances; it means allowing him to use force to alter the status quo in his favor.

Suppose we hear: "The United States should invade East Germany. Naturally the Russians say we must not and that they will fight a war if we invade. But knuckling under to their threats is *appeasement*." The only way to escape such verbal traps is to point to the status quo. East Germany is "theirs." Taking what is theirs is aggression; appeasement is letting them take what is "yours."

For the statesman, a conception of the status quo is the only alternative to chaos. How can the statesman know if his opponent is practicing aggression? How does he know that he himself is not an aggressor? How can he tell if backing down is appeasement—which leads to war—or if a failure to back down is aggression—which also leads to war? Only by developing a conception of what is his and what is not, by keeping his eye on the status quo.

The status quo makes the excitation theory of war largely inapplicable. The excitation theory assumes that nations drift into war because they could see no specific steps which provoked war. It assumed that the road to war was a continuously sloping path and no movement down was different from any other. Newspaper invective, insults, increased armaments, the collapse of a cultural exchange program, receiving a defector, failure to talk at a summit, to sell wheat, to sign a weather data exchange treaty: all these lead to war. If reversed, each of these conditions would be steps to peace. That is what the excitation theory suggests.

But there are specific war-provoking steps. Both sides recognize what they are. The Russians could call us names for centuries without this action causing war. Calling us names is their right and we recognize it. They could recall the Bolshi Ballet, break off diplomatic relations and build more hydrogen bombs. They know that we know such acts are not war-provoking.

But if they cut off access to Berlin or support a North Korean invasion of South Korea or supply communist troops in Laos they know they are risking war. They are using force to gain things that they themselves know are *not theirs*. They are violating the status quo and, in so doing, they are knowingly increasing the probability of war from a negligible level to dangerous proportions.

The path to war is not a smooth slope, but has abrupt steps or thresholds which can be perceived by both sides as violations of the status quo. If hostile powers genuinely seek peace above all else, they have an extremely good chance of avoiding war. They may hate each other, fear each other and hurl insults at each other, but they will have no war if each respects the status quo.

Naturally, if one side is willing to risk war to alter the status quo in its favor, war there may be. But a conscious decision has been made to take the chance. Sometimes war has resulted from such gambles. The Austrians knew that they were risking war in attempting to invade Serbia in 1914. Hitler had to know he was risking war by invading Poland in 1939. Stalin had to know he was risking war by supporting the North Korean invasion of South Korea in 1950. Nasser had to know he was risking war with Israel by blockading the Gulf of Aqaba in 1967. Perhaps these leaders underestimated the risks, but they could not avoid knowing that they were there.

In many other instances, war did not materialize—but it could have. Mussolini had to know he was risking war with Britain and France by invading Ethiopia in 1935. Hitler knew he risked war by remilitarizing the Rhineland in 1936; his troops had orders to withdraw if France responded. Stalin had to know he was risking war in 1948 when he blockaded Berlin. Khrushchev had to know he risked war by placing missiles in Cuba. In each case war was consciously provoked, or risked, by a nation attempting to alter the status quo in its favor.

Determining the Status Quo

How is the extensive web of international rights and possessions known as the status quo created? How do statesmen determine what is "theirs" and what is not?

Earlier, it was suggested that the status quo is a *mutually perceptible* distribution of rights.[1] The stone wall running through the middle of the field is a status quo line because each side knows the other will perceive it. Status quo identifies Hawaii as belonging to the United States because we know that the Chinese know that it does. Mutual perception, then, is the basic characteristic of the status quo. Both sides have to be able to arrive at the same understanding about what belongs to whom.

They will reach such mutual perceptions by applying, even in spite of themselves, the same obvious, inescapable yardsticks of jurisdiction. Although each side may make extravagant claims, conflicting with the public claims of the other, both will agree, "deep down" or intuitively, who has what. This is not to say that either side is satisfied with the distribution. I may fiercely covet my colleague's sports car which I know I deserve more than he does, yet I still know it belongs to him. The Chinese may desire Hawaii, but they realize it is ours.

There seem to be two principles for determining the status quo: *usage,* the most important, and *renunciation.* These two rules, and apparently only these two, provide a mutually perceptible distribution of rights.

"Possession is nine-tenths of the law." This maxim, lawyers tell me, greatly exaggerates the importance of physical possession in determining ownership in civil cases. But in hostile international relationships, where there are no effective legislatures, courts and police forces to create and apply more complicated standards, possession does constitute nine-tenths of ownership. Possession or current usage is something that both sides can perceive, in spite of their hostility and divergent ideologies. China can see we "have" Hawaii because American laws are applied there, the American flag flies there, American troops freely move there, and a Chinese citizen would need American permission to go there. These evidences of possession are so obvious that we know the Chinese cannot fail to perceive them.

The 1967 Egyptian blockade of the Gulf of Aqaba against Israeli shipping illustrates how usage creates mutually perceived rights. For ten years, scores of ships had sailed unmolested through the Straits of Tiran to the Israeli port of Elath. Obviously, the Egyptians had to know it. Therefore, when Nasser blockaded the Straits he realized he was depriving Israel of an existing right and thereby risking war.

An awareness of the usage principle is one reason for the diplomat's traditional caution and conservatism. He realizes, as the layman does not, that bits and pieces of apparently impractical privilege are often important in determining the status quo. Thus, many of our rights in Berlin—such as the presence of Allied patrols on the Autobahn—are not practical but symbolic of our possession of the larger right of access. Giving away these symbolic rights can suggest a diminution of the larger right.

It might seem, for example, that we are foolish holding on to the Guantanamo naval base in Cuba. Clearly, arguments about its importance in the defense of the Panama Canal are obsolete in the space-atomic age. Why should we insist in clinging to this potentially embarassing enclave?

One answer is that the base is an important symbol of Cuba's location within the American zone of responsibility and not the Russian. To withdraw from Guantanamo, even without being under pressure to do so, would suggest a lessening of interest in Cuba and a certain alteration of the status quo. In this way, a new Cuban miscalculation might eventually be produced. A diplomat, it seems, would understand this by intuition and be inclined to "let well enough alone."

The second rule for determining the status quo is renunciation: giving up (or trading) through word or deed something one possesses.

If the United States has a deserted Pacific island which, one day, it announces belongs to the Soviet Union, then it does. And, strangely, we could not the following day claim it back and have it belong to us. One can give (or trade) things away verbally, but unilateral claims on someone else's holdings cannot affect the status quo.

All this makes sense if we consider the mutually perceptible quality of the status quo. It requires only one side to give since the receiving side is automatically assumed to have accepted. Thus, when we say, "The island is yours," we know the Russians accept it. But if we say, "Your island is ours," we have no reason to believe that the Russians also perceive it is ours.

An application of this rule is seen in the Iranian episode discussed earlier. When Stalin signed the 1942 treaty agreeing to withdraw his troops from Iran six months after the end of the war, he renounced his right to station troops there after the stated date (providing the other signatories complied). In refusing to withdraw by that date, he violated the status quo.

The application of the renunciation principle in determining the status quo is limited by an important consideration: to the degree that a verbal renunciation is ambiguous or indefinite it will not be the status quo since it does not establish a mutually perceptible threshold. When the Russians promised to remove their troops from Iran by March 2, 1946, it was a highly specific pledge. Each side could see that the other knew what was expected.

Many times, however, the language of a pledge or promise contained in a treaty will not constitute a renunciation in the status quo sense because it does not identify a mutually perceptible condition. The North Vietnamese, for example, in signing the 1954 cease-fire with the French pledged to guarantee "democratic liberties" in the North (Article 14, Section c). Given the disagreement on the meaning of "democratic liberties" as well as the absence of clear standards for what constitutes a violation of them, one cannot interpret this pledge as a status quo renunciation. France (or South Vietnam) would not have had the right to attack the North claiming violation of this article. To put it another way, France could not have expected the North Vietnamese to be aware of exactly what action would provoke the invasion. The whole point of a status quo line is, of course, that the opponent knows—because he cannot avoid knowing—when he is transgressing.

To what kinds of rights does the status quo apply? There are, after all, many levels of international interaction. Nations customarily trade with each other, they exchange ambassadors, they send tourists back and forth. At what level are the rights which involve war and peace—the status quo—created? Without attempting a dogmatic answer, we can observe that the status quo seems to exist primarily in matters involving territory, or more broadly, spatial relationships. Nations seem to go to war, or threaten war, when geography is involved; an invasion across a border, the orientation of a regime controlling a region, passages through straits or to enclaves.

One obvious reason why the status quo is so heavily based upon spatial relations is, of course, that territory is so vitally important, being the *sine qua non* for the exercise of many other rights. But a second reason is that geographic matters present, by their very nature, mutually perceptible thresholds. The importance of this point can be illustrated by considering several other matters which do not normally form a part of the status quo: invective, commercial relations, espionage, cultural relations, and armaments.

Generally speaking, on these issues a nation may do what it wishes without violating the status quo; that is, actions on these matters are not considered war-provoking. The exclusion of these questions from the status quo does not entirely lie, it seems, in their supposed lesser importance. For they often involve matters of greater importance than rights to bits and pieces of territory. If the Soviet Union builds an anti-ballistic missile system, that is of greater intrinsic significance to us than their snatching a few miles of West German farmland on the East-West border. Yet the latter act would propel us toward a military confrontation, and the former would not. Commercial arrangements and espionage activities may also, on occasion, have momentous consequences in international life. Even invective may be extremely troublesome—as in the Austrian-Serbian relationship prior to 1914.

These matters are excluded from the status quo because they do not afford mutually perceptible limits for what is acceptable or "proper" and what is not. They do not contain obvious sticking-points or thresholds. If the American ambassador in Moscow looks out his window and sees a rocket, is that "espionage"? If he

reports he saw it? And how are the Russians to know he saw it?*
Or, how much wheat must we sell to Russia? What is the "right"
price? If a U.S. congressman remarks that Russian roads are poor,
is that "invective"? If he says it to a friend, how is he to know that
the Russians will know he said it at all? Even on armaments, the
same problem arises: How many submarines is the "obvious" limit
for Russia to have? How many H-bombs? And how is everyone to
know that everyone will know when a limit is exceeded?

It is precisely this problem which the allies after World War
I faced when they unwisely attempted to make the state of German
armaments a part of the status quo by writing it into the Versailles
peace treaty. Germany was obliged to pledge to abolish its general
staff, to limit its standing army to 100,000, its officer corps to
4,000, and to have no tanks or military aircraft. Even though the
limits had been specified, it still proved impossible to enforce
them. The German general staff wore civilian clothes, the air force
pilots trained as civilians. Was the treaty violated? Who could say
for sure?

Moreover, the paper limits set in the treaty did not correspond
to any inherently obvious threshold. If, for example, one could have
armies in only 100,000-man units, then the limit of 100,000 would
have corresponded to a real threshold. But one can have 100,001
men. Were the French to invade Germany to get that one soldier—
even if they knew he was the 100,001st—out of uniform? But if
France allowed this violation to pass, then she would lose her
right to respond on the troop level issue altogether.

The fact that nations generally exclude such matters as
armaments and invective from the list of things over which war is
threatened supports the role we have ascribed to the status quo as
a device to stabilize peace. In their efforts to control the danger of
war, hostile nations have tended to confine the process of bargain-

*This logic apparently escapes the senators who, in commenting upon such
incidents as the seizure of the *Pueblo,* insist on emphasizing that intelligence
gathering was being conducted. The implication of these observations is that we
were somehow at fault and our opponents were partially justified in their action.
But, of course, it is none of our opponent's business what men on our craft in international waters or air space are doing, whether listening to secret enemy codes
or playing craps.

It is diplomatically unsophisticated even to mention the intelligence function
of a seized or attacked craft and thereby suggest the relevance of the function. To
do so reveals to opponents a dangerously hazy grasp of the fundamental issue
involved (freedom of air and sea) and may tempt them into future violations.

ing with the threat of war to those matters on which mutual and stable expectations can develop.

The Great-Power Status Quo

The principles of usage and renunciation enable us to define a status quo existing between a pair of nations. If every nation existed in complete autonomy and separation from every other, then there would be nothing more than thousands of bilateral status quo's, each corresponding to a particular pair of states. There would be an Ecuadorean-Peruvian status quo unrelated to the North Korean-South Korean status quo, which, in turn, would have nothing to do with the Soviet-American status quo.

But as nations become identified or allied with each other and tend to struggle against combinations of other nations, a status quo appropriate to this broader conflict arises. The respective status quo's of each combination of countries become lumped together. Major powers in these coalitions take on the responsibility of protecting, and the right to protect, the status quo of their allies against the allies of the opposing power. In this way, a great-power status quo emerges which transcends the national rights and territories of these powers.

When, for example, the Germans challenged French rights in Morroco in 1911 in the Agadir dispute, the British became deeply concerned not because they had rights there, but because the rights of their ally, France, were at issue. When Austria moved against Serbia in 1914, Russia and France were affected because the Russian identification with Serbia made a violation of the Serbian status quo a Russian problem. And the identification of France with Russia made it a French problem too. When Mussolini invaded Ethiopia in 1935, he did more than violate the Italo-Ethiopian status quo; he violated a great-power status quo which had come about as a result of the British and French identification with Ethiopia, proclaimed in their defense of that country in the League of Nations.

In our day, the great-power status quo—that is the Cold War status quo—involves a combination of *ad hoc* great power alignments and a rigid ideological dimension. In the Mideast, the Cold War status quo has little to do with ideology. Russia has become closely identified with Egypt, the United States is identified with

Israel. Thus, when Nasser violated the Israeli-Egyptian status quo by blockading the Gulf of Aqaba, he also violated the Cold War status quo, given the international identification of the powers with the belligerents. That the Russians were communist had little to do with it. Had Russia been a monarchy or fascist dictatorship—but hostile to us—the sequence of events would still have represented a violation of the great power status quo.

The ideological dimension brings additional elements of clarity and rigidity to the Cold War status quo. First, those nations calling themselves "communist" have been, at least to date, the automatic allies of our major opponents, Russia and China, whenever they engage in conflicts with "non-communist" states. Owing to this close and profound identification, a violation of the local status quo by a communist country against a non-communist state becomes a violation of the Cold War status quo. Conversely, an attack on a communist country by a free-world country is also a violation of the Cold War status quo.

Moreover, the ideological orientation of states is itself a fundamental conflict of the Cold War and, therefore, an important element of the status quo. Our opponents prefer to see "communist" regimes; the United States favors "non-communist" states and opposes the creation of "communist" regimes. While the word "communist" might, in principle, mean anything, it happens to denote mutually perceptible and highly significant characteristics. Our list of "communist" regimes is the same as that of our opponents.

That list represents an important part of the Cold War status quo. If a "free-world" state becomes "communist," or if a "communist" state goes "free," the status quo has altered. One side has gained, the other has lost. If either side employs force to effect such changes, the status quo is being violated; that is, aggression is occurring. And, consequently, the major powers on each side are entitled, with such special exceptions as that of Cuba, to prevent the other from effecting such changes.

Cuba's location in the Cold War status quo (which is, incidentally, analogous to that of Finland) affords an interesting illustration of how the principle of usage produces rights which become superimposed on the communist-non-communist status quo. If the United States should effect an unprovoked attack upon North Korea, Czechoslovakia or East Germany, the Soviet Union would have, following what has just been said, the right to defend these communist countries. But although Cuba is communist, the Soviet Union does not have the same right to defend it.

When it became communist, Cuba was a member of the Rio Pact, the Latin American collective defense treaty signed in 1947. The long-standing Monroe Doctrine against outside penetration in the hemisphere also applied. And we had a military base there. All these circumstances suggested that Cuba was allowed to go communist at the sufferance of the United States and that the Russians did not have the right to defend Cuba.

It appears that the Russians recognized this. When on July 9, 1960, Khrushchev said he would use missiles to defend Cuba against the United States, he said he was speaking "figuratively." In this way, he indicated that he perceived a distinction between Russian rights over Cuba and those over Hungary or East Germany which the Soviet Union would defend more than "figuratively." Thus, a pattern of usage enabled both sides to determine a somewhat anomolous status quo: a communist Cuba which the Soviet Union is not entitled to defend. The Bay of Pigs episode, as pointed out earlier, suggested an alteration of this situation; the missile crisis of 1962 confirmed that it had not altered.

In its broader outlines, then, the Cold War status quo is the sum of the status quo existing between the states identified with our opponents and states identified with the United States. In practice, the states identified with the Soviet Union and China call themselves "communist" although occasionally, as in the case of Egypt or Syria, a non-communist state may also, to a lesser degree, become identified with our opponents. In addition, the Cold War status quo includes the existing division of states into communist or non-communist, and certain rights of each side to act to maintain that division.

It is important to realize that the Cold War status quo, extensive as it may seem, touches only a small part of international relationships. There is a great deal not included in it. If, for example, Ecuador invades and occupies a portion of Peruvian territory, she has violated the status quo with Peru, but the Cold War status quo is not affected since neither country is identified with our opponents. Similarly, a Chinese invasion of communist Mongolia does not touch the Cold War status quo.

If India grows unfriendly toward us and signs a mutual cooperation treaty with the Soviet Union, the Cold War status quo is not altered. But if the closer ties with the Soviet Union should result in increased communist subversion and a communist coup, the status quo will, at the moment India becomes "communist," have altered. This process of "melting" the status quo is discussed in Chapter 8. Or, if India, while closely identified with the Soviet Union, should violate the status quo against a neighbor identified with the United States, then a Cold War status quo issue will arise.

Thus, the status quo language of "ours" and "theirs" does not connote notions of empire or domination; it refers to the rights each side has, *in the eyes of the other,* to act or react on a highly specific set of issues. When we say that South Korea is, in status quo language, "ours" we do not mean that we have, seek or should wish any rights to make South Korean laws, select South Korean leaders, or control their economy or trade. Instead, we simply mean that the South Korean status quo *vis a vis* our opponents or allies of our opponents is also, in a very real sense, *our* status quo. That is, our opponents recognize that *in our eyes* they do not have a right to attack South Korea or otherwise infringe its status quo rights.

The foregoing observations about the status quo do not, of course, constitute a comprehensive treatment. In such matters, there are always more qualifications and applications than space to express them. Moreover, it is clear that some problems involving the distribution of rights cannot be clearly solved by the application of rules of usage, renunciation, and international identification. The exact nature of the Cold War status quo in Laos, for example, is such a tangled matter that our diplomats are reluctant even to discuss it for fear of either renouncing rights which may be ours or claiming rights which are not ours—and thereby provoking a response by our opponents to demonstrate this fact.

Nevertheless, it is clear that, on a broad range of matters, a status quo does exist. Nations do not grope about in complete blindness about each others' rights. There are mutually perceptible thresholds on the path to war. And, in most of the Cold War crises, one does not need to be a diplomatic expert to see what they are and to notice who first crosses them.

It is, for example, a violation of the status quo and therefore aggression for the Russians to attempt to block or hinder Western access to West Berlin. West Berlin is a non-communist territory;

blocking Western access would force it under communist control. To the Russian claim that West Berlin is "theirs" the doctrine of usage provides inescapable evidence that they know it is not. The Russians have not exercised such a supposed right of possession; they have witnessed the Allies exercise such rights.

Had a war broken out over any of the scores of Russian attempts to hinder Western access to Berlin over the past decades, it would not have been a war of excitation. It would have been a war consciously risked by the Russians who sought something they knew was not theirs.*

Characteristics of the Status Quo Framework

The status quo is a distribution of rights and territories which, if respected, will enable hostile powers to avoid war. But what happens, we might ask, if the status quo is violated? The world is full of imperfections. On occasion, the status quo may not be entirely clear to one side. Or an accident or miscalculation may take place. Perhaps an adventurous leader may take imprudent risks. Does the world plunge into catastrophe in such cases?

If so, it would defeat the purpose of the status quo. Statesmen adopt the status quo in order to avoid or at least minimize the probability of war over the possession of rights and territories. It follows, therefore, that they will also seek rules which enable them to control the possibility of war, particularly total war, in treating violations or ambiguities of the status quo. These rules are simple, obvious extensions of the original status quo concept and, as such, have the same inescapable, mutually perceptible quality.

1. *Rule of immediate reaction.* Since de facto possession counts so heavily in determining the status quo, it follows that one must be quick to counter violations or he will lose rights entirely. The aggressor knows he ought to back down to avoid war if you react immediately, since he has provoked the crisis. Wait six

---

*Penkovskiy reported that during the 1961-62 Berlin crisis, Kremlin leaders were aware that *they* were initiating the disturbance of an established status quo—and thereby risking war:

> Many generals bluntly say: "What in hell do we need this Berlin for? We have endured it for sixteen years; we can endure it a little more. One of these days Khrushchev will catch it good! They will hit him in his teeth so hard that he will lose everything!"

The Penkovskiy Papers, p. 207.

months to react and he will expect you to back down since you have "started things."

When, for example, the communists put up the Berlin Wall in August, 1961, it was a violation of the principle of free movement in Berlin, established by over a decade of practice. Since the United States did not rectify this violation of the status quo at that time, we in effect acquiesced in a change of the status quo. Now it would be aggression for us to attempt to knock down the Berlin Wall. Similarly, the Chinese conquest of the Northeast Frontier Agency of India in 1962 was aggression; but an attempt to regain that region today would be aggression. It is now "theirs."

Common sense tells us how long one is entitled to wait before reacting to violations in the status quo: as long as necessary to perceive the violation, make a decision, and carry out a response without stalling. Presidents have to be awakened, Congressmen and allies consulted, appropriate channels explored. As soon as a nation appears to take more time than necessary for a reaction, it is "accepting" the change in the status quo. An illustration of this principle appears in the Iranian episode discussed in Chapter 2. When the Russians requested a one-week postponement of the April 3, 1946 meeting of the U.N. Security Council, Truman was right to refuse. To delay the normal pace of decision-making would have suggested to the Russians that we were accepting the presence of their troops in Iran.

2. *The rule of re-violation.* If an opponent violates that status quo, it is almost always necessary to violate the status quo in return in order to halt or punish the original violation. Responding to an invasion would require attacking the soil of the aggressor; breaking a blockade demands hostile sea action. Naturally, therefore, both sides recognize the right of the other to violate the status quo in reacting to aggression. Such re-violations are understood to be defensive and not aggressive. Thus, the naval quarantine of Cuba during the missile crisis, coming as it did in response to the Soviet attempt to alter the status quo of Cuba, was not aggression but a re-violation. The timid Soviet and Chinese reaction to our bombing of North Vietnam during the Vietnam war suggested their respect for our right of re-violation in response to the attack on the South.

3. *The rule of proportionality and propinquity.* If an East German soldier stumbles over the border into West Germany does

this "violation" of the status quo entitle West Germany to invade? If Chinese Nationalists make a commando raid on the mainland, can Red China drop a hydrogen bomb on Saigon in re-violation?

While hostile powers can recognize each other's right to respond to violations in the status quo, they also perceive rough limits to this right. Beyond a certain point a re-violation becomes aggression. Consequently, if they want to maintain peace, both respect the principle that a re-violation must be proportional to and in the locality of the original violation. Under this rule, South Korea is not entitled to invade North Korea in response to a border raid. To do so would be to employ the raid as a pretext for aggression. But they would be entitled to make a counter raid, proportional to the original violation.

The same idea lies behind the rule of propinquity. Responding to a violation of the status quo by reacting in a totally different geographic area strains the opponent's perception of your act as a re-violation. The action begins to look like aggression, for you are demanding something new and different. The hypothetical Red Chinese bomb on Saigon mentioned above, then, would violate propinquity as well as proportionality. To respond to the invasion of South Korea by invading East Germany, for example, would have violated the rule of propinquity. So would blockading Vladivostok to get missiles out of Cuba. By observing proportionality and propinquity the statesman is saying, "See, I don't want anything of yours; I just want to keep what is mine."

The Berlin Wall episode of 1961 illustrates how this status quo rule shapes policy. When the Russians sealed off the border to East Berlin they violated the status quo. In order to prevent this violation the Allies would have had to re-violate the status quo. Yet there was no re-violation available which observed the rule of proportionality and propinquity. In order to "knock down" the wall, we would have had to invade East German territory—a move well out of proportion to the original violation. And a reaction in another area would not have been consistent with propinquity. Consequently, it was difficult for the United States, following a non-aggressive foreign policy, to prevent the construction of the Wall.

The rule of proportionality and propinquity contradicts the strategic ideal of "massive retaliation": punishing an aggressor with atomic weapons delivered wherever we choose. But, in practice, the massive retaliation principle was never followed even by Secretary of State John Foster Dulles who announced it. The intuitive "rightness" of the status quo rule of proportionality and propinquity overpowered the logic of massive retaliation. When considering the use of atomic weapons to end the Korean War in 1953, Dulles and Eisenhower contemplated a strike not against Moscow or even Chinese cities, but upon "specific targets reasonably related to the area."[2] In response to the shelling of Quemoy in August, 1958, Dulles did not bomb Moscow nor even Peking, but sent U.S. ships to escort Nationalist Chinese vessels to the island.

4. *The rule of alliance responsibility.* Great powers are responsible for the aggression of their allies and must therefore restrain or prevent such aggression. This principle applies even if the power in question gives no physical aid to its aggressive ally. It would still provide a critically important resource: its threat. A failure to observe this rule enables small aggressors to drag great powers into war.

If, for example, control of access to Berlin is given to the East Germans and they cut off West Berlin, the Russians are responsible. It is their back-stopping threat which would give the East Germans the confidence to attempt this deed and which might restrain West Germany and the United States from taking effective counteraction.

But, in the face of this aggression, we would be entitled to take counteraction. Yet the Soviet Union is pledged to assist East Germany which we must attack. In this way a direct big-power confrontation could be produced. Therefore, the Soviet Union must insist that the East Germans not interfere with Berlin access, or publicly refuse all support if the East Germans do not heed the advice.

Similarly, if the Nationalist Chinese attempted to invade the mainland, they would implicitly rely upon our threat to keep China and Russia from reacting with an attack on Taiwan. Nationalist aggression, in this instance, could drag us into war with China and even Russia. For this reason, the United States has publicly pointed out that it has no commitment to assist the Nationalists to recapture the mainland—should that purely hypothetical case arise.

The Russians have not observed the rule of alliance responsibility by repudiating aggressive allies such as North Korea or North Vietnam. Their policy is one of supporting and supplying aggressors; as long as they continue to do this, they must be considered aggressive themselves.

What the Status Quo is Not

While all of us have some notion of a status quo, that is, a distribution of "ours" and "theirs," much confusion and lengthy argument arise in the general public over what this distribution really is. In almost all cases, these debates arise because people employ deficient criteria for determining possession. The status quo, it must be remembered, is a framework which both sides can perceive. It is a framework for maintaining peace. Yet people advance standards for determining the distribution of rights and territories which manifestly will not lead to a *mutual* perception of possession. If ever applied, these standards would lead statesmen to conflicting conceptions and propel them into war.

Criteria of morality and justice are the most frequently heard in connection with international rights. But they are clearly subjective and ambiguous. Hostile powers are bound to disagree on such things. Should nations ever reach a common conception of morality and justice, war will no longer be a menace.

The North Vietnamese cannot claim a right to Laos, Thailand, or South Vietnam because the people there are "oppressed" and require "liberation." They know we shall disagree on such a subjective matter. Nor do we have a right to bring "justice" to the downtrodden East Germans by invading that country. We may believe that barbed wire and machine guns have made that state a prison. Yet it still is "theirs." We cannot claim a right to attack it on moral grounds. Not if we seek peace.

Nor can national or ethnic claims be accepted in determining the status quo possession of rights and territories. That this or that people was once a part of, speaks the language of, or was descended from the same ethnic stock as a particular nation, cannot change its location in the status quo. Such arguments, like moral ones, are subjective and can be pressed by both sides in different directions. Does North Korea belong to South Korea or vice versa? Does the speaking of French in Quebec give France a right to that province?

Legalism is another criterion which cannot be accepted in the status quo framework. An exception to this observation involves the renunciation principle. If a nation has unambiguously given up rights or territories in a document and nothing has happened in the meantime to contravene this renunciation, then this legal document will form a part of the status quo. Thus, the Anglo-Russian-Iranian Treaty of 1942 was part of the status quo since it contained the Russian renunciation of the right to station troops in Iran after a specified date.

There seems to be no other general case where a document itself would, in fact, determine status quo possession in contradiction to usage. If the United States had failed to act immediately in March, 1946, against Russian troops in Iran, the Soviet Union would then have had the right to keep its troops there. That they would be in violation of the treaty would not matter. By allowing the troops to remain, we would have "accepted" them, and the original renunciation contained in the treaty would have been contravened by usage. Once a violation of the status quo has been tolerated, it becomes the new status quo and existing treaties, documents and charters do not affect it.

The reason for keeping legalism out of the status quo is patent: in the great swamp of legal principle, precedent and document, one can find a reed to support any conceivable position. We know this from our experience with domestic law. It is difficult to imagine a claim, however absurd, which could not be buttressed by some kind of legal argument. It might not be a good argument and it might lose in court. But a brief can be prepared. Between hostile states which will not jointly submit to any court decision—and no one can make them submit—all that is left are the briefs: always two of them and always conflicting.

Finally, how the status quo came about has no bearing on what it is. In particular, a given distribution of rights and territories established by force is still the status quo (assuming the time for reaction has lapsed).

It is often thought that only those changes "freely" made by contracting parties should be recognized. Although a pleasing ideal, this principle is impracticable if not inconceivable. Force and the threat of force hang so heavily over the international scene that virtually all concessions and acquisitions by hostile states are shaped by it. To refuse to recognize the changes wrought by force would be to ignore the map of the world today. Moreover, what other map could be substituted? The lines erased by force yesterday were established by force the day before yesterday.

Lest the reader misunderstand, I am not saying that morality, justice, national self-determination, and legality have no place in international politics. These criteria have wide application in shaping our own foreign policy and may be mutually adopted to settle international disputes. Standards of morality and justice affect and should affect our treatment of territorial possessions, dependent allies, former enemies, prisoners of war, poor nations, and enemy negotiators. Criteria of self-determination and legality are often useful for boundary commissions which arbitrate disputes brought to them by both sides.

But when it comes to establishing a workable division of rights and territories between hostile nations, these standards cannot be employed. These criteria will not produce an implicit agreement on who has what rights and territories. Most Americans would undoubtedly agree that in establishing a communist state in Poland, the Russians trampled norms of morality, justice, democracy, legality, national self-determination and non-violence. Yet who would argue that we, therefore, have a right to destroy that regime and should exercise that right immediately? When it comes to the rights of our opponents, we have no difficulty disregarding moral-legal arguments and settling on the status quo. It is in determining our own rights that these arguments sometimes lead us astray.

Why Statesmen Must Sometimes Lie in Order to Tell the Truth

The few basic principles of international threats and the status quo framework just advanced enable us to explain one rather perplexing aspect of the language of diplomacy: the often noted tendency of statesmen to be hypocritical or even lie. It is this tendency which causes many people to mistrust statesmen; it has given diplomacy a poor image. And the popular reaction to the apparent dishonesty of statesmen has given rise to appeals for "openness," and "frankness" in international dealings. While we cannot condone, of course, every act of deception or withholding of information by statesmen, it happens that in some cases deception is actually necessary to achieve honesty.

The proponents of "honest diplomacy" have overlooked that the statesman uses language to communicate threats. This function of language is distinct from that of communicating facts and ideas —which is the way we normally employ words—and therefore requires a different syntax. At the core of this difference between the language of fact and the language of diplomacy is this: the status quo, the framework which, in effect, defines the existing pattern of international rights and hence threats, is created by what each side "recognizes" it is. By honestly announcing what the *facts* of a certain international issue are, the statesman will often be changing the rights and threats involved—and this he may not wish to do. Several general principles may be advanced to illustrate this problem.

> 1. When an opponent is violating or preparing to violate the status quo in a manner not yet publicly known and one is not ready to respond, one does not acknowledge the facts of this action.

When the status quo is violated there are inescapably—as pointed out in the discussion of immediate reaction—two possible responses: the violation can be accepted or opposed. A failure to act at all—or coupled with a perfunctory protest, is acceptance; action —or a threat to act communicated in a warning—is opposition. It is precisely this implacable, unambiguous quality which impels us to adopt the status quo framework: it is difficult to get rights mixed up.

Yet this framework does afford certain elements of ambiguity, and we may expect statesmen to exploit these possibilities as best they can—just as law-abiding citizens will do what they can to find loopholes in inconvenient laws. The statesman discovers that the ambiguity in the status quo framework lies in the fact that you can neither accept nor reject a violation of the status quo until you *know* about it. Until the opponent knows that you *know* he is violating the status quo, you have not reacted, you have neither accepted nor opposed the violation.

Following this logic, it is clear that a statesman who wishes to say to his opponent, "We know you are violating the status quo and we are still making up our minds," can communicate this only by saying nothing and denying knowledge of the violation. For if he says he does know about it, then he is telling his opponent either, "Your violation has created a new status quo and consequently I no longer have a right to oppose it—and will not;" or "I am threatening counteraction—and will, of course, carry out my threat if you do not step back." Normally, of course, such ambiguity and the consequent freedom of action can be preserved for only a few days until the violation becomes clear public knowledge. Then it is necessarily assumed that the defender knows of the violation. Nevertheless, the few days saved can be vitally important in giving the defensive power time to choose a course of action or in allowing new aspects of the situation to emerge.

Illustrations of diplomatic lies told in order to preserve freedom of action abound. On July 20, 1914, the British Foreign Secretary Sir Edward Grey told the German ambassador that he "had not heard anything recently" about an ultimatum Austria was preparing against Serbia. In fact, the British ambassador to Austria had cabled to London, on July 16, considerable information about the ultimatum which he had received informally. The historian reporting this episode scolds Grey for this "diplomatic lying" which, he adds, "unfortunately, was not the monopoly of any one country."[3]

But Grey was actually telling the truth, not an historian's truth but the truth about British policy. If he merely announced his knowledge of the ultimatum without doing anything, then he would be recognizing Austria's right to issue it and, therefore, Britain's intention not to become involved. If, on announcing his knowledge of the ultimatum, Grey issued a warning then he would commit Britain to a reaction when the ultimatum was released. By professing ignorance, Grey stated the British policy: "We shall see how this develops; we have not yet made a decision." ·

This same practice of hiding one's knowledge of facts in order to preserve freedom of action while coming to a decision is found in the American reaction to the Cuban missile crisis. Kennedy withheld his knowledge of the missiles for a week until he had decided what to do.

Three other general principles that govern the manipulation of ambiguity are contained in the following propositions:

2. A refusal to acknowledge one's own violation of the status quo (assuming ambiguity in the public knowledge of the facts exists) weakens the severity of the violation.
3. If the other side also denies knowledge of an unannounced violation, the action practically ceases to be a violation and the status quo in question tends to be "unviolated."
4. Assuming ambiguity in the public knowledge of the

action has been preserved, the violation of the status quo
will "occur" only when the fact of the violation becomes
public knowledge.

These principles lead in several interesting directions. Among
other things, they suggest a fascinating paradox: hostile powers
may, by mutual consent, prevent what would technically be a violation of the status quo from being a violation of the status quo!

The second principle is perhaps not difficult to understand.
When one violates the status quo, it may often be unclear just what
is happening: there can be doubt about the extent of the violation
and also the intent. By allowing this area of doubt to exist, the
violator reduces the likelihood of provoking a response from the
other side. The defender is obligated or expected to counter violations of the status quo; but if he does not clearly know about such
violations, then he is necessarily less obligated to respond. To
announce the violation publicly is to fling a direct challenge in the
face of the opponent: "See, I violate the status quo. What are you
going to do about it? You must do something quickly or I shall
establish new status quo rights."

Naturally, if there is clear public knowledge of the violation as
in the blockade of Berlin or the invasion of South Korea, denial
cannot make the violation any less severe. But often the public facts
of the violation are ambiguous and incomplete. Then the blow may
be softened by public denial. The North Vietnamese, for example,
throughout the Vietnam war, studiously refused to admit that their
troops were in South Vietnam, Laos or Cambodia. In this way,
they hoped to soften the response of their opponents to these violations. It seems likely that, during the same period, the United
States had been involved in sending saboteurs into Laos to hamper
activity on the Ho Chi Minh trail, and we also denied it for the
same reason. We did not wish to say: "I claim a right to do this;
you had better react or it will become my right." This deception
involves keeping the facts ambiguous: disguising the identity of the
soldiers, their weapons, their orders, and their superiors. As more
and more of these facts become public knowledge, the violation becomes increasingly severe.

Notice, however, that telling the factual truth about, for example, U.S. harassment efforts in Laos would have been to lie
about our policy intentions. We did not want to claim a right to
have ground forces in Laos. Our action was a temporary, incidental
measure, contingent upon the activities of the enemy. The only way

to communicate this truth was to lie about our ground activities in Laos.

When a clandestine violation of the status quo is taking place the defender will usually have the resources, both in intelligence and publicity, to expose it and make it fully public. Yet it may choose not to do so. In making the exposure, the defensive power is propelling the issue to a conclusion. If the defender desires to preserve his freedom of action, then he too must deny knowledge of the violation.

When a hostile power effects a clandestine violation of the status quo, it is offering its opponent what can be either a stick of thorns or an olive branch. It is up to the defender to decide which it is. The clandestine violation says, "See, you don't have to worry about anything; we are not contesting the status quo. We acknowledge that what we are doing we have no right to do." This message can be a device to cover up aggression until it is too late for the defender to respond. Khrushchev did not announce he was placing missiles in Cuba. That would have galvanized an American reaction. His hope was to complete the job and then gradually let news of the missiles filter out. Similarly, the North Vietnamese hoped, by denying giving any assistance to the South, to avert our reaction until the fait accompli, a communist South, came to pass. When the clandestine violation will lead to an alteration of the status quo, the defender should normally expose it and react.

But sometimes the clandestine violation leads nowhere. It has a temporary, unintentional character. Or the defender is unready or unable to respond to the violation. He does not want the violation to become the new status quo; nor does he want to react to the violation. In such cases, it is to the advantage of the defender to confirm the denial of the violator and thus make the violation "invisible." If neither side "perceives" the action (and assuming that the facts are not public), then, in effect, the status quo is not being violated. Both sides have cooperated, for reasons of their own, in preserving the status quo even while technically under violation. This cooperation is indeed delicate, for either side can explode it by revealing the facts. Or third parties may erode the suspended violation by progressively revealing the facts of the matter. As the violation looses its ambiguity, it becomes progressively more of a real violation, demanding either acceptance or rejection by the defender.

A simple illustration of this process of suspending a status quo

violation is provided in the aerial espionage on communist countries. We decided, for example, that information to be gained by
flying U-2 planes over Russia was extremely valuable. Nevertheless,
such overflights constituted a certain infraction of Russian rights.
To soften the impact of our activity, then, we released no public
information of the flights and would have denied them. With this
lie, we were telling the Russians the truth, "We know your air
space is yours. What we are doing is a minor infraction; we are not
claiming any rights to attack you or fly bombers over your country or any such thing. And, of course, you are entitled to shoot the
plane down if you can." The Russians cooperated with this fiction,
until the Gary Powers episode, because they could not shoot down
the U-2 and had no effective proportional response against it.

A more complicated episode involving a suspended status quo
violation was the presence of North Vietnamese and Viet Cong
troops in Cambodia in 1966. On May 27, 1966, U.S. Major General Stanley R. Larsen said at a press conference that "We have
enough evidence from prisoners and other sources to satisfy us
that at least four and probably six North Vietnamese regiments
are there [in Cambodia]." The next day, Secretary of State Dean
Rusk denied having such information and the Defense Department
issued a statement denying Larsen's claim, although it admitted
that North Vietnamese units "may occasionally pass across the ill-
defined border. . . . " (Notice how the Defense Department bent
over backward to give the North Vietnamese the benefit of any
doubt: "may," "occasionally," "ill-defined border"—suggesting
the North Vietnamese really wouldn't *know* their own violation—
and "pass across"—suggesting a ghostly floating rather than a
clearly perceptible entrance.) And Cambodia denied that any foreign troops were stationed in her territory. Finally, North Vietnam
also denied its troops were in Cambodia—or anywhere else in
Southeast Asia except North Vietnam.4

What was going on? It seemed that North Vietnamese troops
were in Cambodia, although there was considerable ambiguity
about their numbers, the size of the encampments, whether the
camps were permanent, and who was commanding such troops. But
the countries involved were not seeking to clarify the issue; they all
sought to maintain the ambiguity. Observing this fabric of evasion
and deception, the citizen had further proof of the hypocritical
nature of diplomacy.

If, however, we inspect each country's position with the status quo framework in mind, it appears that each was really telling the truth. North Vietnam denied having troops in Cambodia in order to say, "We recognize we have no right to be in Cambodia so you need not respond to prove that we do not. Our action is temporary and incidental." By telling the truth, Hanoi would have said, "We claim the right to have troops in Cambodia—and, by implication, to attack Cambodia. React immediately or lose your right to react." It seems clear that the North Vietnamese did not wish to claim such a right at that time.

Cambodia, being unable to do anything about the enemy troops on her soil, anxious to maintain a modus vivendi with the communists and fearful of the consequences of an expansion of the war to Cambodia, chose to suspend the status quo. By denying the existence of the troops, she said, "It's all right as a temporary measure but you have no established right to be there." To reveal the truth, without doing anything about it, would simply establish the North Vietnamese right to have troops in Cambodia. Clearly, the Cambodians wished to accord no such right.

The United States, by denying the presence of North Vietnamese troops in Cambodia was saying, "It appears to us that the troops are only incidentally present in Cambodia. They are not being used to attack Cambodia. Hence, we shall tolerate their presence as long as everyone understands they have no right to be there. As soon as we decide their presence is overly inconvenient we shall have the option of announcing the violation and reacting." Our policy was to preserve our right of reaction by preserving the ambiguity of the violation.

To announce the truth would have deceived our opponents about our intentions. If we merely noted the presence of North Vietnamese troops in Cambodia and did nothing, we, according to the rule of immediate reaction, would have lost our right to respond later. We would have said, in effect, "We accept the North Vietnamese right to have troops in Cambodia and therefore we shall not take action against them in the future." Such an announcement would have amounted to a lie since if the North Vietnamese attacked Cambodia or overly abused this sanctuary to carry on the war in Vietnam, we may well have acted. And we wanted the North Vietnamese to keep this threat in mind. If we announced the presence of the troops while issuing some kind of explicit or implicit warning, then we would be threatening imminent action to oppose the violation of the status quo we just "perceived." Since we did not intend to carry the war into Cambodia at that time, our warning would have been a bluff. That is, a lie about our intentions.

The preceding analysis is more than an explanation of some complexities in diplomatic language. It constitutes, in fact, a demonstration of the importance of the status quo as the framework within which hostile states interact.

One way to determine which norms actually regulate human conduct is to reason backward from behavior to the norm that will be consistent with it. The practice of diplomatic deception just examined is a particularly fruitful phenomenon from which to infer the norms regulating the international possession of rights and territories. If one supposes, first of all, that there are no such norms, then we have no explanation for why statesmen should take steps, often to their own embarrassment, to conceal facts. If no international rights existed at all, if everything were up for grabs at any time, then a conspiracy between hostile powers to preserve ambiguity would have no point. If criteria of morality or justice were actually employed, then statesmen would always expose things for a public argument on justice or morality. If legalism afforded the basis for international rights, again exposure, with attendant legal arguments, would be the practice. Yet we have many cases, such as North Vietnamese troops in Cambodia, in which some kind of international transgression is occurring yet no one argues morality, justice or legality. Instead, states are studiously denying the facts. What they *are* doing is manipulating the mutual perceptions of the event.

We can conclude, therefore, that there is a framework regulating international rights between hostile states which has as its central norm that the distribution of rights over which war may be provoked is made on the basis of mutual perception. No other hypothesis seems to fit the facts as well.

Why Intellectuals May Not Recognize Aggression When They See It

Intellectuals mistrust the status quo. It ignores, after all, some of their highest principles: morality, justice, self-determination, the rule of law and the rejection of force. That these principles are ignored in favor of the higher principle of peace they may not apprehend. In rejecting the status quo however, they also reject the only meaningful standard for determining aggression and the only workable basis for peace. Instead, they attempt to employ the numerous moral-legal criteria which, as has been pointed out, lead to subjectivism and interminable debate. The word "aggression" still exists in their vocabulary, not as a violation of the status quo, but as AGGRESSION: a morally repugnant, manifestly illegal, unjust, dramatically cruel deed which, as they perceive it, can be universally recognized as a crime against humanity.

Since events practically never, and then only in retrospect, arrange themselves with such clarity, intellectuals have the greatest difficulty deciding what is aggression. Plagued by all the doubts and ambiguities which the moral-legalistic framework generates, their judgement of an enemy act as "aggression" is an uncertain matter.

The following quotation provides a revealing illustration of the manner in which the intellectual approaches the phenomenon of aggression. The writer dismisses the application of "the good old Munich analogy" to Vietnam thus:

> One thing is sure about the Vietnam riddle: it will not be solved by bad historical analogies. It seems a trifle forced, for example, to equate a civil war in what was for centuries the entity of Vietnam (Marshal Ky, after all, is a North Vietnamese himself and Pham Van Dong, the premier of North Vietnam, is from the south) with Hitler's invasion of Czechoslovakia across old and well-established lines of national division.[5]

The writer has seriously misrepresented the events of Munich. Hitler did not "invade" Czechoslovakia. Great Britain, France, and Czechoslovakia formally granted Hitler sovereignty over the Sudetenland. Secondly, Czech borders were not "old"; the country was proclaimed only on October 28, 1918, and its boundaries established at the Paris Peace Conference in 1919.

Finally, the national division was not "well-established." For many years, the Germans in the Czech Sudetenland, which Hitler wanted, had agitated for union with Germany. Under the leadership of Czech Germans like Konrad Henlein, a wave of anti-Czech, pro-German protest grew. Appealing arguments were advanced: the Sudetenland Germans were an oppressed ethnic minority denied equality in the Czech regime. Hitler, it seemed, was speaking in the name of decency and justice in desiring to protect them. It seemed that vast numbers of Sudetenland Germans wanted to belong to the Reich. Among those who did not believe the lines of national division were "well-established" was *The Times* of London which suggested, three weeks before Munich, that German-inhabited areas of Czechoslovakia should be ceded to Germany. [6]

These issues of justice and self-determination confused the British and French and undermined their resistance to Hitler's demand. Chamberlain thought Hitler's demand was reasonable. Munich represents one of the most ambiguous cases of aggression in history; that is why so few people emphatically opposed it. Many well-meaning, sensible people reasoned that because the division was obviously not "well-established" Hitler's demands were not "aggression." The historian quoted above apparently reasoned from the same premise, but reversed the syllogism:

1. Aggression is an obviously evil deed which has no moral or legal ambiguities.
2. History says Hitler committed aggression at Munich.
3. Therefore Hitler committed an obviously evil deed which had no moral or legal ambiguities; he must have invaded "across old and well-established lines of national division."

This false premise generates the false history.

This is not an isolated example of such thinking as a second, strikingly similar illustration shows:

> At Munich there was clearly an "aggressor." Hitler was on the rampage. Certainly when he marched into Prague he must have known in the back of his mind that he was aggressing by every definition of the term: he was crossing a boundary line, initiating the use of force, using force against the government of Czechoslovakia, and using force against the Czech people, who were clearly almost unanimously opposed to his take-over of their country.*

Again, we see the same errors of historical fact made for the same reason. The writer has misperceived and distorted the events

*Ralph K. White, "Misperception and the Vietnam War," *The Journal of Social Issues,* Vol. 22, No. 3 (July 1966), p. 118. Among the other errors in this passage, the writer has confused Munich where on September 30, 1938, the allies ceded the Sudetenland to Germany with the March 16, 1939 conquest of the rest of the country. This latter move was, incidentally, facilitated by internal dissention in Czechoslovakia: the Slovaks, pressing for complete independence, oriented themselves toward Germany to gain support against Prague.

to create (in his terms) a "diabolical enemy-image" of Hitler and a "moral self-image" for the allies. In this way, "aggression" can continue to have an unambiguous, black-white connotation.

Aggression always has moral and legal ambiguities. One can always see two sides to such issues. By bringing to bear arguments on history, race, nationhood, apparent popular will and justice, the sympathizer can easily construct a defense for any aggressor, no matter how cynical. The statesman seeks to avoid this bog; his only guide is the status quo.

Aggression in Vietnam

Just how easily such a defense can be made is illustrated by the arguments employed by many Americans to excuse a clear case of Cold War aggression: North Vietnamese action against South Vietnam beginning about 1959.

Aggression was taking place against South Vietnam because an outside communist state, North Vietnam, supplied regular and irregular troops, training, military equipment and supplies to assist a communist attempt to capture a non-communist territory by force. The Cold War status quo consists of the communist and non-communist division of the globe. North Vietnam and the allies which supported and supplied her were, therefore, violating this status quo. They were attempting to take something by force that did not belong to them.

Those who defended North Vietnamese action did not seriously dispute the basic facts: the approximately 55,000 (in 1967) North Vietnamese troops in the South; the Chinese rifles, the Russian rockets, the hundreds of tons of supplies, and the Ho Chi Minh trail. Instead, by referring to the following moral-legal principles, they denied that aggression was occurring. In every case, the application of these principles in reverse would give the free world countries rights which these people would never dream of conceding.

1. "Vietnam is all one country. The North has a legitimate right to concern itself with the South."

Under this same right, West Germany, South Korea, Nationalist China, and South Vietnam should proceed to invade their respective communist portions.

2. "The Diem regime was undemocratic and oppressive. The North had a right to help overthrow it."

Turning this principle around would give the United States and its allies the right to attack every communist state in the world, including North Vietnam whose brutal agrarian reform, it could easily be argued, made Diem look like Thomas Jefferson.

3. "The conflict in the South is mainly a civil war. The North Vietnamese are only assisting."

Almost every case of aggression in this century has involved fifth column elements in the defensive state: Austria, 1938; Czechoslovakia, 1938; France, 1940; Iran, 1946. There were communist terrorists in Korea in 1950 when the North invaded. That some local citizens, even an apparent majority, desire outside intervention cannot, in the eyes of an opposing power, justify such intervention.

Turning the principle around would have given the United States the right to send its troops into Hungary to help the uprising there in 1956, and West Germany the right to send its troops to assist the general strike and uprising in East Germany in June, 1953.

4. "The United States started it by sending advisors, supplies, and troops to South Vietnam. The North simply matched our 'escalation.' "

This is an application of the excitation theory and embodies the fallacy of that theory: it fails to recognize that South Vietnam was non-communist territory, and therefore we had a right to protect it. The communists did not have an equal right to take it.

Are we entitled to invade any communist country where Russian advisors, weapons or troops are sent? Should we have invaded East Germany in 1953 or Hungary in 1956 on the grounds that Russian troops were suppressing the rebels, and therefore we had a right to match this "escalation"? In these cases, the free world refrained from acting in the interest of peace. However much we agonized over the slaughter of Hungarian students, we understood that Hungary was "theirs."

That we assist an ally in maintaining itself—even against a purely internal communist movement cannot be a pretext for outside communist attack or assistance.

5. "We may say that the North's attack on the South is a violation of the status quo, but, for them, status quo is a sophisticated and foreign notion. They are simply befuddled nationalists who believe that Vietnam is all one country. There-

fore, in their view, they are not committing aggression."*

But there was overwhelming evidence that the North Vietnamese were fully aware of the status quo in Vietnam and its implications. In 1962, for example, Bernard Fall had this exchange with North Vietnamese Prime Minister Pham Van Dong:

> Fall: But would it not at least be conceivable that some of the almost 100,000 South Vietnamese who went north [of the 17th parallel] in 1954, and whose relatives are now fighting against South Vietnamese forces, would attempt to slip across your border back into South Viet-Nam in order to help their relatives—even without the permission of the North Vietnamese government? Wouldn't that be at least conceivable?
>
> Pham: Sir, in our country one does not cross borders without permission.
>
> Fall: Would not a spreading of the guerrilla war entail a real risk of American reaction against North Vietnamese territory? You have been to North Korea last year, Mr. Prime Minister; you saw what American bombers can do. . . .
>
> Pham (very seriously): We fully realize that the American imperialists wish to provoke a situation in the course of which they could use the heroic struggle of the South Vietnamese people as a pretext for the destruction of our economic and cultural achievements.
>
> We shall offer them no pretext that could give rise to an American military intervention against North Viet-Nam. [7]

Not only did Pham perceive the existing borders but he was aware of the danger he would run in crossing them (". . . pretext"). From his own words, we can see that he perceived a "distribution of rights over which war may be provoked."

Much other evidence confirms this. Why, if the North Vietnamese really believed "Vietnam is all one country," did they studiously refuse to admit they had troops in the South? They did

---

*As an example: ". . . aggression exists when either side uses force on the other side of the East-West boundary line that *we* regard as clear and well-established. In Vietnam, this is the 17th Parallel. And since there are North Vietnamese fighting on our side of that line, we assume that North Vietnam must have commited aggression. For convenience, let us call this the *boundary-line* definition of aggression. (Since they draw the boundary quite differently, they apply this definition quite differently.)" White, p. 107.

not deny having their troops in Haiphong. Clearly, they perceived some distinction between North and South. They drew the same distinction on the bombing issue. When they demanded "an end to the bombing and all other acts of war against the Democratic Republic of Vietnam," they expressed a distinction between bombing around Vinh in North Vietnam and the Iron Triangle in South Vietnam—a distinction inconsistent with the "all one country" proposition.

Not only were the North Vietnamese aware of the North-South status quo; they perceived much finer distinctions. When, in May, 1967, U.S. forces made a sweep in the Southern portion of the demilitarized zone, the official North Vietnamese newspaper, *Nhan Dan,* published a statement calling the action "an extremely serious step of war escalation"[8]—a rather keen diplomatic perception for a band of befuddled nationalists who can't see lines that we Westerners think are important.

It is amusing to see how some Americans, bending over backward to find excuses for the North Vietnamese attack on the South, came up with a point even the North Vietnamese rejected. And, it should be added, the proponents of the "it's all one country" doctrine did not believe it themselves. If they really perceived that Vietnam were all one country, then they would have found no qualitative distinction between sending U.S. Marines on a sweep around Danang or on a sweep around Vinh. Their howls of protest against this latter "escalation" would have revealed that, in spite of themselves, they recognized the status quo quite well. After all, one cannot "invade the North" if there is no "North."

What we have here is the familiar double standard. When opponents challenge our side, "status quo" is a vague, immoral or irrelevant notion: "It's all one country." When we consider a challenge by our side against theirs, then status quo becomes crystal clear: "We can't invade the North."

This frame of mind probably comes from living too long in a defensive nation. One takes for granted one's non-aggressive character and comes to accept the aggression of opponents as normal, natural and, hence, excusable.

To repeat: principles of a moral-legal nature do not sustain a workable distribution of international rights and territories. They are, in fact, a formula for perpetual war. If the United States ever attempted to exercise the moral-legal "rights" which many Americans so readily granted North Vietnam, these people would be the first to protest. There has to be a sense of symmetry. Either both sides claim moral-legal rights to start wars, or arguments of this nature must be denied both sides and the status quo framework respected.

The World Domination Fallacy

We should resist aggressors, one view runs, when they aim at world domination and thereby endanger us. If their aggression seems local or limited, our security is not directly at stake, and we are not justified in waging war to block them. A few days before he went to Munich, British Prime Minister Neville Chamberlain expressed this view in a radio broadcast treating his position toward Hitler's demands upon Czechoslovakia:

> How horrible, fantastic, incredible, it is that we should be digging trenches and trying on gas-masks here because of a quarrel in a faraway country between people of whom we know nothing! . . . but if I were convinced that any nation had made up its mind to dominate the world by fear of its force, I should feel that it must be resisted. Under such a domination, life for people who believe in liberty would not be worth living: but war is a fearful thing, and we must be very clear, before we embark on it, that it is really the great issues that are at stake. 9

A world war should not have been necessary to illustrate the inadequacy of this approach. A little common sense is sufficient to explain why it is futile and dangerous to reserve deterrence for only those nations bent on world conquest.

First, adequate evidence of a nation's "intention" to dominate the world is impossible to obtain at the moment of crisis—or long afterward, for that matter. Verbal statements of intention are surely inadequate, for many national leaders make extravagant claims either to flatter themselves or their domestic audiences. *Mein Kampf,* the writings of Lin Piao or Mao Tse-Tung: such documents are at best warnings. They cannot be firm evidence. Even if we should discover, let us say, in a secret filing cabinet of the Red Chinese policy planning staff, the complete plans for world domination, would such plans themselves constitute the unequivocal intentions of that nation? Would the United States be justified in bombing China to rubble the day after such plans were discovered? Clearly not. The "intentions" of national leaders can never be known with certainty until they have faced the particular opportunities and risks in each case and have acted.

Even if a hostile nation has made one or two aggressions, we are still unable to determine if it seeks the world. Any aggression could always be the last, but how can this be proven? Promises made by the aggressor are clearly inadequate. Even secret knowledge of files which have no more aggressive designs in them does not help because leaders may change their minds—or new leaders may emerge with new designs.

Second, the world domination question is irrelevant since war with an aggressor would be produced long before he came near conquering the entire world anyway. Britain decided to go to war against Germany over Poland. Would it have made any difference to the millions who died in that war to discover, after the war, a document, signed in Hitler's blood, that Poland was absolutely the last territory he wanted? Poland was the straw that broke the British back; whether there were twenty more straws or none to come if the British had not acted is both unknowable and irrelevant. Our problem in the Cold War is similar: whether the communists "intend" to conquer the world is irrelevant. We would have a war to stop their aggression long before such a design were unequivocally established. When we are ready to fight for South Korea it is pointless to wonder if, having conquered the rest of Asia, the Chinese would stop at Hawaii.

Finally, the world domination approach to deterrence ignores the role of the deterrent power in creating or blunting the aggressive orientations of hostile states. Indeed, the defensive power is assumed to play no role, as if it projected no threat. It calmly watches the world scene and then, in a moment of careful and considered judgment, it labels a hostile power "out for world domination" and goes to war. This view assumes that aggressors single-mindedly draw up their plans of conquest without regard for the risks and opportunities involved.

But surely this is not the case. The defensive power obviously plays a decisive role. If it is weak and hesitant, then a potential aggressor is encouraged to advance; if it adopts a firm strategy of deterrence then the hostile power grows more cautious.

Chamberlain's tragedy was his failure to understand that *he* could have chosen to project a firm deterrent threat and that his failure to do so enabled and encouraged Hitler's aggression. For Hitler was not, as a contemporary writer puts it, "The man on the bicycle who could not stop, a madman commanding vast military force and requiring immediate and visible success."[10] This interpretation is at variance with the facts. When, for example, Hitler remilitarized the Rhineland on March 7, 1936, he did not possess "vast military force" but was astonishingly weak. Having recently decreed conscription, he had not even 28 complete divisions while France, Poland and Czechoslovakia together had 90 standing divisions and a mobilized capability of 190 divisions—to say nothing of Russian and British capabilities.[11] As the head of the German Home Defense Department, Alfred Jodl said later, "Considering the situation we were in, the French covering army could have blown us to pieces."[12]

And Hitler knew it. He conceded to his nervous generals that German troops would be withdrawn if the French undertook military opposition.[13] Hitler later reminisced:

> The forty-eight hours after the march into the Rhineland were the most nerve-racking in my life. If the French had then marched into the Rhineland, we would have had to withdraw with our tails between our legs, for the military resources at our disposal would have been wholly inadequate for even a moderate resistance.[14]

This is not the orientation of a "madman" "on a bicycle who could not stop" but of a rational aggressor responding to the opportunities and risks put before him. Moreover, even if Hitler had been an unstoppable madman, he still had his generals to contend with. At the remilitarization of the Rhineland, Field Marshal von Blomberg, the commander, reserved "the right to decide on any military counter measures" should the French act. By this he meant retreat of German forces.[15] Even as late as the Munich crisis of September, 1938, the chances of a successful military coup against Hitler were good if only the allies had resolutely opposed him and thereby forced either a German retreat—and disgrace for Hitler—or a move directly to war which the generals, knowing the still inferior German position, might have openly resisted.[16]

War was not inevitable. Germany was not on an inexorable collision course with the allies. It was the weakness and cowardice of its opponents which transformed Germany the potential aggressor into Germany the rabid aggressor.

We should be wary, then, of statements like the following:

> And, if Mao rather than Ho is the Asian Hitler, even the Chinese have neither the overwhelmingly [sic] military power nor the timetable of aggression nor, apparently, the pent-up mania for instant expansion which would justify the parallel.[17]

World War II constituted, in effect, the most atrociously expensive research grant in history. We paid a fabulous sum to test certain theories about how war comes and how peace can be maintained. We ran the experiment and collected the results. Yet now, with a disconcerting disregard for the facts so dearly purchased, some are slipping into the same misconceptions and sophistries as before.

As I just noted, prior to Munich, Hitler did not have "overwhelmingly military power," and it is therefore misleading to suggest that he did. As was Germany, Red China, now in an inferior military position, is arming rapidly (in a short time she will probably have ICBM's and submarines with nuclear devices which may threaten our cities), and has made up for her lack of capabilities with a high level of determination. In the 1930s no one had— or could have had—solid evidence that Hitler had a "time-table of aggression" (even in retrospect it seems unlikely that he did[18]) and it is presumptuous for an historian to suggest that, without benefit of hindsight, he would have had such evidence. Nor could it be known that Hitler had a "pent-up mania for instant expansion." When Hitler moved into the Rhineland, many thought that it was only the Germans' "own back garden."[19] Yet, when we see China subdue Tibet or attack the Indian Northeast Frontier Agency, many excuse it with precisely the same reasoning: it is the Chinese backyard.

Finally, it is a fatal error to suggest that nations either have or have not a "pent-up mania for instant expansion" which has nothing to do with the action of other states. Such a view ignores the enormous impact of deterrent threats on aggressors. Whether the communist Chinese are expansionist or not will depend heavily upon our threat to oppose their expansion. If we contract our deterrent posture in Asia and thereby create opportunities for aggression by China and its allies, we shall probably have that aggression. There is little doubt that, after the radioactive dust had settled, there would be historians to chide us for not realizing that China had a "pent-up mania for instant expansion."

Discussions, then, of who is "mad" and who has or has not plans of world conquest in his files should be avoided. We would be ill-advised to sit quietly behind our guns until a nation seeking world domination appeared and then go to war. Such a policy is unworkable and, worse, constitutes a self-fulfilling prophecy.

The alternative is to watch the status quo and defend it against the assaults of our opponents. In this manner, we shall prevent any potential aggressor from seriously believing in, let alone attempting, world conquest. And we shall thereby avoid the terrible war which would be necessary to prevent it.

Non-Coercive Alterations of the Status Quo

The theme of this essay is the problem of aggression and deterring aggression and, in consequence, little will be said about the many other modes and levels of international behavior. We ought not to leave the subject of the status quo, however, without making a few observations about how hostile powers may jointly and peaceably alter the status quo between them.

Hostile states are engaged in a bargaining process. Each has, as its primary resource, its threat of war. It is for this reason that alterations in the status quo are so important and so delicate: they reflect on the coerciveness of each side's threat. That is, the status quo is significant not only for its own sake but as an indicator of each side's willingness to face war. It follows, therefore, that if some way is found to prevent changes in the status quo from reflecting relative fear of war, statesmen will gladly undertake such changes as they find mutually convenient.

In the abstract, we can identify two distinct contexts for alterations of the status quo: coercive and non-coercive. A coercive alteration is aggression. It consists of demanding something under penalty of war if it is not relinquished, or simply attempting to take it by force. The defensive power which permits a coercive altera- tion is assumed to be—and probably is—yielding in order to avoid war and, consequently, its deterrent threat will suffer. A non- coercive alteration is one in which war and the threat of war are renounced, explicitly or implicitly, by the side requesting the alteration. Since the threat of war is removed from the context, neither side has its threat at issue.

In a coercive alteration of the status quo, the demanding power is saying, in effect, "I want this. I shall use, or am using, force to get it. The only way to stop me is to use force." In a non-coercive alteration, the demanding power says, "I want this. I know it is yours and I will not use force to get it, but can't we make an arrangement?" Between friendly states, a non-coercive context is assumed almost as a matter of course. Each country will, of course, be bargaining with the other, but the threat of war is not a resource for either side. Instead, non-violent inducements and penalties are involved: tariffs, propaganda advantages, good will, commercial benefits and so on. When Mexico and the United States sat down to negotiate the Chamizal border dispute, settled in 1967, no one had to take elaborate steps to renounce the use of force. Everyone automatically assumed that it was renounced.

But with hostile powers it proves difficult to remove the threat of war from the context. Their history of intense rivalry, clashes and confrontations involving war or the threat of war overshadows their relationship and consequently will, unless great care is taken, color all adjustments in the status quo they might make. The statesman, if he is not alert, may lead his opponent to believe that a certain adjustment was made out of his fear of the other's threat of war, even though the statesman himself may believe the fear of war had nothing to do with his concession.

Two ancient rules of statecraft serve to protect the diplomatist from falling into this error:

1) Never negotiate under an ultimatum;
2) Always demand compensation for an alteration in the status quo achieved by your opponent.

If one agrees to negotiations after the opponent has issued a threat of war in an ultimatum, then it will seem dramatically clear that both your very presence at the negotiations as well as the outcome were compelled by your fear of war. Hence, even if one desires to have negotiations, he should not enter them under an ultimatum— not if he intends to make a non-coercive settlement in which his threat is not tested and weakened.

This same issue underlies the practice of compensation. To give something for nothing in return might have no implication if the two nations were friendly. If they are hostile, however, always seeking for symbols of each other's fear of war, an unequal outcome will reflect a greater fear on the part of the donor. Consequently, a non-coercive alteration of the status quo between hostile states ought to involve "compensation," something given in return. This still applies even if the donor power really wishes to give the piece of status quo outright (Quemoy comes immediately to mind). The primary function of compensation is not to acquire the value of it, but to demonstrate to opponents and third parties that the alteration was genuinely non-coercive, that one was not at a bargaining disadvantage owing to one's greater fear of war. Notice, thus, how even the manner of "peaceful" alterations in the status quo between hostile powers is shaped by their problems of protecting the credibility of their respective threats of war.

The Cold War status quo, then, is not immutable. Non-coercive alterations are possible and often desirable; it is the unilateral alterations which create grave problems and which must generally be resisted. In the post-war period there have been a few such non-coercive alterations, perhaps the most important being the Austrian neutrality agreement of 1955. In its broadest outlines, this settlement provided for the withdrawal of Russian troops from the Eastern section and Western troops from the Western section and a pledge that Austria would not join any military alliances. And so, to the Austrians' great pleasure, all military occupation was ended and the nation became sovereign and fully united.

This settlement was a non-coercive one. There was no threat of war hanging over the bargaining table; no ultimatum had been issued. Of course, hard bargaining took place, with each side withholding and granting this or that concession. The outcome of the negotiations also confirms the non-coercive character of the settlement: each side received approximately equal compensation for what it gave up. Aside from the arrangement of many smaller matters, the Soviet Union relinquished its right to a portion of the territory of a non-communist country but received, in turn, Austrian exclusion from NATO. In view of the then recent rearmament of Western Germany, and our threat to do the same with Western Austria, the neutrality of Austria was a useful quid pro quo for the Russians.

We must be cautious, however, about expecting too much from non-coercive settlements. Most of the time when we have "gone to the negotiating table" over status quo issues (remember cultural, commercial, and armament matters do not form part of the status quo) the context has been coercive: war was being threatened or was actually in progress. No one should have supposed, for example, at the time of the 1961-62 Geneva negotiations on Laos that the context was non-coercive. The fact that we attended such a conference as well as its results were taken to mean, and correctly, that the United States was not willing to fight a war to keep half of Laos out of communist hands. The "negotiating table," therefore, is not the automatic solution for our problems. Appeasement and the subsequent loss of reputation can take place there quite readily.

It should also be remembered that, owing to the ideological character of the Cold War status quo, we are much more constrained in the scope of possible non-coercive settlements than earlier was the case. We cannot, as was done years ago, trade one slice of territory for another, a piece of the Congo for rights in Morocco. People live in these slices and neither side can condemn them to living under the opposing ideological system. Imagine, for example, trading South Vietnam for North Korea.

Although some possibilities for non-coercive alterations of the status quo exist, the basic Cold War frictions will not, for some time and then only gradually, be amenable to peaceable solution. We must live with these uncomfortable situations and insist that our opponents do the same.

Chapter 5

THE DEMONSTRATION OF WILL

One has not made a threat until his opponent believes that he can act and that he will act. The United States with its great population, gigantic economy, sophisticated military technology, and atomic arsenal, has the material capacity to inflict intolerable penalties upon any aggressor. That is, were preventing aggression simply a matter of having the resources to make aggression prohibitively costly, we could prevent it. All our enemies know we have such resources.

What they do not know and what they are continuously attempting to estimate is our willingness to use these resources. What sacrifices and what risks are we willing to accept to oppose their aggression? How deeply do we cherish the values to be challenged in this or that situation? What is our level of determination or will? Their answer to this question defines the coerciveness of our threats. Consequently, demonstrating to our opponents that we have the will to make sacrifices and take risks to oppose their aggression is a major problem of American foreign policy. It is a recognition of this problem which causes American statesmen to act in a manner which the layman often fails to understand.

Why Divisions in the Communist World
Do Not Affect Our Deterrence Strategy

Russia and China are at loggerheads. Polycentrism is becoming increasingly evident in the communist world. Surely, many have reasoned, these changes should produce some corresponding shift in our deterrence policy. But they have not. Our Secretary of State still talks about "communist aggression," and we act as if a communist victory were undesirable no matter where it took place.

The change in our policy which people customarily suppose should result from communist divisions is a lessening of our efforts to deter aggression of smaller communist states and to thwart purely internal communist subversion. Russia and China, this view runs, are our only real enemies, the only states capable of the massive aggression which would result in a world war. We should allow, therefore, the smaller communist states to do as they please. Even if, through aggression, they succeed in establishing communist regimes in neighboring countries, little harm will come to us. North Vietnam, for example, whether it succeeds in establishing communist regimes in Laos and South Vietnam or not, can never threaten us, so why should we worry about its aggressive activities? Deter and oppose Russian or Chinese aggression, yes; the other communist states, forget about them.

This position is undermined by a critically important point: we cannot deter Russia and China without acting against lesser communist states which attempt aggression. The Russian or Chinese perception of our determination to oppose them is shaped by what they see us do against our other opponents, particularly "communist" opponents.

This observation is not so strange as it might first appear. Reputations are, first of all, public. One does not have to act directly against every possible adversary to communicate a threat to each one. A nation which takes strong action in one case against one opponent is, quite reasonably, assumed to be more likely to take similar action against another opponent. Nations and national leaders are judged to be "daring" or "timid," "courageous" or "cowardly." They establish these reputations by acting firmly or timorously in a few cases. Hitler's bold moves in the Rhineland and against Austria and Czechoslovakia gave him a reputation for forcefulness and determination throughout Europe. Even though the Poles had a treaty of non-aggression with Germany, they began to worry. What we do about the aggression of one opponent offers other enemies an indication of our determination to oppose them.

This principle is particularly important in the Cold War framework. Communist perceptions divide the world into communist and non-communist camps. There is for them (and for us) an understanding of "we" and "they." The United States is regarded as the backbone of the non-communist ("capitalist-imperialist") enemy. The communists believe, not without reason, that we dislike communism, and that we oppose its extension because we do not like it and believe it is hostile to us. When a country calling itself "communist" (and recognized as "socialist" by other communist states) commits aggression, we are expected to oppose it. Our failure to respond would suggest that we are not so willing to oppose "communist" aggression in general and, therefore, we would be more likely to let another communist nation, such as Russia or China, succeed elsewhere in aggression.

Our opponents are not the only ones estimating our determination. Our allies are doing the same thing and they are doing it by making the same obvious assumption: our present reaction to one challenge, because it indicates our commitment to the values at issue, is a guide to our future behavior in other places where similar values would be challenged. A Thai view of our Vietnam involvement in 1968 is illustrative:

> "If you Americans negotiate your way out of South Vietnam by turning the country over to the Communists," says one prominent Thai, "you will then overcompensate in Thailand, assuring us that we are the new line of defense and pledging your word and power to us." Then, after a pause, he adds: "But don't have any illusions—no one here will believe you."[1]

The Russian and Chinese leaders believe, correctly, that our willingness to take risks and make sacrifices to oppose them is, in large measure, a function of how strongly we are committed to defend the values challenged by those identified as "communists." Therefore, the more "anti-communist" the Russians or Chinese think we are, the more they assume we shall have the will to resist *their* aggression. And we demonstrate this "anti-communism" by acting against their ideological allies elsewhere. If a President is "hard on communism" in Laos, that is one more reason to believe that he will be "hard on communists" in the Dominican Republic or Berlin. Indeed, the American president who vigorously attacks the local American communist party would thereby indicate a somewhat greater willingness to resist aggression by "communists" abroad.

If we select American leaders who have a harsh view of communism in general—Barry Goldwater for example—we would expect them to react quite firmly toward the "communist" attempt in South Vietnam. If we select leaders with a more tolerant attitude toward communism—Senator William Fulbright, for example —we would expect them to be less willing to oppose "communists" in any particular situation. In Senator Fulbright's case, our predictions would work fairly well. He opposed the Bay of Pigs invasion before it was even attempted; he opposed American action in Vietnam; he opposed American involvement in the Dominican Republic. A few days before the border between East and West Berlin was closed in August, 1961, he felt that the East Germans "had a right to close it."[2]

If Mr. Fulbright were President and we were Russian strategists deciding in September, 1962, if the United States would respond to the presence of missiles in Cuba, we might conclude from his other stated positions that of all possible presidents, Mr. Fulbright would be the one least likely to oppose us. We put missiles in Cuba. And receive the shock of our lives, for Mr. Fulbright advocated an invasion of Cuba in this case.[3] A dreadful miscalculation would have occurred.

If opponents are using a certain scale (such as degree of anticommunism) to predict your behavior, then you must act within the dimensions of that scale if you wish them to predict your behavior correctly. This principle is all but ignored by those who freely recommend "new approaches" and "flexibility" in American foreign policy. Once a nation has accepted a deterrence policy, its actions are severely constrained by its own values and traditions and the opponents' framework for perceiving its actions. To ignore these constraints is to undermine, or at least alter in an unintended fashion, the deterrence posture.

The traditions, perceptions and expectations which define threats between hostile states are not arbitrary or superficial. They have their roots in the underlying conflicts which give rise to the hostile relationship; they develop over many years in response to the channels the competition has taken. Since nations do not grow hostile through the whim of one leader or a single chance misunderstanding, it follows that it is beyond the power of any particular statesman to terminate a great power hostility or dramatically reshape the manner in which threats are perceived, and, hence, the way in which they must be communicated. The best he can do is make cautious, marginal moves toward the reduction of hostility—always keeping in mind that success in this direction cannot be had unless the other side, having modified its goals, also moves in the same direction.

The relationship between hostile powers resembles, in several respects, a tug-of-war with two opposing teams attempting to pull the other into a lake which separates them. To make the analogy closer, let us assume that members of each team are chained to the rope. The struggle began with the presumption that each side sought to pull the other into the water. But after several hours of inconclusive tugging, let us suppose one team desires to end the match as a draw. If it greatly relaxes its position, it will probably end in the lake. The other side, believing that the tug-of-war is still being carried on, will conclude that its opponents have weakened and will redouble their own efforts. Or, even if the other side suspects that the first side is voluntarily relaxing as a gesture of good will, it may still desire victory and simply take advantage of the yardage gained. If the first side calls out to the other that they want a truce, that too can be interpreted as a sign of weakness, of fatigue.

The captain of the side seeking a draw, therefore, must be sensitive to the nature and tradition of the conflict in order to communicate accurately and safely to his opponent. Whatever *he* may think at the moment he has to remember that the conflict *has* been a tug-of-war, that each side *has* been pulling the other toward the lake, and that both sides have taken this struggle seriously. The other side will interpret his actions with these facts in mind. If he suddenly announces that he finds the conflict silly and stops pulling, he will quickly be yanked into the water. To bring about a successful truce he must use verbal signals and tiny relaxations on the line with the full awareness of how, in the light of the ongoing conflict, these actions will be interpreted. And, of course, if his opponents wish to continue the tug-of-war, then it is beyond his power to bring about a truce.

The significance of one's actions lies, then, not in the reasons one has for them but in the interpretation placed upon them by opponents. An interesting illustration of this principle is reported by Sir Edward Grey, British Foreign Secretary from 1905 to 1916. In the decade prior to World War I, Germany had expanded her navy. The British responded to the German increases with expansions of their own, while, at the same time seeking to allay the hostility by conciliatory gestures toward Germany. But at least one German leader, Naval Minister Admiral Von Tirpitz, misinterpreted the British intent. Writing after the war, referring to Von Tirpitz's Memoirs, Grey noted:

> Von Tirpitz now attributes our readiness to make agreements with Germany about the Bagdad Railway and the Portuguese colonies to the increase of the German Fleet. The growing strength of that fleet was, he thought, making us more conciliatory. It was I who negotiated and initialled the last versions of those two Agreements. The whole transaction was in my hands, and I *know* that the growth of the German Fleet had nothing whatever to do with my attitude. The sole motive was a desire to show that we were ready to meet German aspirations, wherever we could reconcile them with British interests and engagements. [4]

We can see, in light of this illustration, why the task of establishing better relations with a hostile power acquiring new armaments is particularly delicate. Unless one approaches that power with great caution, carefully preserving the appearance as well as the reality of symmetry, of a quid pro quo relationship, the hostile power may misinterpret conciliatory gestures as signs of fear before its new weapons. This problem is apparently not grasped by those who fervently appeal for dramatic, unilateral American gestures of conciliation toward a Red China rapidly acquiring a nuclear arsenal.

Finally, communist military alliances, explicit and implicit, give our actions toward small communist states a direct indication of our posture toward the large ones. No small communist state is without a backstopping, protective threat from one or both of its "socialist" big brothers. No small communist state would engage in aggression without that threat. Our posture toward these small states is, in large part, shaped by our fear of that protective threat. If in 1965, for example, Russia and China had publicly promised to do nothing if we invaded North Vietnam and destroyed the communist regime there, then the war in Vietnam would have come to a rapid end. Under our unopposed threat to eliminate North Vietnam as a communist state, the North Vietnamese would have been obliged to draw back from their attack on the South.

It is therefore correct to say that whenever a small communist state undertakes aggression, it is an extension of Russian and/or Chinese power. The men, the guns and the rice may be domestic but the backstopping threat is external. It follows, therefore, that our behavior toward small communist states will give Russia and China an indication of our determination to oppose them. If we allowed the North Vietnamese to capture South Vietnam, it would be presumed, correctly, that we remained inactive because, in part, we feared the danger of escalation into a war with China. We would be telling the Chinese that we would rather tolerate aggression than get into a war with them.

An even better illustration of this point is Cuba. The Bay of Pigs landing was superficially a matter between only the United States and Cuba. It might have demonstrated only that we chose not to employ our own forces to destroy Castro. But the Russians had voiced various threats to defend Cuba "with rockets" if we should invade. Clearly they had some interest in Cuba. By failing to support the invaders, we suggested to the Russians that we were frightened of *them*.

These observations help to explain why, for example, State Department officials say that China is the real enemy in Vietnam. They do not mean, of course, that we are shooting at Chinese troops. Rather, that we are protecting the credibility of our threat to act against China if she attempts aggression. We can also see why State Department officials speak of "communist aggression." Once one understands the relationships involved, it becomes a meaningful phrase. "Communist aggression" is a shorthand way of saying "aggression by a state which is linked to Russia and China by perception and alliance patterns in such a way that our action toward that aggression will provide an important indication of our willingness to respond to aggression by Russia or China—or other states linked by the same perception pattern."

The Myth of the Myth of a Monolithic Communist Conspiracy

One of the recurring themes in critiques of American foreign policy is the charge that the State Department has not noticed the divisions in the communist world, that it is obsessed with a belief in a monolithic communist conspiracy. On the surface, such a charge appears unconvincing. The people in the State Department have gone to college; they spend their working days poring over reports, articles, and books on communist countries and communism. When one meets State Department personnel they appear to be well-adjusted and moderate in their views—indeed many, if not most, are liberals on socio-economic matters. One would not readily suppose that they were abysmally misinformed on world affairs or in the grip of a psycho-pathological prejudice.

Yet it *is* supposed and argued repeatedly, as the following excerpts illustrate. Both writers are college professors:

> . . . the obsession of American policy-makers with what they still see as monolithic communism has blinded them . . . 5
>
> The clichés about a centralized communist conspiracy aiming at monolithic world revolution are still cherished in the State Department, in spite of what has struck lay observers as a rather evident fragmentation of the communist world.6

How does this belief that the State Department accepts the myth of monolithic communism arise? Why does it persist? The root cause appears to be the failure of lay observers to understand threats and their implications; that is, a failure to understand a central dimension of American foreign policy. High State Department officials say things such as "communist aggression" or "extension of Chinese power" or "the world-wide significance of aggression in Vietnam" or "the larger design." And they act as if aggression by "communists" in one place were somehow connected to other "communists." Once one understands the problem of demonstrating will and how this problem resolves into matters of perception systems, alliances, and backstopping threats, these statements and actions make sense. If one does not understand the implications of a deterrence policy, they are perplexing; and one falls back on detraction: State Department officials are misinformed and narrow-minded.

The notion that if one's opponents are not united, they are, for that reason, less dangerous is a gross oversimplification. A wolf pack is not monolithic; nor is it an organized conspiracy. Wolves sometimes fight each other. Yet if a lonely traveler is pursued by a pack of wolves in the forest, he has to worry about each one. If one cub, harmless in itself, begins nibbling at his snowshoes, the traveler had better strike back. Otherwise others, which had paced quietly in the background, will suppose that the prey is weakening and may close in.

It is therefore misleading to forcefully announce that communism is "no longer" monolithic, as if the fact had dramatic consequences for our deterrence policy. It does not. It is naive to allege that State Department officials are unaware of divisions in the communist world known to outsiders for years. The idea that American policy-makers believe in the myth of a monolithic communist conspiracy is itself a myth. The function of this latter myth seems to be that of blocking the intelligent analysis of American foreign policy. The critic need not take what American statesmen say and do seriously, as requiring a thoughtful explanation; he has already "explained" their behavior: they are stupid.

The Strategic Value Theory

Most Americans would agree that we should fight a war to prevent the forcible communist conquest of Britain, West Germany, Japan, India or Australia. There is considerably less agreement on whether we should oppose a forcible communist attempt against Laos, Nigeria or Quemoy.

Typically, the debate on what we should defend is carried on within the framework of a "strategic value theory" of defense policy. American action in a particular case is justified to the degree that war-making capability is falling into the hands of our opponents. If the country about to fall into communist hands has sizable natural resources, a developed economy, a large population or a strategic geographic position, then our resistance is correspondingly justified. The underlying reason for this concern about "heartlands" is the assumption that in the event of a large, future war, our opponents will have greater military capability and, therefore, be more likely to defeat us. Even before this war, our fear of losing it would weaken our bargaining position and cause us to retreat before the demands of our enemies.

As an explanation for the behavior of hostile states, the strategic value theory is inadequate. It does apply in some cases, and in others it is a secondary factor. But it cannot be offered, particularly today, as the primary explanation for the observed tendency of hostile states to defend the status quo.

The strategic value theory has gained wide acceptance, in part, because it emerged in the pre-atomic era when it frequently did correspond to reality. Many territorial acquisitions did substantially enhance the military position of the aggressor against his opponents. Indeed, almost all the Axis aggressions prior to World War II had this effect. Hitler's remilitarization of the Rhineland enabled him to build fortresses there against a possible French attack; Austria added to Nazi economic and human potential; Czechoslovakia had the Skoda armaments works and an army which would have been joined with the allies in a war.

But, looking further back, there are many crises and cases of aggression which clearly did not involve a significant redistribution of war-making potential between hostile states. Practically none of the pre-World War I confrontations can be convincingly explained by arguing that substantial human or economic potential was in dispute. The Austrian annexation of Bosnia-Herzegovina on October 6, 1908 affords a typical illustration. Before the annexation, these regions were already under Austrian occupation and administrative control. Thus Austria already had whatever geostrategic or tributary benefits which the possession of these small, impoverished areas would confer. Indeed, the administration of the hostile populations of these territories so drained Austrian resources that they could be considered a military liability to the Austro-Hungarian empire. Significantly, it was in Bosnia, at Sarejevo, where the Austrian Archduke Ferdinand was assassinated on June 28, 1914.

If nations operated on a strategic value theory of defense policy, the annexation would have gone unnoticed. It did not. It produced a serious international crisis the shock waves of which were felt for years afterward. In particular, the annexation created "a dangerous and irremediable state of tension between Austria and Russia . . . [and] produced a deep rift in Austro-Italian relations."[7] Further, it produced a tightening of the Triple Entente of Russia, England and France against the Central Powers. The annexation provoked a European crisis not because significant military potential changed hands but because it was an Austrian violation of the status quo to the disadvantage of Russia.

The status quo in this case had been established by renunciation thirty years earlier at the Congress of Berlin in 1878 (and later reaffirmed in the Constantinople Agreement of 1879).[8] The Austrians agreed that while they occupied Bosnia-Herzegovina, the Turkish government would have "sovereign rights" in these territories. Illogical and ephemeral as this dual arrangement might seem, it was recognized by diplomats throughout Europe, including the Austrians, as the status quo.

Violation of this status quo was offensive to Serbia and, therefore, offensive to Russia which was identified with Serbia. The Russian inaction in the face of this violation was a "humiliation," that is, a blow to Russia's reputation as a determined actor willing to defend its interests. The Russian ambassador to France, Nelidov, expressed the consequences succinctly:

> A public exposure of this kind of our weakness has made a most painful impression upon our friends and must encourage our opponents to present the most impossible demands to Russia in the firm conviction that we shall yield. [9]

The annexation of Bosnia-Herzegovina produced a decline in the coerciveness of the Russian threat. It was this threat which served to inhibit aggression by Russia's opponents; a decline in its integrity encouraged, as Nelidov correctly anticipated, further thrusts in the future, including the Austrian ultimatum to Serbia of July, 1914, which led to general war.

The strategic value theory explains international confrontations in the pre-atomic era only some of the time; in the nuclear age, it applies even less. It is only with the greatest difficulty that we can conceive of a future war in which the strategic value of countries kept out of communist hands would have a decisive effect. If we are considering future limited wars, then, almost by definition, one ally more or less could not be critical to success. Limited war is characterized by an under-utilization of U.S., free world, and communist war-making potential. In limited wars there are U.S. allies not contributing, U.S. men not mobilized, and U.S. weapons not employed. The 50,000 South Korean troops that fought in Vietnam have certainly been a great help. If we had not opposed North Korean aggression in 1950, these troops would not have been there. Yet their presence was not decisive. We could have raised 50,000 more troops of our own, or for that matter, 5,000,000 more. Or other allies could have contributed more troops. With so many slack resources lying about in the limited war situation, it is unrealistic to consider any particular outside contribution as decisive. Limited wars are won, lost, or drawn not because one side or the other runs out of men or weapons but because one side is more or less determined and courageous. Of course, allies with military and economic potential are often a useful asset in many limited war situations, and occasionally they can be quite important. This is particularly true when one has only a modest level of determination to begin with. But rarely would they have a strategic value commensurate with the costs of the war which we would fight in their defense.

If one considers the nuclear or total war possibilities, the contribution of potential allies becomes even less significant. In a nuclear duel between the superpowers, whether the Laotian army is on our side or theirs will make little difference in the outcome. Such a duel would almost certainly be arrested before either side exploded all its atomic weapons; courage and determination, not manpower, would form the basis for a settlement. Or, if the United States capacity were strained in fighting a conventional war, it would always have the option of using atomic weapons. Again, determination would substitute for manpower.

In some cases, strategic geographic considerations would be involved in our decision to defend certain countries. One could argue that by our losing Laos, for example, the communists would gain long borders with Thailand, Cambodia and South Vietnam. Thus, an infiltration campaign may more easily be mounted against these countries in the future. Yet again, this consideration, while important, cannot be decisive. If we had the will to assist these countries in defeating infiltration attacks, we certainly could do it. It would be more difficult and more costly with the exposed border but not beyond our military capabilities.

The military-strategic value of this or that distant land, therefore, is generally of secondary importance in the atomic age. The loss of such lands to our opponents would not decisively affect our ability to defeat our enemies in a future war. With our great, and increasing, abundance of military potential the question "How many divisions have you?" is becoming less and less relevant, and "How determined are you?" correspondingly more important in establishing strong or weak international bargaining positions.

It follows, therefore, that the strategic value theory, which proposes that we do (and should) decide to defend particular territories on the basis of their military potential, is inappropriate. We can see this by a quick glance at the conduct of American policy for the last two decades. It is absurd to declare that we stay in Berlin, Guantanamo, Quemoy, and Matsu because these points have significant strategic value. It is unconvincing to argue that our opposition to communist aggression in South Korea, Laos, or

South Vietnam springs mainly from a desire to protect a human, economic and military potential which is vital or even important to the survival of the free world or the security of the United States. Indeed, one is hard-pressed to show that all of Indochina would weigh significantly in the balance of military potential between the superpowers.

Thus, if we seek an explanation for why nations behave as they do, the strategic value theory is clearly incomplete:

> Hostile powers tend to oppose moves by each other and each other's allies to alter the status quo because they oppose the redistribution of war-making potential which would result from the successful alteration.

This proposition cannot account for most international confrontations, particularly in recent years. The alternative theory defended in this essay seems more consistent with the actual behavior of hostile states:

> Hostile states tend to oppose moves by each other and each other's allies to alter the status quo because they desire to avoid the loss in threat coerciveness (or reputation for determination) which would result from the successful alteration.

The strategic value theory, then, should not be used as the primary justification for opposing or not opposing aggression in a particular case. The critic of American action in Vietnam who points out that it "is not a region of major military and industrial importance" is alluding to the strategic value theory and, therefore, raising a secondary, even peripheral, issue. If all we were worried about were regions of "military and industrial importance" then we would not have stood firm in Berlin, Laos, South Korea, or Quemoy.

Exposing the shortcomings of the strategic value theory also undercuts the relevance of the monolithic-polycentric communism issue. The reason we opposed the expansion of an assumedly "monolithic" communist movement was not that resources of vital importance to our own security in the atomic age were falling to our opponents. We were attempting to protect our threat to resist the aggression of our adversaries—as hostile nations have done for centuries. Therefore, to show that Russia or China are less likely to be aided by the resources of other communist states in some future war is beside the point. We were not worried about those military resources in the first place. The discussion, for example, about Ho Chi Minh being an "Asian Tito" is academic for our Vietnam policy. Whether North Vietnam is a "puppet satellite" or an "autonomous communist state," our action in South Vietnam would have, in either case, almost identical consequences as a demonstration of our general willingness to carry out our threats.

This inspection of the strategic value theory enables us to clear away some of the confusion surrounding the phrase "balance of power." When the statement is made that between two hostile states (or alliances of states) there exists a "balance of power" two quite distinct meanings may be applied. One, perhaps, the most common usage, is that the two sides have an approximately equal supply of men, weapons and economic resources so that the outcome of a war between them is in doubt. That is, the meaning given to "power" is a summation of the physical resources of each side.

If we recognize that power, or the ability to influence the behavior of other states, consists of threats, a different interpretation of "balance of power" is warranted. One component of a threat is certainly the capacity to act—that is, military potential. But a threat has another element, always important in the past, overwhelmingly so today: the opponent's perception of one's courage or will. "Balance of power" would then refer to the relative coerciveness of each side's threats, keeping in mind that today, this coerciveness largely consists of the reciprocal perception of will. Thus, a world situation in which each side had approximately equal fear of the other so that deterrent threats were equally credible on each side would represent a "balance" of power. As one side came to have threats of decreasing credibility, then an "imbalance of power" against it could be said to exist.

When we hear, then, that an American retreat in Vietnam would cause the "balance of power" to tip (more) against us, the statement can be either absurd or sophisticated, depending upon how one understands "power." If one means that the military resources we would lose would put us in a significantly more disadvantageous position in fighting a future war with Russia or China, then the statement is highly unconvincing. But the statement does make sense if it says a retreat would, by demonstrating a lower level of will, weaken our other deterrent threats. In general, balance of power statements often make much more sense if one substitutes "balance of threat credibility."

Yet another meaning of "balance of power," widely used by 19th century statesmen, is simply "status quo"—that is, the great-power status quo. When diplomats called the Austrian annexation of Bosnia-Herzegovina an "alteration of the balance of power" they meant it was an alteration of the existing great-power status quo.

At first, it might seem that these two definitions of "balance of power"—balance of threats and status quo—are quite distinct. But in fact they are two sides of the same coin. Since the value of a threat cannot be estimated independently, it must be deduced from the changes presumably caused by threats: alterations in the status quo. We know that the nation with the more coercive threat is able to change the status quo in its favor; therefore, if a nation does alter the status quo in its favor, it is assumed to have the more coercive threat. When Hitler altered the status quo over Czechoslovakia in 1938 to the disadvantage of France and Great Britain, he also demonstrated that his threat was more coercive than that of the allies. To decide who was more determined to face war, France or Germany, observers did not need to carry out extensive opinion polls or in-depth psychological research; they simply had to glance at changes in the map.

The balance of threat credibility ("balance of power"), then, is in practice revealed by the direction and nature of changes in the status quo ("balance of power").

Why the Size of the Country Is Less Important Than How Our Opponents Get It

Indonesia is a country with an area of 576,000 square miles and a population of 100 million. South Vietnam has 66,000 square miles and 16 million people. Let us suppose, as nearly happened, that Indonesian communists effect a successful coup, and, literally overnight, the country becomes a communist state. Let us also suppose that the United States failed to send ground troops to South Vietnam in 1965, and the Viet Cong-North Vietnamese destroy the South Vietnamese army and gain control of the country. Indonesia has gone communist; South Vietnam has gone communist. From the American point of view, which would be worse?

If our policy were to keep areas of economic and military potential out of communist control, then clearly the loss of Indonesia would be worse. If our policy were merely to protect specific groups of human beings from the unhappy consequences of communism, then, again, the loss of Indonesia would be more unfortunate than the loss of South Vietnam. But if the American objective is, as I argue, to sustain a credible threat to oppose our opponents' aggression, then the conclusion is reversed. Losing Vietnam would do us the greater injury. It would more dramatically undermine our deterrent threat.

This conclusion follows from an examination of what our failure to respond in each case would demonstrate about our willingness to oppose violations of the status quo. In Indonesia, we would be presented with a *fait accompli*. We wake up the next morning, and the country is communist. Our only opportunity to respond would be to invade and destroy an established communist regime. We never had an opportunity to oppose communist *expansion* or *aggression*. Consequently, our threat to oppose communist aggression would not have been explicitly challenged. (The loss of Indonesia would still, of course, be a serious reverse).

In Vietnam our deterrent threat would be more clearly tested. First, we had made a number of explicit statements that we would defend South Vietnam—letters of assurance from Presidents Eisenhower and Kennedy, and SEATO. Second, the communist attempt was not an overnight coup, but a long, drawn-out guerrilla war in which the rebels were clearly identified as "communists" and supported by our opponents. The United States had ample opportunity to act to prevent a communist victory. For a period of years, the world—our opponents and allies—would be asking, "Is the United States sufficiently determined to prevent the forcible expansion of its opponents?"

Finally, the North Vietnamese role in the struggle became so evident that the Vietnam war could no longer be realistically called an "internal matter." By the beginning of 1965, the North Vietnamese had sent, in addition to supplies and personnel which were integrated into Viet Cong units, entire military units of their own. The struggle therefore involved an "outside attack," that is, aggression. Hostile troops were within the territory of an ally and were fighting the troops of that ally.

Our failure to respond in Vietnam, then, would have seriously impaired our general deterrent threat. We had ample time to respond; the guerrillas were known to be "communist"; the communist states were clearly identified with them; and outside attack by a communist state was obviously taking place.

This hypothetical Vietnam-Indonesia comparison is yet another illustration of the basic principle being advanced in this chapter: the justification for American action abroad must be made in terms of the extent to which it demonstrates a will or lack of will to oppose aggression by our opponents, that is, of the extent to which it affects the coerciveness of our threat.

This principle provides a framework for analyzing and explaining many points of American defense policy. One quite difficult issue is the connection between outside support for a communist guerrilla movement and the extent to which American action is justified. This matter arose over Vietnam. For some, whether we should have been in Vietnam hinges upon the outcome of a debate on how much outside assistance the Viet Cong received: guns, men, combat units, and training. This matter has been argued longer and with more hairsplitting than necessary.

The real issue in Vietnam was not whether it fulfills some technical standard of ours for "outside aggression." It is, what would our opponents conclude about our will from our action or failure to act under these circumstances? The outstanding question raised by the Vietnam struggle was: Is the United States being challenged to demonstrate willingness to prevent an armed communist attempt to alter the status quo? Clearly it was. Thus, to a considerable degree, our threat was tested simply by the protracted nature of the conflict and the manifestly "communist" identification of the insurgents. Even if no outside aid at all was involved, the credibility of our threat to oppose *aggression* was being tested.

Since aggression was actually involved, then, presumably, our threat was more dramatically tested. But we must be cautious. *We* may be able to distinguish between local communist efforts and outside communist aggression. *We* might like to have our opponents believe, "We shall tolerate local action but resolutely oppose outside aggression." But it is doubtful that such a distinction would be understood and assimilated by our opponents—at least not with much clarity. Our failure to prevent an autonomous *alteration* of the status quo would reflect upon our willingness to oppose an (outside) *violation* of the status quo. The communists assume

—correctly, to a large extent—that our opposition to aggression stems from our commitment to values challenged by the advent of communist regimes; and the strength of this commitment would be tested in our reaction to the autonomous alteration of the status quo.

The reverse is also true for ourselves. If Russia should tolerate an anti-communist revolution in Hungary which had no outside support whatsoever, we would begin to speculate about their commitment to communism. We would be tempted to conclude that they would be less likely to oppose, for example, a South Korean invasion of North Korea. This conclusion would remain even if they announced, after the hypothetical Hungarian episode, that they would implacably oppose anti-communist *aggression*.

Even if, in a general way, the United States could communicate to its opponents a distinction we might like to make between internal and external attempts to alter the status quo, it is clear that the distinction will not bear much refinement. We have, particularly in Vietnam, made our opponents understand that active outside support for a communist insurgency increases the chance of American involvement. To this extent, we have succeeded in "communicating" an internal-external distinction. Yet establishing the precise levels of outside involvement which will trigger our response is, as a practical matter, impossible. The different classes of outside support are not commensurable and will not have the same effect in each case. If two dozen Chinese rifles are enough to enable communists in Kuwait to capture the country, then this outside assistance is too much. We ourselves would not want to establish precise limits on the amount of outside aid which defines "aggression" and hence provokes American action. In any case, there would not be enough wars or involvements to communicate whatever limits we established. The communication of one's willingness to go to war under certain circumstances is extraordinarily difficult and expensive. It is no good just saying that we shall respond if A, B, or C degrees of outside support are involved; we would have to fight a war to establish each limit as a real—not paper—one.

Our threat was tested in Vietnam because we had a clear opportunity to prevent a "forcible," "communist" attempt with "substantial" outside communist support to gain control of a non-communist territory. To argue further whether 5 or 15 tons of supplies came weekly from the North, or in what precise sense the

Viet Cong are connected to Hanoi, is to develop distinctions which we could not communicate in threats to our opponents. If we had deserted Vietnam because, let us say, only 17 percent of the Viet Cong were trained in the North, and we announce we definitely would fight if that figure had been 25 percent, our opponents will not believe it. They will conclude that we lacked the will to fight a tough war to hold on to a piece of the non-communist world. And they would undoubtedly be correct.

This discussion on the demonstration of will enables us to unravel some rather complicated aspects of American policy toward Cuba. Many Americans have been perplexed by our position toward Cuba. "Why," they ask, "do we go half-way around the world to fight communism in Vietnam when we have permitted a communist state right on our own doorstep?" In effect, two questions are being raised: 1) why don't we destroy the communist regime in Cuba now; and 2) why didn't we prevent Cuba from going communist back in 1958-1962?

We do not attack Cuba today because it is not our policy to violate the status quo. For the moment, Cuba is a communist state outside the Soviet defense sphere. An American invasion of Cuba, while it would not justify a Russian response, would undo much of our accomplishments in convincing our opponents that we are willing to live and let live. They would find disturbing the deliberate destruction of communist Cuba. It would indicate an aggressive orientation on our part and necessitate closer alliances in the communist world, greater defense expenditures, greater hostility, more suspicion, and a stiffened resolve to oppose anything that appears of benefit to the United States.

Earlier, I argued that the excitation theory of war was inappropriate because there exists a status quo which gives each side an effective measure of the aggressive or nonaggressive character of its opponent. It followed that we should disregard all the "encirclement" claims of our opponents since we both had a meaningful measurement of who was encircling whom: the status quo. If we violate the status quo then we are, in fact, aggressive.

If the world is ever to move away from a continuous existence on the brink of war, it will have to be on the basis of the status quo. Both sides will have to respect the existing, mutually perceived distribution of rights and territories. Thus far, the United States and its allies have a highly commendable record in this respect. We have demonstrated that we shall defend the status quo against aggression but that we shall not violate it. We have established, therefore, a principle which our opponents can clearly recognize and adopt when, and to the extent that, they find the risk of war more frightening than the prospect of expansion. To erode this principle would condemn the world to a future of unregulated aggression in which any nation takes what it thinks it can get away with.

It is true, of course, that an invasion of Cuba would enhance the credibility of our deterrent threat. So would an invasion of Red China. Our opponents would reason that if we were willing to *take,* we certainly would be willing to *defend.* Indeed, this is our view of the communist threat. But to argue in this fashion loses sight of why we wanted a credible deterrent threat in the first place: to insure the greatest long-run chances for peace. A violation of the status quo not only produces a war, or risks war; it undermines the only basis on which peace may eventually be constructed: the status quo.

One might put it another way: a deterrent threat is not an absolute value. The United States does not, nor should not, do whatever increases the coerciveness of its threat regardless of the consequences. It has been argued here that a credible deterrent is so important that we should be willing to make considerable sacrifices for it. Yet clearly there are limits to what we should pay. Under most circumstances, aggression lies beyond those limits, first, because it is ordinarily much more costly and more risky than fighting defensive wars, and second, because it upsets the world order we seek to create.

Why we did not oppose the Cuban drift toward communist rule is a somewhat similar question. American policy-makers were faced with the following situation. When Castro was in the hills he was known to be a "democratic reformer." He was supported by several American newspapers. He was not identified as a "communist." The American people and their government looked benignly upon Castro. We curtailed military assistance to Batista six months before Castro won. Then, through a series of subtle changes, the regime—which first appeared as a democratic revolution—was transmuted into a communist one. Moreover, the regime was not generally understood to *be* communist until after it, in fact, *was.* Consequently, the United States had little opportunity to oppose an alteration in the Cold War status quo. Up to a certain period—about May, 1960—no alteration in the status quo had apparently occurred. As we began to realize what had happened, the status quo was already somewhat altered, and American action would have had aggressive overtones.

If we return to the basic justification for American action abroad—maintaining the credibility of our deterrent threat—it appears that the Cuban episode ought not to have seriously undermined our deterrent. When he was in the Sierra Maestra, Castro was not identified as a communist nor was he assisted by other communist countries. Indeed, the communist world was not cheering for him. It would therefore seem to follow that our willingness to oppose our opponents was not being tested. The Russians, Chinese or North Vietnamese would draw no very clear conclusion about our willingness to oppose them from our failure to act against a "bourgeois-opportunist." The Cuban revolution did not appear to test our willingness to oppose the aggression of our opponents, and, for this reason, there would seem to have been little justification for acting against it before it succeeded.

Yet the issue is still more complex. After Cuba was recognized as "communist," the communists were likely to misinterpret and misunderstand the situation in a way which did undermine our threat. First, to the extent they believed that we would never tolerate a communist regime in the Western Hemisphere, and certainly not in Cuba, our toleration of this regime did reflect poorly our general determination to oppose their expansion. Second, it is quite probable that our opponents would gloss over the fact that Castro was a "democratic" guerrilla and loosely assume that here was an illustration of the successful conquest of power by a communist guerrilla movement *to which we did not respond.* On the basis of this experience, the Pathet Lao, Viet Cong, and North Vietnamese could easily have concluded that we would not act against them in Southeast Asia. After all, many Americans asked "Why do we go half-way around the world to fight communism in Vietnam when we have permitted a communist regime on our own doorstep"—implying that our action in Vietnam was inconsistent with our inaction in Cuba. Certainly, therefore, opponents could fall victim to the same line of argument and expect us to be "consistent" on the Vietnam issue.

Once again, we encounter the vitally important principle: a

threat is not what you *say* it is but rather what the opponent *believes* it is, based upon *his* interpretation of your behavior. In Cuba we wanted to say, and tried to say 1) we do not violate the status quo; 2) we shall oppose and have the will to oppose a communist guerrilla attempt to alter the status quo if it is supported by other communist states. However, our opponents, to some extent, probably misinterpreted the Cuban episode as reflecting a lack of determination to oppose their aggression.

Should we have acted against Cuba in 1960 or 1961? That is, would the costs and moral agony of toppling Castro been worth the more credible deterrent threat and a subsequent possible reduction in future communist thrusts—in Laos, Vietnam, the missile crisis, and Berlin? The answer involves weighing the costs of acting; the impact of acting or not acting on the expectations of our opponents and allies; the probability of future aggression; and the probable course and cost of our response to that aggression. It is sufficient to show how difficult the question is; fortunately we are not compelled to answer it. The policy-maker must.

Chapter 6

THE DIMENSIONS OF COMMITMENT

How and why does the United States get committed to defend certain countries? This question has been raised with particular urgency by some critics of the American involvement in Vietnam. The United States, they agree, could not withdraw defeated from Vietnam after 1965 since such a dramatic retreat would seriously weaken our threats elsewhere. But, they insist, at some earlier time we could have retired with little or no cost to our reputation. Indeed, we might have chosen never to make a commitment back in 1954-55 when we first extended American assistance and SEATO treaty protection to South Vietnam. According to this argument, the war in Vietnam was the result of the short-sighted diplomacy of earlier years.

Underpinning this argument is a mistaken assumption about the nature of threats and their credibility: that a great power can freely select the specific threats it wishes to make. A nation following an ongoing deterrence policy does not have this freedom. Obligations or commitments are, to a large extent, thrust upon it. It has values which are challenged by opponents; it has set precedents in defending them. These values and precedents create expectations about the nation's future behavior. And that is, analytically, what threats or commitments are: the expectations of others. Leaders can, of course, refuse to meet these expectations and suffer a corresponding loss of reputation. But it is not in their power to eliminate, without cost, a specific threat.

To understand this conclusion it is helpful to examine the nature of the most general threat we project: to defend any free-world country against outright communist attack—should our

assistance be necessary to defeat the attack. Few people realize
that we have such an obligation—so few, in fact, that it is
politically unhealthy for an American Secretary of State to emphasize it on nationwide television. Grilled before the Senate
Foreign Relations Committee TV hearings in 1966, Secretary of
State Dean Rusk allowed the senators to believe that we were
committed to protect only those countries covered by collective
defense treaties:

> Senator Aiken. And are we bound to fight communism
> wherever it exists?
> Secretary Rusk. No, sir, no, sir, we are not, we are not.
> We are not talking about fighting communism for the
> purpose of destroying communism as such as a social
> or political organization, if that is what people want.
> But what we are talking about, I believe, Senator, is
> that where Communist countries undertake to com-
> mit aggression against those to whom the United
> States has undertaken a clear commitment in an alli-
> ance, that there we have a duty to assist our allies to
> meet that aggression.
> Senator Aiken. That would include what, about 80 or 90
> countries in the world?
> Secretary Rusk. No, sir. This would include just over 40
> countries.
> Senator Aiken. Only 40?
> Secretary Rusk. That is right.[1]

> Senator Mundt. You said one thing I know a lot of
> Americans are going to be pleased to hear—you said
> that we are not committed to fight Communist coun-
> tries every place that they emerge. We are limited to
> 40 or about 40.
>   I think it would be good to have you place in the
> printed record the list of those 40 countries.
> Secretary Rusk. I will be glad to.[2]

In fact, however, we do project a threat to defend any free-
world country against communist attack, and we would normally
have to carry out that threat if it were clearly tested. Although
Rusk was carefully guarding himself from being called a "policeman of the world," he did indicate the broad extent of our obligation to resist communist aggression:

> Secretary Rusk. [Pax Americana] . . . is not our policy.
> We do not have worldwide commitments to all 117

countries with whom we have relations. We have some 42 allies, very specific commitments to those allies.

Now, it is true that, in the appropriate way in the United Nations and elsewhere, we would presumably give sympathy and support to those who are victims of the kind of aggression which would have worldwide implications.[3]

Later, in a prepared statement before the Preparedness Subcommittee of the Senate Armed Services Committee, Rusk announced our policy more firmly:

Whether or not we have . . . a treaty with a particular country, the presence there of a U.S. base clearly signifies an interest and concern on our part with the security of that country.

* * *

No would-be aggressor should suppose that the absence of a defense treaty, congressional declaration, or U.S. military presence grants immunity to aggression.[4]

Rusk was not announcing a new American deterrence policy with these words; he was merely recognizing an obligation that has grown up over the past decades without our being able to prevent it.

It is easy to see how such unsought obligations can arise. A threat is what your enemies expect you might do. If, in view of your past behavior, they expect you to do something that you, in fact, do not want to do, you still have "made" a threat. In some cases, of course, it is possible to let the enemy go ahead and find out that he had mistaken your intentions. But when a nation is locked into a global deterrence policy against one or more hostile powers, it becomes dangerous not to live up to the expectations of one's opponents, regardless how these expectations were created.

An analogy might be drawn from the old West where a man's position and worth were closely tied to his ability and willingness to use his guns. Lightning Joe is coming to Dry Gulch to apply for the job of sheriff. The day before he arrives, a rumor spreads around town that Lightning has challenged Rough Pete, the fastest local gun, to shoot it out in front of the saloon at high noon on the day of his arrival. Lightning, who never made such a challenge, arrives on the eleven o'clock stage to find Pete oiling his guns and the entire town gathering around the saloon to watch the duel. Can Lightning refuse to live up to the expectations of the townspeople, even though he did not intend to create those expectations? If he refuses, would he get the job of sheriff? Or, even if he got it, would Pete and his gang respect him and avoid tangling with him?

The United States has a similar problem. Just by being what we are and having acted as we have in the past, we have created expectations which we cannot safely ignore. In particular, our opponents believe we have an interest in preventing the expansion of communism everywhere. Or, to say the same thing differently, the political partition of the globe into communist and non-communist countries is an important part of the great-power status quo. It is something we have been fighting about; it is something we are *expected* to be likely to fight about. That is, we have threatened to prevent its forcible alteration by our major opponents or their allies.

It ought to be emphasized that our opponents are not "misperceiving" when they conclude the United States is hostile to the expansion of communism. The overwhelming majority of Americans do dislike such expansion, for communist regimes negate important American values. It is easy to overlook this by adopting a superficially hard-headed view of the goals of American policy. Some excerpts from George Kennan's prepared statement before the Senate Foreign Relations Committee on February 10, 1966, illustrate this danger. At one point Kennan observed:

> I see in the Vietcong a band of ruthless fanatics, many of them misled, no doubt, by the propaganda that has been drummed into them, but cruel in their methods, dictatorial, and oppressive in their aims, I am not conscious of having any sympathy for them. I think their claim to represent the people of South Vietnam is unfounded. A country which fell under this exclusive power would have my deepest sympathy . . . 5

It is difficult to square this view with his opening remark:

> The first point I would like to make is that if we were not already involved as we are today in Vietnam, I would know of *no reason* why we should wish to become so involved, and I could think of several reasons why we should wish not to. 6

Mr. Kennan himself enunciated one reason why we should become involved: our "deepest sympathy" for those who might fall victim to the "cruel" methods and the "dictatorial" and "oppressive" aims of the Viet Cong. And, it must be immediately added, the Viet Cong were not an isolated force, unrelated to our opponents, Russia and China. They were closely identified with and supported by these opponents. And they were attempting to implement the values advanced by these opponents—the same values we found ourselves opposing in other parts of the world.

Our opponents may expect us to make efforts to protect the ideological status quo, but is there any need to conform to their expectation in a given case? After all, if *we* do not really want to protect a certain country, surely we should not have to do so just because our opponents believe we would. Let them attack and discover that we really had no intention of defending that country. They would soon learn that they had incorrectly generalized about our threat in this case.

Unfortunately, we cannot adopt this view for the same reason Lightning Joe could not. We have a reputation to protect. If everyone believes we have made a threat, even when we have not sought to in a particular case, then a failure to act would show a lack of determination. The communists will not conclude they were mistaken about our desire to oppose their expansion. They would continue to believe that we wanted to see them fail. And they would be correct. Our failure to act would communicate that we lacked the determination to oppose them, that we lacked the courage to fight a dangerous, costly war with them in defense of our interests.

But the threats we *want* to make will work only if enemies believe we have the determination to carry them out. The integrity of these threats depends on the same reputation tested in the "unintended" threat.

These reflections suggest, then, that to a large extent the United States does not have the freedom to choose which threats to make, which countries to defend. The obligation to resist the aggression of our opponents and their allies overtakes us as a consequence of our worldwide position as the enemy of the communist powers and defender of the values they challenge. We may choose not to meet this obligation in a particular case, of course, but not without impairing, to some extent, the credibility of our many other threats.

With these observations in mind, we can understand the dilemma U.S. policy-makers faced in Indochina in 1954 after the collapse of French power in the area. A formal denial of a U.S. interest in the area would not have been a wise or viable policy. It would not have been wise, because the United States was too strong and too deeply involved in deterring and fighting communists around the world to convincingly declare "no interest" in Indochina. Such a statement would have been manifestly inconsistent with the entire course and conduct of our general deterrence policy. A formal proclamation of non-involvement would have been interpreted as a statement of "no contest." It would communicate that we lacked the determination to fight a war to prevent communist expansion in that area. Such a display of timidity would weaken our threats elsewhere. Even today, those who argue that we should not have "become committed" give as a reason the war that we fight as a consequence of the commitment. So our opponents would have interpreted our declaration of non-involvement correctly: we would rather tolerate their aggression than fight a war to stop it.

A proclamation of non-involvement in 1954, aside from being dangerously unwise, probably would not have been viable. An American president, watching Laos and South Vietnam fall to the communists would begin to feel the deterioration of the American reputation. Although he might boldly proclaim no interest in the area, after a few countries had fallen the president (or another president) would reverse this position and act in order to preserve the general credibility of our threat.

As evidence for this conclusion we need only note that no American president has ever tolerated the loss of even two countries in succession to aggression by our opponents. Indeed presidential tolerance for alterations of the status quo has been much less than that. President Truman responded to the attack on South Korea even though we had made no explicit pledge to defend it. When the event was upon him and he had to weigh the effect inaction would have on the American reputation, Truman concluded he could not accept the loss. President Eisenhower was on the verge of intervening in Indochina in 1954 to forestall a communist victory; and, in this case, the element of outside aggression was minimal, and it was French prestige that was primarily involved.[7] President Kennedy, facing the guerrilla attack on Laos in 1961-62, apparently decided he could not permit the entire country to fall to the communists; the most he would concede was, in effect, about half the country. With Cuba, where no outside aggression took place, two Presidents seriously considered opposing this alteration of the status quo: Eisenhower in preparing the invasion force and Kennedy in sending it. And here, the status quo was only half-changing since Cuba remained outside the Russian defense sphere. Presidential actions to prevent possible alterations of the great power status quo in many other places—Quemoy, Berlin, Iran, Greece, the Congo, the Dominican Republic—further illustrate just how narrow is the practical range of tolerable alterations in the status quo.

Inspection of the behavior of four different Presidents over a 23-year period suggests, in a crude way, the approximate amount of retreat which does not intolerably damage our deterrent threat: about one-half of a small country. To put it another way, to protect their general deterrent threat adequately, Presidents have found that they almost always must act against an overt communist attack on any single free-world nation; they usually must act against a local communist rebellion in a single country if that rebellion receives outside support; and, frequently, they must act against a purely internal communist revolt. One can predict with some confidence, therefore, that no American president would stand for the successive loss of Southeast Asian countries to our opponents. It is highly unrealistic to imagine that an American president would stand by while Laos, South Vietnam, Cambodia, Thailand and Malaysia came under clandestine or open communist attack. He would soon perceive the disastrous effect such unopposed aggression was having on the American threat and would be impelled to prevent it. Thus, a proclamation of non-involvement in Southeast Asia would not be tenable.

Indeed, the Southeast Asian problem in 1954 closely resembled the Korean: a partitioned area, one sector of which was communist. The Korean episode taught us to expect the communist regime would seek a forcible reunification of the country. It also taught us that, in fact, the United States could not accept the loss of reputation and the encouragement given to aggression which would follow such a successful reunification. Debaters these days glibly dismiss the "domino theory" as an empty cliché, but no responsible statesman, then or now, could do the same. In the absence of an American threat it was quite possible, indeed probable in view of efforts already made, that the communists would capture Laos and South Vietnam. Following these victories, it would be quite possible, again, even probable, that the communists would attack Thailand and Cambodia. After two quick victories, encouraged and supplied by the Chinese and probably the Russians, would it be reasonable to suppose that local communist aggressors would suddenly stop at the borders of Thailand and Cambodia?

Realizing that we could not serve the area up to our opponents on a platter, then, what could we have done? We might, of course, have let matters drift and countered aggression as it occurred. But a creative statesman would seek some way to avoid war. Since we could not wisely or practicably withdraw, the only alternative was to project as forceful a threat as possible in the hopes of deterring aggression altogether.

This threat took the form of economic and military assistance to the Southeast Asian countries and an energetic, solemn announcement of our intention to defend South Vietnam, Laos, Cambodia and Thailand, an announcement so solemn that it would appear we could not get out of it even if we wanted to. The SEATO collective defense treaty stated:

> Each party recognizes that aggression by means of armed attack in the treaty area against any of the Parties or against any State or territory which the Parties by unanimous agreement may hereafter designate, would endanger its own peace and safety, and agrees that it will in that event act to meet the common danger in accordance with its constitutional processes.

At that time the United States Senate accepted the grim logic of this threat. The Committee on Foreign Relations said in its report on the SEATO treaty:

> The committee is not impervious to the risks which this treaty entails. It fully appreciates that acceptance of these additional obligations commits the United States to a course of action over a vast expanse of the Pacific. Yet these risks are consistent with our own highest interests. There are greater hazards in not advising a potential enemy of what he can expect of us . . .

To a certain extent this strategy was successful. There never has been an open, Korean-type invasion of any of the treaty countries. The communists had learned that we could and would fight a successful war against such an invasion. But they doubted, understandably, that we could or would resist aggression by guerrilla infiltration.

Why a Collective Defense Treaty Is Not a Piece of Paper

As just suggested, our obligation to resist the aggression of our opponents flows from circumstances not easily or wisely altered: the values we hold which our opponents challenge, the precedents we have set in defending those values, and our strength. Simply by standing and standing so tall we cast a threat. We may choose, however, to make our threat more compelling in particular cases. The enemy already believes that we *might* react if he attempts aggression. But we can cause him to believe that we *probably will* react. The object in strengthening a threat is, of course, to discourage further aggression and thereby prevent war.

Converting a threat of *might* to *probably will* involves depriving yourself of your freedom of choice. It involves showing your enemies that you are more automatically bound to respond to their aggressive moves than before. A nation can adopt several different practices to bind itself to a response and thereby increase the credibility of particular threats. One device is to station troops in the country likely to suffer aggression. If attacked, these troops will fight. If they cannot hold their own, the nation that sent them will probably send reinforcements. In this way, it will end up defending the country.

Another method whereby a nation may strengthen its threats is to bind itself to action through a formal treaty. In a solemn, long-negotiated, long-debated document which purports to be the "law of the land," a nation promises to defend certain areas that might fall under attack. It is common knowledge, of course, that treaties between nations are often broken. Contracts between individuals within a state are enforced by courts with their police power. But treaties between nations can seldom be enforced because there is no world police force to do it, nor, it might be added, the moral or ideological consensus on which such a police force could be built. Consequently, when a nation finds a particular treaty obligation onerous or unprofitable, the country is likely to set aside the treaty and do what it wants to do. Experience shows that nations sign treaties when they consider the agreement beneficial and honor them only so long as is convenient. It is generally accurate, therefore, to view treaties as pieces of paper which have no force of their own.

Apparently following this understanding, Senator Eugene McCarthy in the 1966 hearings before the Senate Foreign Relations Committee tried to get Secretary of State Dean Rusk to agree that the SEATO treaty was peripheral to our Vietnam involvement:

> Senator McCarthy. All this talk about our legal obligations under SEATO comes very close to being irrelevant, does it not?
>
> Secretary Rusk. No, sir, Senator. I cannot—I must confess I find it very difficult to understand the idea that a treaty is sort of a legal technicality or irrelevant when the treaty itself says if there is an armed attack—in this particular case against South Vietnam—we will do something about it. I just do not see the irrelevance there.
>
> Senator McCarthy. It is irrelevant to the question of whether or not we should be there, is it not. It may be an additional legal justification for our being there, but apart from the legalism, does it have any great bearing? [8]

The Senator, it appears, misunderstood the nature of collective defense treaties. These are not, except in a most unusual sense, documents which formalize an arrangement of mutual benefit. They are not like international agreements to limit the number of whales taken from the sea, or to exchange weather data. Such arrangements are contracted because they appear mutually beneficial. If one side discovers that the arrangement is inconvenient it will find a way, often *de facto,* to violate the agreement.

A collective defense treaty, on the other hand, must be honored precisely when it proves inconvenient. It is a threat and for the most part, a unilateral American threat to defend certain countries against communist attack. It is our strongest verbal communication of "You shall not." Keeping this threat credible, therefore, is vital. If our most solemn pronouncements do not accurately reflect our intentions, then what words, what documents will?

If we cannot convincingly tell potential aggressors that we will intervene, our problems of deterring aggressors and avoiding war increase enormously. When our words, particularly our solemn words, cease to be convincing, opponents are encouraged to *guess* that we might not defend certain countries, no matter what we say. If they guess right and we do not react, we lose the country and suffer a further decline in our threat. If they guess wrong and we do fight back, we have war. Either way we lose. Our job, it seems, is not to let them guess at all. They must *know* we mean what we say.

Collective defense treaties, then, have little in common with ordinary international agreements. They are American threats and should be regarded as such. They cannot, for example, be subjected to legalistic interpretation. Defense treaties are not legal documents; they are political statements of intention, of will. In spirit, they threaten an American response to the aggression of our opponents. Should our policy change or our courage fail, there are dozens of legal loopholes to justify our inaction in the face of aggression. We could claim that the regime involved was not legitimate, that there was no armed "attack," that there was no "common" danger.

But our enemies know that we can slip out of any defense treaty on legal technicalities. They know we have sharp lawyers and clever dialecticians who can rationalize any actions in terms of a treaty. What they want to know is: will we use these people? Do we have the determination to stick to the spirit of the treaty or will we slither out to avoid war? If they learn that we will adopt legalistic escape routes, then the collective defense treaty loses its meaning as a threat of war.

Either a collective defense treaty is a real threat which commits us to defensive war and thereby deters aggression; or it is a meaningless document communicating no threat because we shall wriggle out of it when the time comes to fight the necessary war.

Why the Decision to Honor Defense Treaty Commitments Should Be Based Neither on Prudence nor Wisdom

Following his line of questioning on the unimportance of SEATO in our Vietnam involvement, Senator Eugene McCarthy arrived at this conclusion:

> Senator McCarthy. Then the question is really not basically one of legality or of illegality, is it? It is a question of whether it is wise and prudent to be there,

of whether we are pursuing a wise and prudent policy,
of whether we know what we are doing and of
whether we have any idea as to how this is going to
come out.[9]

At first glance this position seems sophisticated and realistic.
One is asked to evaluate the Vietnam involvement coldly and ra-
tionally on its merits. The danger with the "wisdom and prudence"
approach is that it gives us a choice we must not permit ourselves.
If we are to deter enemies with defense treaties and other documents
as threats, these enemies must believe that our response to aggression will be automatic and inexorable. If we allow ourselves the
luxury of deciding to keep only those commitments which are convenient, prudent, or limited we undermine our threat.

Suppose at some future date Hanoi or Peking or Moscow are
considering an energetic guerrilla infiltration campaign against
SEATO-protected Thailand. If they know we shall respond automatically, without worrying about "how this is going to come out,"
it is almost certain they will not try. But if they believe we shall
weigh the matter "prudently," that we will consider the loss of life,
the danger of escalation or nuclear war, the inflation back home, the
relative strategic importance of Thailand, the viability of a free Thai
government, and the possible length of the war, the chances for
aggression increase enormously.

Indeed, most tests of military alliances would force us to act in
a manner which would normally seem imprudent and unwise. If the
Russians threaten, as they have on more than one occasion, a possible nuclear war unless we relinquish West Berlin, the dictates of
prudence would counsel retreat. Could any policy-maker who risked
total war for a few square miles of real estate be called "wise"?
If our enemies could depend on us to be wise and prudent about our
commitments, we would be in a dangerous situation. Either, actually
being wise and prudent, we would concede slices of the free world
rather than fight the open-ended war which they threaten; or, not
being wise and prudent at some point when our enemies thought we
would be, they would engage in aggression, we would counter and
we would probably have war. Again, either way we lose.

It is important, then, to fulfill defense treaty obligations in as
automatic a fashion as possible. In practice, of course, one does not
always react automatically because one lacks the courage or
capabilities to do so, or one cannot find a proportional response.

But insofar as one fails to act readily for any such reason, a price is paid in a weaker threat. This observation runs counter to the oftheard injunction for a "flexible" foreign policy. Those who urge flexibility in the matter of honoring defense commitments have not understood threats and deterrence. The whole idea behind a threat is to deprive yourself of your freedom of choice, to show enemies that aggression *must* provoke your response. A "flexible" threat is simply a weak threat.

When Khrushchev put his menacing, provocative pressures on West Berlin during 1961-62, he must have had some hope that the United States was not automatically committed there. He would not have embarrassed himself by threatening to sign a peace treaty with the East Germans nor would he have repeatedly risked war in the many provocative thrusts unless he thought he might succeed. In part, he believed our commitment was uncertain, I have suggested, because he saw us "prudently" reexamining our SEATO threat in Laos and witnessed our "wise" policy of "non-provocation" in the face of aggressive Soviet moves in Berlin. Fortunately, Khrushchev finally decided that we might not be bluffing in West Berlin, that we might go to war if he made a drastic move. But we shall never know how close the Russians came to disbelieving our threat to defend West Berlin, how close they came, for example, to signing a treaty with the East Germans and, thereby, escalating the crisis to include a blockade.

That we have fought a costly war in South Vietnam to carry out our threat there cannot but enhance the credibility of all defense commitments around the world. The next time an adventurous Kremlin leader thinks about pressuring us in Berlin he will remember Vietnam. He will have to remember that the Americans, wishy-washy and weak-kneed as they sometimes seem to present themselves, have a capacity for carrying out their threats to defend countries, no matter how difficult such a defense might be.

Recently, many have lamented the Russian opposition to our role in Vietnam as an unfortunate obstacle to cordial relations. But it would be wiser to ask what Vietnam tells them about our threats, for the road to peace between hostile powers is through credible threats which insure a mutual respect for the rights of each, not handshakes, smiles and cordial dinners. One reporter, attempting to illustrate the unhappy consequences of Vietnam on communist attitudes wrote:

At Mamaia, the Russian resort on the Black Sea, I
shared a beach umbrella with a high-ranking communist
economist. "We never believed the Americans would go as
far as this," he said gloomily; "sending hundreds of thousands of soldiers to South Vietnam, bombing the north,
contemplating years of fighting."[10]

That communist leaders did not believe we "would go as far as
this" is why, in fact, we had to fight the war in Vietnam. Russia
and China, in encouraging and supplying North Vietnam, thought it
would be a low-risk strategy to infiltrate the South; so did the North
Vietnamese. They assumed we would be wise and prudent. That this
war teaches the world how far we will go to back up our threats is a
great assurance against further aggression and war.

Commitment Reduction

We have recently been hearing an appeal, voiced with growing con-
viction, for a decrease of American commitments around the world.
This position, which might be termed "neo-isolationist," holds that
the United States has attempted to be the "policeman of the world,"
imposing a "Pax Americana" around the globe. Instead, it is
argued, we should contract our area of concern and reduce our
commitments abroad.

A proper discussion of this position requires an examination
of the nature and causes of the existing American policy of intervention abroad. As I have suggested, the underlying objective of our
foreign policy is to maintain a credible deterrent threat. Therefore,
American involvement is desirable when and to the extent that our
failure to act will weaken this threat. Fortunately, in most international disputes our threat is not directly tested and we need not—
and do not—intervene.

First, there are disputes between non-communist countries,
neither of which is closely identified with the communist powers.
Since regardless how the dispute is settled, no alteration of the Cold
War status quo will take place, we may play a passive or merely
mediating role. Illustrations of such conflicts include India's conquest of Portuguese Goa in 1962, the war between Pakistan and
India in 1965, the dispute between Great Britain and Spain over
Gibraltar, the Greek-Turkish dispute over Cyprus in 1967, and the
war between El Salvador and Honduras in 1969. And, of course,

disputes between communist countries do not lead to our intervention, since again the Cold War status quo is not at issue. If Russia and China wish to fight about communist Mongolia, we shall be on the sidelines.

Secondly, there are many conflicts which might result in an alteration of the status quo against us but which the countries themselves can handle without our direct military involvement. Communist guerrilla movements in Greece, the Philippines, Venezuela, Peru, Colombia and Guatemala have been combatted by the countries themselves. The June 1967 Arab-Israeli war had important Cold War overtones in view of the close dependence of Egypt on the Soviet Union; the United States could remain aloof because Israel, the object of Soviet-supported aggression, could take care of itself.

It is therefore inappropriate to characterize the U.S. role as that of "policeman." A policeman intervenes to protect the citizen whether the citizen is able to protect himself or not. American policy has been one of assisting actual or potential victims of an attack when it appeared that they could not defeat the attack alone.

Unfortunately, there are no illustrations of a communist attack on a free-world country which could defeat such an attack. The reason is not difficult to discover: our opponents, understandably, choose targets where they are likely to succeed. If the Cubans would be foolish enough to attempt an invasion of Brazil, I do not believe we would find American ground troops resisting it.

It is important to remember, however, that our objective is to see that aggressive opponents are denied success. To the degree that this purpose can be achieved without our military involvement, well and good. (Of course, our back-stopping threat to counter the Soviet Union or China could never be dispensed with.)

We can agree, then, with the position which former Defense Secretary Clark M. Clifford reported he took in March of 1968:

> . . . the United States had entered Viet Nam with a limited aim—to prevent its subjugation by the North and to enable the people of South Viet Nam to determine their own future . . . we had largely accomplished that objective. Nothing required us to remain until the North had been ejected from the South, and the Saigon government had been established in complete military control of all South Viet Nam.[11]

Of course, there is room for disagreement on the application of this position: whether it is prudent to make a highly publicized announcement of it in the middle of negotiations; and whether a withdrawal of American troops too soon or in too large numbers would demoralize the South Vietnamese, encourage the North Vietnamese to redouble their efforts (no longer anticipating any reaction from us), and thus bring about the subjugation of South Vietnam by the North.

In examining possible American intervention in the internal political struggles of other countries, we must again consider the relationship of these struggles for international alignments. When, as is usually the case, forcible changes of government do not endanger the Cold War status quo, we need not and do not intervene. There have been scores of such coups, revolts, and rebellions around the world. The 1967 coup in Greece is an interesting illustration because, in this case, many Americans supporting the neo-isolationist view inconsistently urged that the United States oppose the junta and thus play a *greater* role in internal Greek politics. The Bolivian social revolution of 1952 was another violent change of government which, since it did not involve an alteration of the international status quo, led to no American military action. Indeed, the Eisenhower administration cooperated with and assisted the subsequent revolutionary regime.

When the internal violence appears to lead to a change in the Cold War status quo, a "non-communist" regime about to be replaced with a "communist" one, then, for reasons I have already explained, our threat is affected and American involvement may be necessary if the problem cannot be handled locally.

It is therefore inaccurate to suggest that the United States has been militarily involved in most of the international disputes around the world. We have not. It is not our policy to be. If such widespread intervention is what the neo-isolationists fear, then they have no fundamental disagreement with existing American policy.

To a large extent, however, the recent appeals for a reduction of American commitments arise from a somewhat different and much more specific complaint: the war in Vietnam. It is mainly this war which has given rise to the isolationist sentiment; it is in terms of this war that the case for commitment reduction is argued. Quite simply, the contention is this: the Vietnam war came about as a result of a commitment; the way to avoid such wars in the future is, obviously, not to have so many commitments.

This logic has ominous overtones. A "commitment" as it has applied to Vietnam is an American threat to respond to communist aggression. To "reduce our commitments to avoid future Vietnams" means, then, to reduce or eliminate our threat to oppose aggression in certain places. If certain non-communist countries are attacked by the communists, the neo-isolationists seem to say, we should let them seize these countries.

This position comes dangerously close to being a policy of appeasement: we should tolerate the aggression of our opponents rather than risk war to oppose it. No one is arguing for reducing our commitments to Ecuador or Uruguay. The reason is manifest: Ecuador and Uruguay are not under communist attack nor likely to be in the immediate future. Therefore we shall not have to fight a war to defend them. Where the neo-isolationists apparently want our commitments reduced is precisely where we may have to fight a war to honor them—particularly in Southeast Asia. They cannot have it both ways. If they believe that a country will not be attacked, then there is little need to worry about the consequences of our "commitment." No war will take place. But if they fear that a country might be attacked, then, unless we are to practice a policy of appeasement, a deterrent threat is obviously necessary.

Polarization

The first thing that must be understood about specific American commitments is, then, their high degree of inflexibility. They are largely the necessary consequences of a general deterrence policy. They cannot be made, unmade or altered freely and independently, without consequence to other threats and our world-wide posture. We cannot have deterrent threats *a la carte.*

A threat does not arise simply from the pledge contained in a collective defense treaty. Such statements are primarily an attempt to make firmer and more precise a threat that has already emerged. A commitment originates in a conflict which involves an actual or potential alteration of the Cold War status quo. One is expected to do something about such an alteration and this expectation is the genesis of the commitment. It follows, therefore, that if the statesman is seeking to avoid commitments, his opportunity to do so will not be found in situations where the status quo is already endangered unilaterally by his opponents—or by actors identified with his opponents. In such cases *it is not within his power to prevent a commitment from arising.* If Russia attacks Ghana with a paratrooper division, we are expected to respond. Not to respond results in an alteration of the status quo, a "victory" for them, a "retreat" for us and a weakening in our general deterrent threat.

It helps in understanding this point to introduce the notion of "polarization." Polarization is the process of hostile powers becoming located on opposite sides of a conflict—so that a great-power status quo issue arises. The passive term "polarization," instead of "taking sides," is used to describe this process because great-power status quo issues can emerge without the deliberate action of one side and even against its will. Because each power carries along with its threat posture an extensive and inescapable framework of value, precedent and tradition, any dispute (no matter who specifically creates it) which fits this framework becomes polarized. Thus, a great power is often drawn into a bargaining situation in which its threat is being tested, not through the specific decision of its leaders, but by what it has stood for and whom it has stood against.

When, for example, the Pathet Lao, with North Vietnamese and Russian backing, were overrunning Laos in 1961, we were, inescapably, on the other side. To have announced "we like the Pathet Lao too; they are true social reformers" would mean "we give in." The so-called "neutralization" arrangement of 1962 did not depolarize the situation: there are still communist forces threatening the country and we are still expected to oppose them if they push too hard. Similarly, in South Vietnam, the "communist" identification of the insurgents, not to mention the assistance given to them by North Vietnam, polarized the conflict and thereby created a U.S. commitment long before the United States sent ground troops in 1965.

If neither side in a dispute is communist, polarization is less likely, but it can still occur. Our opponents can ally with one side, and, thereby, force us to take the other. Probably the conflict between non-communist states which most clearly involves the Cold War status quo is that between Egypt and Israel. The Soviet Union, through its massive military and economic aid and its pledges to defend Egypt has taken up Egypt's international interests. Egyptian aggression would be carried out with Soviet arms, Soviet money, Soviet approval and a Soviet back-stopping protective threat. Successful Egyptian aggression would become, indirectly, successful Soviet aggression and would consequently reflect poorly on our general willingness and ability to counter the advances of our opponents. Therefore, the Russian support of Egypt has strengthened a counter-American identification with Egypt's enemy, Israel. Or, to put it more accurately, it has greatly increased the importance of defending Israel—should such a defense prove necessary.

It does not seem, given our policy of not supporting aggressors —and Egypt, desirous of violating successive status quo's in the area, had to be considered an aggressor—that we could have avoided the polarization which took place in the Mid-East. The Russian decision to actively support the Arabs made the Arab-Israeli conflict an issue of great power competition.

Our ability to prevent polarization and the attendant growth of commitments is, therefore, quite limited. But not completely. Upon occasion there are certain steps we may take to prevent a Cold War status quo issue from arising. One general rule which may sometimes be applied is this:

If a conflict might become polarized, support the side most likely to be that which your opponent will take.

In order for the United States to apply this rule successfully, the following must be true: the conflict must, of course, be still unpolarized; we must know which side would become the opponent's; that side must accept our support; it cannot be aggressive; the other side must be constrained by ideological or practical considerations from being a possible ally of our opponents. If this last condition does not hold, then by aiding one side, we merely drive the other to the opponent and polarization takes place even more quickly.

Clearly, the above principle will have only infrequent application; but yet there are occasional illustrations of its use. In July, 1967, there was a revolt led by Belgian, French, and Spanish mercenaries against the Congolese government of Joseph Mobutu. Congolese government radio denounced this attack of "imperialists" from "Western" countries. It alleged that two plane-loads of mercenaries had flown from Belgium (a "Western" country and closely identified with the United States as a member of NATO). Congolese trade union leaders called upon the government to re-view"relations with Belgium and other countries that may be implicated in this aggression." The atmosphere was explosively—and perhaps demagogically—anti-Western.[12]

The danger existed, therefore, that the Congolese government, seeking support against its real or imagined "Western" enemies, would turn toward the Soviet Union. At the same time, if there were a wave of anti-white atrocities, condoned by the Congolese government, these would create hostility toward the Congo in the United States and Western Europe. As time went on, with the Soviet Union pouring arms and advisors into the Congo, that state could become closely identified with the communists. Then any dispute in which the Congolese government became embroiled —another Katanga, mercenaries "invading" from a neighboring country, a border dispute with any of the nine neighbors, or an invasion by, or against, any of these countries—would be a polarized dispute with the Soviet Union actively supporting the Congo and the United States implicitly on the other side.

To prevent complications of this nature, the United States issued a statement of support for the Congolese government and sent, as evidence of this support, three C-130 cargo planes to provide logistic support for the Congolese government troops in their fight against the rebels. Since it was impossible for the "Western" mercenaries and the Soviet Union to cooperate, the Russians kept out of the dispute. We had supported the only side likely to shift to our opponents and had thus kept the delicate Congo situation unpolarized.

Strangely, many Americans, both hawks and doves—including Senators Russell, Fulbright, Case, and Mansfield—attacked this Congo policy in the belief that such activities would "pave the way for 'another Vietnam.' "[13] They apparently believed that the sending of American men and equipment abroad produced *ipso facto,* a "commitment." In this case, however, the effect was the opposite: to prevent commitments from arising.

We must, therefore, take our eyes from the mere formal acts which often—but not always—enhance or further define a specific threat. In refusing to send assistance or sign a particular defense treaty, one does not avoid projecting a threat. Conversely, as just shown, sending assistance may, on occasion, be a method of forestalling the development of a commitment. The origin of any specific commitment—that is, expectation—is found in the nature of the Cold War struggle: who our opponents are; their objectives; and our general policy toward those objectives.

Overcommitment

For some time now, various communist leaders around the world have been urging all communists to rise up and begin anti-American "people's wars." The Chinese have been the voluble firebrands. Defense Minister Lin Piao's argument is:

> The peoples of Asia, Africa, Latin America and other regions can destroy . . . [U.S. imperialism] piece by piece, some striking at its head and others at its feet.

> * * *

> When the U.S. aggressors are hard pressed in one place, they have no alternative but to loosen their grip on others. Therefore, the conditions become more favorable for the people elsewhere to wage struggles against U.S. imperialism and its lackeys.[14]

Such remarks have stimulated discussion in the United States on the problem of "overcommitment." The question is raised: Could we meet all of our commitments if they were tested simultaneously? What if the communists follow Lin Piao's advice and start striking everywhere? Must we triple our defense establishment to prepare for such an eventuality?

When someone gives advice, it is wise to observe whether he follows it himself. China advises communists to embroil the United States in many wars and thus sap our energy. Presumably, then, she ought to begin this campaign herself by attempting to invade Laos, Taiwan, or India. Such moves would probably lead to a U.S. response and would therefore tie us down in war elsewhere. But China does not invade.

The Chinese fear that to become embroiled in a war with us would be risky and unprofitable. Although they would like to see someone distract the United States, they will not sacrifice their men, weapons, and cities on the altar of their doctrine.

If China will not follow her own advice, who else will? Should the North Koreans expect anything but a losing war if they invade

South Korea? And so each communist regime will assess the
dangers. Each believes that *it* will be punished and unsuccessful;
each assumes the United States will probably react to an attempt
at aggression and punish it besides. It may be true that if there
are two Vietnams underway, a third might succeed. That is not the
relevant point. The important question is: Which enemy will dare
to be the *second?* If the United States keeps the apparent costs of
aggression prohibitively high for every potential aggressor none
will act.

It is instructive on this matter of overcommitment to examine
the specific background of the Lin Piao document. It was not an
incidental tract, but, as Stefan Possony has persuasively argued,
stated the program of a Maoist initiative then under way on a
world-wide scale, "a concerted effort to bring about a tri-continental people's war."[15]

In 1965, the Chinese promoted or at least strongly encouraged
a rash of efforts against free-world countries: the formation of the
Thai Patriotic Front; the attempted communist coup in Indonesia;
the planning of the Tri-Continental Conference in Havana; the
initiation of a guerrilla effort by North Korea against South
Korea; the resumption of guerrilla activity in the Philippines;
Che Guevara's visit to China and subsequent guerrilla activities
in Latin America; the shipment of arms to African countries;
close coordination with highly sympathetic African leaders, including Kwame Nkrumah of Ghana and Ben Bella of Algeria;
the selection by Peking of a Congo guerrilla leader; and the
fanning of the Indonesia-Malaysia confrontation and the
Pakistani-Indian war.

The key to this "strategic initiative" was the expected victory
of the Viet Cong in South Vietnam in 1965. The Chinese ardently
supported this effort with a giant pro-Viet Cong rally in Peking
on February 10, 1965. The North Vietnamese, in an effort to
hasten the expected victory, introduced entire units into the South
in late 1964.

Coinciding with this general offensive was an effort to bolster
China's resources. Fifty million tons of grain were purchased from
the West to establish a food reserve, the military budget was increased by about one-third, and China exploded its second
nuclear device, an operational bomb dropped from a TU-4 bomber.

China was not interested at that time in committing her own
military forces to the general effort, but apparently preferred to

test the possibilities (e.g., the likely American response) indirectly. Had there been no response and had the offensive succeeded, then the probability of direct Chinese involvements would have risen enormously.

But when the United States intervened in force in Vietnam in 1965 (defeating communist forces in every major encounter), the hopes for communist victories were chilled around the world. The U.S. action encouraged Laos to authorize U.S. air strikes against Vietnamese forces in its territory; the anti-communist generals were encouraged to resist and defeat the attempted communist coup in Indonesia; the guerrilla attempt against Thailand was sidetracked. Most importantly, the U.S. action in Vietnam exposed to the Chinese the folly of treating the U.S. as a paper tiger and ignoring its military potential. The more cautious elements in China, including "professional" military circles sensitive to the military realities being recorded in Vietnam, were greatly strengthened to resist Mao's "adventurism." A profound split developed in the ranks of the Chinese communist party.

The cultural revolution, launched in 1966, can be seen as Mao's destructive (and basically unsuccessful) attempt to eliminate opponents emboldened by the communist failure in Vietnam.

"The U.S. intervention in Viet Nam (and the Dominican Republic) during 1965," Possony concludes, "prevented the outbreak of a gigantic tri-continental people's war. Rarely in history has the mere assertion of will and power been so successful."[16]

It might seem that having succeeded so well in disrupting the Maoist people's war offensive by intervening in Vietnam in 1965, we could have therefore withdrawn in 1967 or 1968. But it is well to consider how the offensive was nurtured. The years 1959-1964, and especially 1962-1964 were punctuated by numerous developments favorable to the communists which the United States was unwilling or unable to prevent: the loss and the arming of Cuba; the partial communist victory in Laos and the withdrawing of the SEATO commitment from Laos and Cambodia; a rapidly deteriorating situation in South Vietnam following the death of Diem in 1963, and an apparent American decision to withdraw;*

*Possony notes the White House Declaration of October 2, 1963, and Defense Secretary McNamara's statement that the battle could "only be won by Vietnamese themselves," p. 156. To which should be added Lyndon Johnson's election campaign statements to the same effect.

and the increasingly close and fruitful ties China was establishing with numerous Third-world nations, including Indonesia (Sukarno), Ghana (Nkrumah), Algeria (Ben Bella), Pakistan (Ayub Khan), and Cambodia (Prince Sinanouk).

Exhilarated by these developments, aware of numerous foci of incipient guerrilla activity from the Congo to Venezuela, and facing an apparently timid and incompetent America, the Maoists forged their strategy.* It would have been profoundly unwise for us to foster a similar climate in the late 1960's by withdrawing defeated from Vietnam.

The appropriate response to a Lin Piao-type offensive, therefore, is not to conserve one's resources and refrain from battle, for that policy is what stimulates such a broad offensive in the first place. By continuing to hold back, one only intensifies the offensive. Instead, the statesman must discourage widespread attacks by deploying his forces in response to an early challenge.

Of course, it is true that when forces are used in one place, they are unavailable for action elsewhere. And, even though one has vast reserves, it may be inconvenient or awkward to mobilize them. Finally, depending on the state of domestic opinion, the nation may be psychologically unready or somewhat unwilling to fight in a second plaçe. These, then, are certain weaknesses in our deterrence posture which fighting in one place might create. But there is also a vitally important gain.

The overcommitment argument incorrectly assumes that national power at any point on the globe is purely a function of the military capabilities one can bring to bear at that point. If, for example one has soldiers fighting at point A, then one is necessarily weaker at points B and C because the soldiers fighting at A are not available for these other actions. But national power involves the *threat* of war, and a threat is a function of the opponents' perception of both your capability and your determination. Since by fighting at point A the nation demonstrates its determination, its threat to defend B and C can become *more* credible, that is more coercive—assuming, of course, that it has capabilities left to apply in these other places.

---

*The only significant communist reverse in this period, the missile crisis, did, it is true, chasten the Russians. But the Maoist people's war strategy was designed to avoid just such confrontations and therefore the missile crisis need have had little impact on their plans.

When Britain and France avoided war with Mussolini over his invasion of Ethiopia in 1935, they conserved their military resources but their international power, the coerciveness of their threat of war, declined. They demonstrated their lack of will to oppose a violation of the status quo by a hostile power. When Hitler moved into the Rhineland in March 1936, it was not the military capability of his opponents that he doubted; he knew it was overwhelming. He disbelieved their threat to oppose this violation of the status quo because he doubted their *will* to act. During the later 1930s British and French power steadily waned not because they committed troops to battle, but precisely because they did not. Although their military capabilities were increasing their apparent willingness to fight—as perceived by Germany, Japan, Italy, Spain, Rumania, and Russia—diminished.

Whether or not the United States is overcommitted, therefore, depends heavily upon the condition of our threat. If it is widely believed that we will steadfastly oppose aggression by our opponents, we shall need only a moderate level of forces to sustain our position. But if our enemies start guessing that we might not respond just here or just there, then even the largest army will prove inadequate. We will find ourselves embroiled in a rash of wars provoked by aggressors who thought they might not be resisted.

It is therefore misleading to assume that 500,000 American servicemen in Vietnam create a gap in our deterrence posture. On the contrary, by fighting in Vietnam, they compensate for the strictly numerical gap in our defense that they represent. They are showing our opponents that our threats really mean something. They are restricting the horizons and aggressive ambitions of our opponents. And so we shall not need two million men to hold back a Russian invasion of Europe, or a Chinese invasion of India. Our threat does those jobs for us. If we grow so worried about "overcommitment" that we refrain from placing our troops in small wars to carry out our threats, then we are likely to end up with more and larger wars on our hands. Then, indeed, we shall be overcommitted.

There is the danger, of course, that a foreign military involvement may, through its adverse effect on domestic opinion, weaken the national will to oppose the aggression of opponents in the future. This is a real problem, as the growth of isolationist sentiment in this country in reaction to Vietnam indicates. But although there is a risk of domestic antagonism to action abroad, it does not seem wise to forego involvements solely to avoid this risk. A consideration of the Vietnam involvement is illustrative.

Before the fact, when decisions had to be made and policy laid out, there was no good way of knowing that this particular confrontation would follow its particular course with the attendant result on national opinion. The risk of an adverse public reaction goes along with every confrontation. The extent of the public disenchantment depends upon the course and duration of the confrontation as well as the popular perceptions of the issues involved. And none of these things are easily predicted. The president who studiously avoided confrontations from fear of a possible adverse public response if everything did not go well would have to avoid them all.

Moreover, in avoiding the Vietnamese conflict we would not have been getting away free. Both in Southeast Asia and worldwide our threat would gravely suffer. There would have been new challenges and new tragedies lurking behind them. If the American people were going to shrink from the sacrifices a deterrence policy entailed, they soon would have had the opportunity to do so, regardless of (indeed, because of) our retreat in Vietnam. And if we continued to avoid conflicts out of fear of a possible public resistance, our threat would be as surely and completely undermined as it would be by the most extreme domestic reaction to any conflict.

The danger of overcommitment and that of adverse public reaction to foreign involvement are similar problems. Of course the statesman must be concerned about these difficulties and he must attempt to avoid or resolve them. But he cannot allow these issues to become the central considerations in the management of a deterrence policy, for to do so is to lose sight of the meaning and purpose of that policy. One continually steps backward in the fear that one is not entirely prepared or not completely assured of indefinite public support; and meanwhile one's international position deteriorates more dangerously than it would if one had fought even in unfavorable circumstances.

Chapter 7

THE UTILITY OF COURAGE

To compile a list of all the specific threats the United States projects at any moment would require several volumes. And even then it would not be complete. One would have to look at the world through the eyes of other national leaders—opponents and allies—and try to see what they believe about our future behavior under different hypothetical aggressions or status quo alterations. One would have to list all these hypothetical circumstances and determine, in each case and for each set of national leaders, the expectations they hold about our possible behavior. It would be an exercise in combinations and permutations.

Yet all these many threats have a common denominator: it is the United States which is making them, and the expectation of their being carried out depends upon the perceived determination of this country to do so. We are like a bank funding many different debts. Each debt is different in size and perhaps interest rate. But they all rest upon the assumed capacity of the bank to supply the money. If the bank defaults on one loan, its ability to fund the others comes under suspicion. This is not to say that all the other creditors will conclude that the bank will default on their loans too; they realize that some debts are more important than others and the bank probably defaulted on its least important obligation. It may still be able to pay off the others. All we can say is that it becomes more probable that another creditor will press for immediate repayment—which will, of course, further worsen the bank's position.

Our specific international threats have, like the debts, different values. The probability that we shall respond to a Russian invasion

of West Berlin, whatever it is, is probably greater than the probability of our response to a Chinese guerrilla infiltration campaign
against Burma. But the two specific threats are linked by the
common denominator of American determination. If we do not
respond to the Chinese effort against Burma, it does not mean that
we shall not respond to the attack on Berlin. But it will be taken to
mean that we are *somewhat less* willing to respond in Berlin. Since
it is American determination which stands behind every one of our
specific threats, this determination is being tested or estimated
whenever we act or fail to act in support of any of these threats.
For this reason, the singular form, the American threat, is used in
this essay to emphasize our opponents' perception of our underlying
determination to oppose their aggression.

When grappling with deterrent threats and the task of keeping
them credible, there is always a temptation to seek an easy way
out. Surely, one supposes, there is a safer way to maintain a credible threat than all this sacrificing and taking of risks. Can there
be some device or procedure which can be substituted for American
lives?

The answer to this question, of course, has to be "no."
Frederick the Great, in his instructions to his generals, explained
the problem this way:

> If we imagine that every motion of ours will oblige
> the enemy to move also, we are decived. It is not merely
> by changing our position, but by the manner in which it
> is effected that we must expect to force him to decamp.
> Specious appearances will have no effect upon an experi-
> enced commander. Your dispositions must be *real,* and
> such as will reduce him to the *necessity* of changing his
> situation.[1]

If our opponents are really to believe that we shall sacrifice
American lives and risk terrible destruction to oppose their aggression, we must, for all practical purposes, be in fact willing to
do so. We cannot say we are firm and be cowardly, for our words
will be a "specious appearance." In managing a deterrence policy,
there is no substitute for courage. A nation cannot follow a more
dangerous and wasteful course than to be projecting a worldwide
threat—as we are unavoidably doing today—and yet manifest a
lack of courage to sustain it.

When One Must Say: "Well, then, it is war."

In a speech to the German Parliament in 1871, Minister of Foreign Affairs, Otto von Bismarck, described an episode which typifies the problem American statesmen confront today:

> It is well known that the French ambassador entered my office as late as August 6, 1866, with the briefly worded ultimatum: "Either cede to France the city of Mayence, or expect an immediate declaration of war." I was, of course, not one moment in doubt about my reply. I said to him: "Well, then, it is war."*

When the opponent offers a choice between war or retreat, the statesman chooses, without hesitation, war. Or, to put it more accurately, he chooses a process leading to war if the opponent will not relent. This may have been easy, one could argue, in earlier days when war exacted only modest sacrifices. How can we choose "war" with all its terrors today? How, in the nuclear era, does one muster the courage to say "Well, then, it is war."?

To a large extent, the roots of courage lie in understanding that *the opponent can have a war whenever he chooses*. If he desires war, it is not within our power to prevent it. He simply has to attack something he knows is "ours": our own country, territories, or allies or related rights, that is, the status quo. Since our opponent knows how to cause, or at least risk, war, then the choice to begin or not begin war is up to him and he knows it. Hence, when faced by an ultimatum of retreat or war the statesman should calmly say—and mean—"it is war." If the ultimatum was a bluff, then no war results and no retreat is made. If the ultimatum was real, then the resulting war was actively risked by the enemy and the responsibility for it is his.

The 1961-62 Berlin crisis illustrates the error of holding oneself responsible for a possible war provoked by an aggressor. Khrushchev, in word and deed, was threatening a war over Berlin in order to panic us into yielding. Panic us he did. Illustrative of

---

*Kuno Francke, ed., *The German Classics* (20 vols., Albany, New York, J. B. Lyon Co., 1914), Vol. X, p. 183. This incident happened to have a happy ending as Bismarck recounts: "He proceeded with this reply to Paris. There they changed their mind after a few days, and I was given to understand that this instruction had been wrung from Emperor Napoleon during an attack of illness."

the fright was George Kennan's comment, reported by Schlesinger: "I am expendable, I have no further official career, and I am going to do everything I can to prevent a war. . . . the only thing I have left in life is to do everything I can to stop the war."2

But Kennan was apparently assuming precisely what the United States should not have assumed: that *we* should have done anything to prevent a war. Khrushchev was threatening the war, deliberately and consciously. He knew what the established Western rights in Berlin were; he was simply attempting to deprive us of those rights under his threat of war. In such circumstances, one does not plead for "negotiations"; one calmly closes the file: "When you wish to discuss exchanges for mutual benefit, come back and we shall explore the issue; since you merely wish to take what is ours under a threat of war, go ahead and start your war."

It is dangerous to believe that we can do anything to prevent war when an aggressor wishes to risk it, because there is one thing we can do and a panicky search will lead right to it: retreat. It should not be necessary to explain again why it is unwise to let an enemy believe we shall retreat if he threatens war.

How to Talk Ourselves into War without Really Trying

In recent years, some American politicians have been worrying about Thailand. They see North Vietnam infiltrating guerrillas into that country; they fear we may have to fight there. "We ought to know what we are getting into," they ask. "Are we going to have another Vietnam?"

In one sense this question merely requires a factual response. As such, it can be answered with considerable confidence, assuming no dramatic change in the policy we have followed for the last two decades. Yes, indeed, we shall have another Vietnam in Thailand—or even a bigger war—*if an opponent wishes to provoke it.* Our threat to resist aggression there is quite clear. Beyond the general threat to defend non-communist nations from communist attack, Thailand has acquired numerous other guarantees of our commitment: the SEATO collective defense treaty; public assurances such as those given by the Kennedy administration on March 6, 1962: "The Secretary of State . . . expressed the firm intention of the United States to aid Thailand, its ally and historic friend, in resisting Communist aggression and subversion." American bases in Thailand indicate our interest in the defense of Thailand and, finally, the Thai troops which have fought in Vietnam further increase our obligation to help Thailand if and when it should need help. Our threat to defend Thailand is especially firm; we have deliberately made it so in order to deter communist attack.

It is unlikely, of course, that those asking "Are we going to have another Vietnam in Thailand?" are unfamiliar with this factual answer to their question. Rather, it appears that this question is a rhetorical way of advancing an interpretation of the Vietnam war: The United States has got into a costly and unfortunate war. South Vietnam really isn't worth such a war. Other possible wars in Southeast Asia are likely to be costly, unfortunate and not "worth it." Therefore, we should learn our lesson and never again become involved in such a war.

This view is perhaps the most dangerous, most destructive interpretation that could ever be placed upon our involvement in Vietnam. The war in Vietnam represents one case—a relatively infrequent case, as a matter of fact—where our threat has been seriously questioned. Our struggle is one to maintain this threat which has worked silently and efficaciously to prevent aggression in many places. That we should make such sacrifices in Vietnam is the best evidence we can offer our opponents that we shall oppose them if they attempt aggression elsewhere. The correct interpretation of our action in Vietnam is, therefore, that it shows what we can and will do *and do again* to defend our position. To reverse this interpretation, to tell the world that we shall never fight again in Southeast Asia is to weaken our threat and encourage aggression. It is difficult to imagine a more senseless way to squander the American blood that has been shed in Vietnam.

Of course we would prefer not to fight another war in Thailand. But our opponents would rather not fight such a war either, particularly if they understand that their struggle will be costly and unsuccessful. If one grants that, in view of our commitment to Thailand, we would eventually come to that country's defense, would it not be wiser to convince the communists of our response at the outset? We should not "sucker" them into a good-sized war in the belief that the United States would not respond with talk about "never fighting another Vietnam," and then respond. We should let our opponents understand, loud and clear, that, if necessary, we shall indeed repel their aggression.

The problem of peace in Vietnam involves precisely the same issue. No matter what the ultimate nature of a settlement in Vietnam (except a complete defeat) the threat of American intervention will be necessary to stabilize it. If the Viet Cong are included in a Saigon government—admittedly an unlikely arrangement—what is to keep them in it when they can always return to the jungle and start fighting again? If we withdraw our troops in exchange for a cessation of infiltration, what will make the North Vietnamese keep the bargain? An American threat to repeat the entire performance.

The surest way for American politicians to weaken this threat and undermine the chances for future peace in Vietnam is to announce that Vietnam was a "mistake," a "blunder" which should never be repeated.

Aside from its pernicious effect upon our threat, the view that the Vietnam war must be a mistake embodies the unhealthy assumption noted above: that *we* should always have done something to avoid a war. If we are fighting a war, this view runs, *we* must have managed affairs badly. From this assumption flow many allegations that some American leader—Eisenhower, Dulles, Kennedy, Rusk, or Johnson—should have done something to avoid the war in Vietnam. This view completely ignores the enemy and his role in creating a war. We are simply trying to hold on to the noncommunist world. If an opponent wishes a war with us, all he has to do is try to take some of it away. If we are not to retreat, there will be a confrontation. Thus, if one is looking around for someone to blame the Vietnam war upon, Ho Chi Minh ought to be considered a likely candidate.

How Voicing Fear of War with a Potential Aggressor Increases the Likelihood of War

To those who do not see American foreign policy as a system of threats, the principles we must follow often seem paradoxical. An illustration is the proposition that if we become overly anxious for peace and express great fear of war, then peace becomes less likely. Conversely, if we face the prospect of war with courage, we are more likely to have peace. As an ancient dictum runs: "If you desire peace, prepare for war."

The logic behind this principle is quite simple. If one is sustaining a deterrent threat, this threat will prevent aggression and war insofar as the enemy believes his aggression brings a forceful response. The more we are observed to fear war, the less our opponent will expect us to engage in war to counter his aggression; that is, the less credible our threat.

This principle had a direct application to the matter of possible Chinese intervention in the Vietnam war. Clearly, there existed a possibility that the Chinese might, on a massive scale, aid North Vietnam and the Viet Cong. How could American policymakers discourage the Chinese from making such a move? It was most important to make it perfectly clear that if the Chinese entered the war we would not withdraw but confront them without hesitation. The Chinese had to believe that we were ready, willing, and able to counter any move they might make. If they believed this, the probability of their intervention would be reduced.

Several members of the Senate Foreign Relations Committee would not accept this view. Instead, they freely voiced their private fears of war with China—even possibly exaggerating their fears for dramatic effect:

> Senator Morse. . . . But my last point, Mr. Chairman, is this fear that wakes me up in the night time and time again. I think we are following a stumble approach here in regard to this matter, until we will finally stumble into a war with Red China. [3]

> Chairman Fulbright. . . . I think, General, in all honesty, behind the concern of many of us, is not just Vietnam. There is the possibility, or even probability, of this situation escalating into a war with China. We always hesitate to talk about these things, but that is one of my concerns.
> I would regret to see us continue this war to the point where we became engaged in an all-out war with China. Many people who are wiser than I am believe that this [is] a possibility. [4]

> Senator Gore. Well, Senator Fulbright suggested to you, as others have, that a very deep concern on the part of certain members of this committee and a great many Americans, is whether this war in Vietnam will be escalated until a war with China becomes almost inevitable. [5]

Such remarks, if they were repeated widely enough, might finally have been accepted in China as an American position. Perhaps the Chinese never considered entering Vietnam until they "perceived" a wave of hysteric fear of Chinese intervention in the United States. Or perhaps the Chinese were seriously considering entering Vietnam but had postponed a decision fearing U.S. retaliation. These remarks (which could be distorted and exaggerated in the Chinese communications network) might have caused them to diminish their reservations. They would begin to expect us to retreat when they entered the war since we were (apparently) so desperately frightened of getting into a war with them. But we would not have retreated and war would have resulted. Those who loudly voiced their fears of a U.S.-Chinese engagement, instead of realizing they had helped bring it about, would then have told us "we told you so."

Of course we do not wish a war with China—or with anyone else, for that matter. That is not the issue. When high American public officials announce that they fear war under certain circumstances, they are not merely noting an unfortunate but inescapable aspect of the situation. They are, whether they realize it or not, offering a reason for altering our policy, for doing or not doing something. They are saying, in effect, that it is right and proper for us to allow our fear of war to influence our policy in this case. But if the danger of a larger war exists because we are attempting to block the aggression of our opponents, then our fear of this larger war cannot be allowed to have the obvious policy implication: retreat. And we must not let our opponents suspect that it does.

In Vietnam, for example, we could not let the fear of war with China or Russia affect our determination to stay. For, stripped to its essentials, the question was: Do we have a right to support an ally under attack or do the major communist powers have the right to demand our retreat by threatening war? Ironically, many of the same people who found it absurd to consider the communist attack on South Vietnam, "an extension of Sino-Soviet power" wanted to pull out of there because they feared a confrontation with China or the Soviet Union.

Should we, then, never fear war? Surely there are limits to the utility of courage. An obvious one is aggression. The courage which sustains a policy of making unprovoked attacks on the status quo is a reckless, dangerous courage. Secondly, one should not be so unafraid of war that he responds to violations of the status quo with unnecessary haste. Many times one may build the threat of response slowly, leaving the opponent time to reconsider and retreat. Finally, the fear of war should temper one's re-violations of the status quo in response to aggression so that they are in meaningful proportion to the original thrust.

After surveying American policy over the last two decades, it is difficult to argue that we have exceeded these limits of useful courage. American policy has not been aggressive. Neither we nor our allies have seriously attacked or undermined the Cold War status quo. Our reactions to the violations of our opponents have been slow, cautious and usually less° than proportional. The Blockade of Berlin of 1948-49 did not provoke a military reaction but only an airlift. We did not carry out an immediate air strike against the missiles in Cuba in 1962, but utilized a symbolic blockade. When China shelled Quemoy in 1958, we did not launch a counterattack. Our response in Vietnam has also been hesitant and reluctant: it cannot be argued that the United States plunged abruptly into the war in Vietnam at the first sign of an enemy threat to the status quo. Indeed, we have established such a tradition of caution and restraint that our opponents can virtually depend on our taking a cautious response. The Russians know that if they sail an intelligence ship into our waters or buzz planes flying into Berlin, nothing serious will happen. Cuba knows that if she sends a small boatload of terrorists to Venezuela, nothing will happen. The North Koreans expect to go unpunished if they send a small terrorist squad into South Korea. Our problem in the Cold War era certainly has not been an excess of courage, a reckless, devil-may-care attitude toward the dangers of war which leads to over-reaction.

Indeed, Americans have grown so accustomed to our tendency to under-react that they often forget we even have a right of re-violation. The public debate on our bombing of North Vietnam and the right readily conceded to the Soviet Union and China to respond to this bombing illustrate this forgetfulness. The starting point for a discussion of how severely we are entitled to treat North Vietnam cannot be, as many suppose, what Russia or China will stand. Instead we have to ask: what is the minimum punishment we can give the North to cause them to adequately respect our position in the area? For it is we who are defending and the North Vietnamese—and their allies—who are aggressing. So if it is true, as some have suggested, that Russia or China will intervene before allowing the North Vietnamese effort in the South to fail, we are driven to accept the position: Well, then, it is war, their war.

It is surprising to see how easily and readily many Americans

give China and Russia the right to assist and defend North Vietnam. Were the situation reversed these people would not hesitate in
condemning our action. Suppose the South Koreans began a highly
successful infiltration campaign against North Korea. China and
Russia begin to intervene to prevent this attempted alteration of the
status quo. If military advisors were not enough, they would send
troops. If the South Koreans were still successful, China would begin to bomb South Korean supply lines, then power plants and
petroleum installations. Under these circumstances, would the
United States be entitled to encourage the South Koreans, send a
billion dollars of aid, and extend a threat to enter the war if South
Korea were invaded because of its aggression?

Obviously not. We would, long before the situation reached
these proportions, have told the South Koreans to get out of the
North and inform them that we would cut them off without a penny
and without a protective threat if they did not. They would be
violating the status quo and trading on our threat to do so. This we
would not permit. We must expect, indeed, demand that our opponents have an equal regard for the status quo.

To be peace-loving, then, contributes to peace if one lives in an
aggressive nation. In a nation following a defensive deterrence
policy, urgent cries for peace tend to increase the danger of war.
It is one of the subtle ironies of modern history that the pacifists
have appeared in the wrong country at the wrong time and therefore
have consistently contributed to war. In the 1930s Britain and
France needed all the courage they could muster to deter Hitler
and Mussolini and thereby prevent a major war. The pacifists who
sapped their will to resist aggression should have been in Germany
to weaken Hitler's aggressive courage. In the postwar era pacifists
have been badly needed in Moscow, Peking, Pyongyang, and
Hanoi. Yet, oddly enough, they are exclusively concentrated in the
free world—which has trouble enough screwing up its courage to
sustain the deterrent threat which protects the peace.

Why a Nation Should Never Announce a Limit on the
Resources It Will Employ in Carrying Out Its Threats

A threat to defend a particular nation against aggression would
seem to be a limited commitment. The objective of such a threat
—preventing a communist attack on that nation—is indeed limited

and specific. Yet we must be prepared to use all necessary measures to carry out this threat. To place a limit on our involvement any- where weakens our threat and encourages war, particularly larger or longer wars.

Suppose we announce—or let it be thought—that in defense of South Korea we would send only 200,000 men, that we would fight a war for only two years and we would not, under any circum- stances, use atomic weapons. Our threat would still have some deterrent value, of course, but it also tempts potential aggressors to attack or threaten to attack at a level greater than our an- nounced limit in the expectation that we shall retreat. China, for example, could be tempted to send 200,001 troops (or whatever necessary to overpower our contingent) or prolong the war beyond our two-year limit. Had we announced no limit, aggression, if it had occurred at all, may well have resulted in a shorter, smaller war.

Our experience with the Vietnam problem provides numerous illustrations of our failure to understand and accept the inherently unlimited nature of the threat we were making to defend South Vietnam. A number of Senators and Congressmen who originally supported the Administration later deserted this policy saying, in effect: "I never expected it would come to *this.*" But any of our threats could come to *this*—or something very much worse. The possibility of escalation lies behind every confrontation. It has to. Otherwise opponents will threaten major war, often by taking dangerous or even irrevocable steps in that direction, with the expectation that we will yield.

Many Americans have been deceiving themselves about the nature of the sacrifices which their threats imply. Congress boldly and easily passes SEATO which pledges, as clearly as words can say it, American action against aggression, and then when the promised war has to be fought, we hear: "I didn't realize . . ."

The White House generally allows this unrealism about threats and war to persist, probably because it fears that the American public has not the courage to face the issue squarely. In his speech at Akron University on October 21, 1964, President Johnson, while saying that we would "help our Asian friends" resist Chinese ambi- tions, announced that "we are not about to send American boys 9 or 10,000 miles away from home to do what Asian boys ought to be doing for themselves." That statement was poor diplomacy.

Insofar as it was assimilated abroad as a suggestion that we would never send ground troops to Vietnam, it could only demoralize the South Vietnamese and encourage Hanoi and the Viet Cong to press for a military victory. By undercutting our own threat of intervention, it would place a compromise settlement in Vietnam further away.

Was the statement good domestic politics? I fear that it was. The American public seems so thoughtlessly desirous of peace that it virtually pleads for its presidential nominees to promise to keep the country out of war—any war for whatever reason. In August, 1964, our policy was—or ought to have been—that if the situation in South Vietnam continued to deteriorate, we would send troops and do whatever else was necessary to cause the communist effort to fail. Is it politically expedient to tell such a thing to the American public?

If we are often deceived about the course of American foreign policy, it is largely because we wish to be deceived. We find war senseless and detestable; our leaders must reflect our sentiment. Molded by this culture, a Wilson, a Roosevelt, a Johnson declares that there will be no war. Shutting its eyes to experience and history, the press, the radio and television interprets this as a promise. Rejoicing, their readers and listeners clutch this "promise" to their breasts. Across the world, equally eager to be deceived, opponents make another interpretation of the declaration. And so "a lie" is born.

The matter of limits on the involvement in Vietnam also came up in the Senate Foreign Relations Committee hearings in early 1966. This time the search was for some promise, some pledge from the administration about the ultimate level of U.S. troop involvement. The senators should not have sought nor expected an answer to their question; in this case they, properly, did not get one. One senator finally wrung this reply from Secretary Rusk:

> I am not going to say that this country has accepted in advance a certain point beyond which it will not go in meeting its commitments, because that is subject to the greatest misunderstanding. And when we say in this country, as we do, because it is true, that we don't want a larger war, it is just possible that there are those on the other side who are saying, "Ah, that means that we can have a larger war without an increase in risks."
>
> Now, how do we insure that the other side faces up

to the recklessness and the danger of the decisions that they may be making, if they want to make this into a larger war? 6

These are sobering words. We have to be willing to take all necessary steps to carry out our pledge to defend the smallest place. Otherwise we encourage our opponents to outmatch us. The business of deterrent threats is rather like playing poker with the sky as limit: if we have to play—and we do—we must bring to the table enough cash to match whatever the opponent might bet.

The motorcyclist rounding a sharp, slippery curve at high speeds faces a difficult decision. He must bank sharply to take the curve, yet leaning at such an angle he fears that his wheels may slip out from under him. His natural reaction, therefore, would be to apply the brakes so that the machine may traverse the rest of the curve in a more upright position. Since the application of the brakes causes the tires to break contact with the pavement, this natural reaction would produce a skid and spill the rider onto the road. The rule is, then, that one must never brake on a slippery curve. Although it seems the safe thing to do, braking actually produces the skid one seeks to avoid.

In its world position today, the United States is astride a motorcycle halfway round the slippery curve. What is the safest way to avoid disaster? Instinct counsels us to apply the brakes, to strive directly for peace, tolerate aggression and thereby avoid war. That course will lead toward more and larger wars. By retreating, we shall weaken our deterrent threat, and, as a result, many other aggressions, confrontations, and wars—now prevented by our threat—will come to pass.

Somehow we have got to find the courage to face the possibility of sacrifice and war. For without this courage our threat will not be *real,* as our enemies will quickly perceive.

Chapter 8

PRESTIGE AND WORLD OPINION

The President of the United States is making a visit to Bugistan. He is ascending the red-carpeted steps of the governmental palace to greet the Prime Minister. Just before he reaches the top of the stairs, his hand outstretched, the President slips on a banana peel, falls back down the steps, and tumbles headlong into the Fountain of the Laughing Virgins. Does this incident damage American prestige?

Unfortunately, the term "prestige" is too vague to permit a clear answer. The "prestige" of the United States is mentioned in connection with winning the Olympic Games, integrating schools, sending a man to the moon, pulling out of Vietnam, receiving an insult from Charles de Gaulle, and manufacturing records by Elvis Presley. Such an amorphous mass of meaning, while useful for the journalist dashing off a piece on "America in the World Today" for the Sunday supplement, corrupts our thinking and undermines the practical examination of foreign policy. By themselves, words like "face" or "prestige" are confused. For useful discussion, a specific meaning must be split off.

Perhaps the most important idea behind "prestige" is the coerciveness of a nation's explicit and implicit threats to defend its international interests and counter the advances of opponents. This is the meaning of prestige as it occurs in diplomatic language, particularly of earlier days. Other terms also referred to threats and events which affected their integrity: "face," "national honor," "reputation," "loss of face," "humiliation," and "insult." It is in reference to threats that I would propose these terms be used. Of course, anyone may use terms as he wishes to define them. But, generally speaking, writers who use the above words do not define them at all. Consequently, the concept of threat coerciveness becomes hopelessly tangled up with other ideas and we are never clear just what is meant.

The following statement, for example, can be true or false, depending upon the meaning given to "prestige":

> The Soviet Union's intervention in Hungary in 1956 is instructive. . . . The Soviet Union put the success of the intervention above all other considerations, and succeeded. Its prestige throughout the world suffered drastically in consequence.[1]

If "prestige" refers to the credibility of a nation's threat, then the statement is apparently false. The Soviet Union demonstrated its willingness to employ force to keep Hungary in its camp. In acting thus, the Soviet Union enhanced its threat to defend its other interests, particularly in Eastern Europe. If "prestige" means the "approval" of non-communist governments or peoples, then the statement is probably true.

Unfortunately, terms such as "face" or "humiliation" suggest the private dueling code of bygone days when aristocrats developed an exaggerated notion of personal honor. Hence when "honor" or "prestige" are mentioned in foreign relations today they are sometimes thought to refer to silly, outdated conceptions which the modern, mature nation should ignore. Intelligent policy-makers, it is thought, should put aside childish notions of "pride" and conduct their business practically. One aspect of practicality is thought to be the ability to turn one's back on the affronts of an enemy—just as the modern man would simply refuse to duel with an enraged nobleman.

We can observe this overtone of meaning entering the criticism of U.S. involvement in Vietnam voiced by George Kennan, former U.S. Ambassador to Russia. He recognized that the American threat in that area would be undermined by U.S. withdrawal with some possibly dangerous consequences:

> A precipitate and disorderly withdrawal could represent in present circumstances a disservice to our own interests, and even to world peace, greater than any that might have been involved by our failure to engage ourselves there in the first place.[2]

Yet certain inconsistencies enter his position. He commended earlier withdrawals of the French and British from certain areas of the world and suggested we might attempt the same in Vietnam:

> In matters such as this, it is not in my experience what you do that is mainly decisive. It is how you do it; and I would submit that there is more respect to be won in the opinion of this world by a resolute and courageous liquidation of unsound positions than by the most stubborn pursuit of extravagant or unpromising objectives.[3]

What does this statement mean? In one sense it is a truism: by definition, "unsound positions" should be liquidated and "unpromising objectives" not pursued. No one would urge the contrary. The entire argument lies in deciding what is "unsound" and what is "unpromising." But, it appears, Mr. Kennan intended more than a truism. He was suggesting—and this phrase has been quoted as suggesting—that retreat can also be a virtue, that there is "respect" to be won in making a gentlemanly exit. This conclusion is apparently reached by applying the dueling analogy: approximately every fifth show of the TV western, *Bonanza,* ends up with the hero courageously and maturely declining a showdown.

But national prestige is not a silly, outdated objective. A credible threat is a vital national resource. The main issue in our Vietnam involvement was maintaining our threat. It was therefore highly misleading to suggest that an American withdrawal from Vietnam would not affect our reputation, that, indeed, it would enhance it. An American withdrawal from Vietnam, in the face of a clear communist attempt, with substantial outside communist support, to gain control of this non-communist area could only reflect poorly on our willingness to make the sacrifices our threats imply. And, in point of fact, the overwhelming reason why opponents of U.S. involvement wished us to withdraw was the sacrifice we had to make to stay there. No amount of obfuscation can make it otherwise.

Then Mr. Kennan suggested that it is not "what you do" but "how you do it" that is decisive. Again language obscures the harsh realities. When all is said and done, *how* we retreat from Vietnam or stay there is of secondary consequence. The question is: *what* are we going to do, stand or yield, make sacrifices or fail to make sacrifices? It is illusory to suggest that we can make up for a lack of determination by elaborate conferences, complicated pro-

PRESTIGE AND WORLD OPINION

cedures or abstruse protocol. An "orderly" or "gracious" retreat is still a retreat. Our enemies will not be deceived about it; we should not deceive ourselves.

It is true that under certain circumstances a nation may withdraw from positions without weakening its threat: whenever the withdrawal cannot be interpreted as a lack of capability or will. Thus, in 1946, the United States gave the Philippines independence without losing prestige. Nothing in this withdrawal suggested that the United States lacked the determination to defend its interests. There was no military pressure being applied to force our withdrawal. If, however, a strong communist guerrilla movement had been pushing us out, it then would have been inadvisable to retreat. The Vietnam conflict, representing as it did a direct challenge to our deterrent threat, inescapably affected our prestige.

Mr. Kennan's apparently inconsistent attitude toward Vietnam, and its relation to our prestige, prompted Senator Symington to press the matter:

> Now, I would like to go back to another point on page 5, if I may, where you talk about France giving an impressive exhibition of statesmanship in withdrawing from north Africa; and about the British wisely and tolerantly liquidating great portions of their colonial empire.
> Do you feel that the position of the United States in the world today, with our unprecedented economy and our obligations, whatever they may be, to free people, is comparable to that of the British today?
> *Mr. Kennan.* Well, it is sufficiently comparable so that I should doubt—and this is all that I meant to say with that statement—I should doubt that we would be receiving any bitter reproaches from the British over giving up an individual position like this, even if we were to do it, because *they have been all through this,* as have the French and others. And, incidentally, as far as that is concerned, *this sort of loss has usually been digested somehow or another.* [4]

Here we see the danger of understanding threats only by intuition as diplomats sometimes do. One is seduced into contradictions. Earlier, Mr. Kennan told the committee that a retreat from Vietnam could have dangerous consequences; now we are told not to worry, for such losses are usually "digested somehow or another." The error lies in a misapplied analogy. Mr. Kennan observed France and Great Britain withdraw from large areas of the world without any subsequent disaster and reasoned that, therefore, we could do the same. An analysis of the threats in the two situations reveals this parallel to be false.

Neither Great Britain nor France project, except in a secondary way always backstopped by the American threat, a deterrent threat against communist aggression. Their smaller economies, their deficient military establishments and their lower level of concern preclude a major deterrent role. If the French were to promise to defend Cambodia or Thailand in the event of a communist attack, that threat would not be worth peanuts. The same has become increasingly true for the British. It is the American threat which deters the aggression of the communist powers and allies; these other states have an international deterrent so feeble that any further retreats they might make are of little consequence.

Closer inspection of just how British and French retreats were "digested" reveals our different role. When in February, 1947, Great Britain relinquished the task of defending Greece, then under attack by communist guerrillas, the United States, in the Truman Doctrine, took up the task of supporting Greece. When French influence was destroyed in Southeast Asia in 1954, again the United States picked up the job of deterrence. It is misleading, therefore, to suggest than an American withdrawal from Vietnam would be digested as were the retreats of European countries. *There is no larger free-world nation to pick up the marbles.* It is doubtful that Mr. Kennan would have arrived at this conclusion had he isolated the notion of threat credibility from vague words such as "respect."

The proper French-British parallel to an American retreat in the world today would have to be a situation where there was no other country to replace the French and British threat. Such a situation did exist in Europe in the 1930s. When these countries, in failing to oppose the aggression of their opponents, allowed their threat to wane, no one else took up the burden of deterrence. In these circumstances, the loss of a country such as Czechoslovakia, for example, was not harmlessly "digested somehow or another."

A study of Mr. Kennan's thinking on these matters is particularly instructive because he is both a diplomat and a scholar of international affairs. Strangely, what Kennan the diplomat knows by habit and experience about "prestige," that is threat, is not communicated to Kennan the scholar. One of the most intriguing examples of this gap between theory and practice is found in his discussion of containment policy. Writing in his *Memoirs* Kennan expressed the limits which he felt the containment idea, propounded in his "X-Article," should have had:

> A third great deficiency [of the "X-Article"] . . . was the failure to distinguish between various geographic areas, and to make clear that the "containment" of which I was speaking was not something that I thought we could, necessarily, do everywhere successfully, or even needed to do everywhere successfully, in order to serve the purpose I had in mind. Actually, as noted in connection with the Truman Doctrine above, I distinguished clearly in my own mind between areas that I thought vital to our security and ones that did not seem to me to fall into this category. My objection to the Truman Doctrine message revolved largely around its failure to draw this distinction. Repeatedly, at that time and in ensuing years, I expressed in talks and lectures the view that there were only five regions of the world—the United States, the United Kingdom, the Rhine valley with adjacent industrial areas, the Soviet Union, and Japan—where the sinews of modern military strength could be produced in quantity; I pointed out that only one of these was under Communist control; and I defined the main task of containment, accordingly, as one of seeing to it that none of the remaining ones fell under such control.[5]

Kennan, writing as a scholar, propounded an application of the strategic value theory. But in practice, he ignored it. Later in the *Memoirs* he recounts his reaction to the invasion of South Korea:

> It was clear to me from the start that we would have to react with all necessary force to repel this attack and to expel the North Korean forces from the southern half of the peninsula. I took this position unequivocally on that first day and in all the discussions that followed over the ensuing days and weeks. I also took occasion to emphasize, on that first occasion and on a number of others, that we would now have to take prompt steps to assure that Formosa, too, did not fall into Communist hands; for two such reverses coming one on the heels of the other, could easily prove disastrous to our prestige and to our entire position in the Far East.[6]

A statesman-like summary of the problem. But what does it have to do with the academic formulation of the containment policy given before? Neither South Korea nor Formosa were in one of Kennan's five heartlands; yet he unhesitatingly urged that we go to war in their defense to protect our "prestige." If we make the meaning of "prestige" explicit, we can see Kennan's advice was sound. The attack on South Korea was a violation of the status quo and, hence, a dramatic challenge to our threat. If we did not wish our reputation to be destroyed—with the subsequent increased danger of aggression elsewhere—we would have to respond. The five heartlands version of the strategic value theory becomes irrelevant.

This conflict between the diplomatic and scholarly view of defense policy in the same individual reflects the general gap that exists between scholars and practitioners in international relations. If we were to select the term which contained the key to this conflict, it would be "prestige." For their part, the practitioners use this word daily but without stopping to make explicit what they really mean by it, namely, the coerciveness of their nation's threat of war. Scholars of international relations, consequently, find "prestige" a vague term which, therefore, cannot have a central place in their thinking. As a result, the scholar often overlooks the profound importance of threat and its many implications in governing the relations between hostile states.

Another illustration of confusion arising from the careless use of threat terminology is the following injunction offered by a professor of international relations:

> I think our policy [in Vietnam] violates one of the basic rules of diplomacy—which is never put yourself in a position from which you cannot retreat without losing face and from which you cannot advance without grave risks.[7]

At first glance, this advice appears to be sound, old-worldly wisdom. But let us look more closely. If "losing face" means impairing the credibility of your threat or reputation for action, then the advice is logically impossible to follow. Making a threat means creating an expectation of action (or reaction). Failing to carry out the threat, that is, failing to live up to the expectation, necessarily weakens the threat. Hence, by definition, every threat is the taking (even implicitly or unintended) of a position from which one cannot retreat without losing face.

A glance around the world makes this clear. We have made a threat to defend West Berlin. Would not a retreat there cause us to "lose face"? If the North Koreans invade South Korea, would we not be in a position from which we cannot retreat without "losing face"? The only way one can avoid being in a position where retreat means losing face is never to project any threats, that is, never take any positions. And then, of course, one has no "face" to lose anyway.

The above advice, therefore, cannot possibly be a "basic rule of diplomacy." It suggests that a statesman, if only he were wise enough, could make a credible threat without risks or sacrifice. Impossible.

World Opinion and a Deterrence Policy

For the few general observations we have to make on the subject, we do not need an elaborate definition of "world opinion." The following will serve our purposes: the sentiments which other peoples and their governments hold about the United States. Do they admire us or despise us; do they approve or disapprove of our country and its policies?

At first, one might suppose that world opinion has, or should have, little to do with deterrence. The projecting of threats is a matter of capability and will; it seems unconnected with the attitudes other governments might have toward us. Who cares, one might argue, if we are hated, despised or scorned by other governments and other peoples; the important thing is that, under the appropriate circumstances, we be feared.

Such a view is too hasty. The opinions of other governments and other peoples have important consequences for our ability to carry on a successful deterrence policy. First, it is useful to have allies to join with us in making threats and to assist us in carrying them out. Although the United States is, and must be, the central pillar of any deterrence alliance, the contribution of allies should not be disparaged. The troops of South Korea, Australia, Thailand, New Zealand, and the Philippines in Vietnam, for example, representing more outside military help than we received in Korea, have been a useful contribution. Were they not there, our burden would have been that much heavier. Should we be hated and despised by these nations, they would be less inclined to join such a common effort.

An even more important link between world opinion and a successful deterrence policy concerns alterations in the status quo through a process of "melting." Aggression is not the only way in which the great-power status quo can change against the will of a major power. An individual country may undergo a regime and alignment change to such an extent that it alters its location in the status quo from the side of one power to its opponent. Carefully defined, melting of the status quo is the autonomous alteration of a state's location in the great-power status quo with the approval of the existing regime(s) in that state. Notice that "melting" does not apply where the existing regime requests aid from the power with which it is aligned to combat some internal (or, of course, external) attempt to destroy it. When melting takes place, the regime itself "wants" to shift its alignment.

The losing power in a melting situation is faced with a difficult problem. To arrest the process at an early stage, it would have to invade against the existing regime—a gross violation of the local status quo. If it acts later in the melting process, when the regime has already shifted toward the camp of the opponent, then it will be violating both the local status quo and, to varying degrees, the great-power status quo. Although it would seem that adverse melting—not constituting a case of aggression—ought not to affect a power's threat, in practice it does. One has lost something of value; opponents have scored a gain. One seems unable to preserve one's interests; opponents are exhilarated.

The melting of the status quo would typically involve both successive decisions of an existing government, and transformations of that government. Beginning with a clearly identified non-communist state, for example, one could end up with a clearly identified communist one through something like the following steps:

1. The government "cools" in its attitude toward the United States;
2. It accepts a small amount of Soviet economic assistance;
3. It accepts Soviet armaments and a Soviet military mission;
4. It severs diplomatic relations with the United States;
5. The Soviet Union formally pledges its support and protection for the state;
6. Through the Soviet embassy and military mission com-

munist or pro-communist groups are encouraged and coordinated;

7. The prevailing pro-communist atmosphere discourages the activity of anti-communist groups;

8. In response to the demands of pro-communist forces and a promise of greater Russian assistance, the Prime Minister appoints a communist Minister of Interior;

9. Pro-communist forces enact a successful coup against the incumbent regime;

10. All opposition is outlawed; the regime declares itself "Marxist-Leninist."

There is, of course, nothing inevitable about the above pattern, or others one could describe. But a sequence like this can take place. The result is a fundamental alteration in the status quo, yet at no point could we have properly employed force to prevent it. The country is "entitled" to take each step; nothing we can reasonably call "aggression" is taking place. A glance at past situations in Ghana and Indonesia and now Syria and Egypt shows that this melting of the status quo is a real possibility.

In Cuba it happened. Between 1959 and 1962 a substantial alteration of the status quo took place. Yet at no point did we have an option to prevent this alteration that did not involve at least a violation of the local status quo. This change, however, had implications for our deterrent threat. As suggested earlier, the Cuban transformation very likely reflected poorly on our determination to resist aggression by guerrilla infiltration elsewhere, and encouraged our opponents to believe that the tide of history was flowing more strongly their way.

We might note, incidentally, that our opponents can also face melting problems. The transformation in Czechoslovakia in early 1968 is an excellent illustration. The regime was voluntarily altering in a manner disadvantageous to Russia with its communist ideals and to the delight of the West. Had the transformation succeeded, Russia's reputation for defending its ideological and geostrategic interests would have suffered a decline. As we saw, the Russians, however, are much less hesitant than we are to protect their reputation by violating a local status quo.

The statesman, therefore, must constantly work to prevent alterations of the status quo through melting. It is not enough to oppose forcible aggression with force. While he is patiently awaiting the next dramatic enemy thrust, the statesman may have the status quo quietly melted out from under him *with deleterious consequences to the credibility of his threat to oppose aggression.*

World opinion therefore impinges upon a deterrence policy in this fashion: the attitudes of other governments and their citizens toward the United States affects, in part, the ease with which our opponents may melt the status quo. If we are stingy, rude or barbaric, we make our task more difficult. If we are admired and well-liked, marginal penetration of our opponents will be made more difficult. Hence, we can see why, in a general way, it is desirable for the United States to be courteous, generous, and fairminded in its dealings with other nations. Economic and military assistance, reduction of tariffs, settling of outstanding disputes: such policies, carefully employed, contribute to a successful deterrence policy.

We can say, for example, that had all Cubans, including Fidel Castro, loved and admired the United States, the transformation which took place in Cuba could have been avoided—and all the dangerous consequences that followed from it. Yet, what exactly could we have done? Economic assistance? Perhaps, but how much? Perhaps we should have decreased the sugar quota to force agricultural diversification, but that would not have been popular. Perhaps—and this is quite possible—there was nothing we could reasonably have done which would have altered the opinions of Castro and his colleagues.

In some cases, the futility of attempting to please all nations all of the time is readily apparent. If a nation is aggressive so that our assistance is assistance to an aggressor, we shall find our relations with that country deteriorate. We do not and should not assist an aggressor; as we attempt to restrain him by witholding aid, he turns to our opponents—who have a more liberal view of his aggression. It was therefore unavoidable that our relations with Egypt, which sought the destruction of Israel and Sukarno's Indonesia, which prosecuted an attack against Malaysia, should have deteriorated.

The statesman, then, will try to keep the governments and peoples of the world friendly toward his country. In pursuit of this goal, he realizes that he often cannot know how to achieve it, and that in other cases it is simply impossible to please everyone.

But what of war? Here, it is commonly believed, a direct

contradiction arises between the apparent demand of world opinion and the requirements of a deterrence policy. A deterrence policy involves threatening and fighting wars; "world opinion" is supposed to oppose war and condemn all those who engage in it. Our Vietnam involvement is often supposed to illustrate the dilemma. We might fight in Vietnam to sustain our deterrent threat; yet world opinion, it is said, opposes the war and holds us at least partly responsible. Therefore, the conclusion runs, we are losing more than we gain by fighting in Vietnam.

Down this road one hesitates to travel. So very much depends upon the "facts" one has. It is, first of all, characteristic to perceive "world opinion" in one's own image. If one opposes the Vietnam involvement then "world opinion is turning against us"; if one adopts the opposite position then "the world respects our defense of this little country." In making such allegations, neither side has anything approaching satisfactory evidence nor the most elementary rules for drawing conclusions from this evidence. How many people around the world even hold an opinion on Vietnam? How intensely held is this opinion? Will it last or be forgotten? Will it change? How much will that opinion affect their future behavior? Does American action in Vietnam have anything to do with such opinion, or were certain people already anti-American? Is this opinion freely formed or created by a controlled mass media? How much does public opinion count in government policy? The French people were apparently sympathetic toward Israel in the 1967 war, but de Gaulle found it possible to side with the Arabs. These problems have to be resolved before useful statements about world opinion can be made.

There are further weaknesses in the typical world opinion arguments for American withdrawal from Vietnam. One thread in these arguments runs like this: "All those countries opposed to our policy in Vietnam are opposed because our action is unwise or immoral." Underlying this conclusion is the assumption that nations adopt positions toward another nation's policy solely on the merits of the specific policy. More often than not, this assumption is incorrect. Nations are eminently selfish organizations. Their positions on this or that issue are determined by their own long-term goals. Thus, the opposition of Egypt or Syria to American action in Vietnam does not flow from anything we do in Southeast Asia; it is a consequence of the Arab-Israeli dispute and our position in it.

One of the most important issues which affects the posture of other nations toward us is their own security. It is fear, not love nor admiration, which causes many nations to adopt a pro- or anti-American position. The basic questions each nation asks are these: What is the danger of communist attack? Would the American threat be sufficient to deter such an attack? Can the possible communist attack be prevented by leaning away from the United States and toward the communists? The answers each government gives will, in many cases, determine its posture toward the United States. Thus, the South Koreans and Nationalist Chinese see themselves as likely targets for aggression, and unavoidably so. They cultivate good relations with the United States to insure our support. Finland realizes that the United States cannot protect her and therefore takes pains not to offend the Soviet Union. In 1947, Finland considered sending delegates to the European Conference on the Marshall Plan. The Soviet Union was displeased by this prospect. Finland declined to participate.[8] From such action one could have inferred nothing about the inherent wisdom or morality of the Marshall Plan.

In Southeast Asia the effect of the balance of fear on the attitudes of Asian governments toward the United States has been dramatic. It almost seems that the entire area is a field of weather vanes pointing first one way and then another, depending upon which threat—the communist threat of aggression or the U.S. threat of defense—appears most credible. Thus, Thailand was deeply disturbed by the American inaction in Laos in April, 1961:

> When the Thai leaders became aware of America's decision not to intervene, they were astonished and even angry. . . . If the United States was not prepared to accept its responsibilities by defending Laos against a Communist takeover, Thai leaders concluded, what reason was there to believe that it would be any more prepared to defend Thailand when it was faced with a similar threat?[9]

Shortly thereafter,

> There were renewed discussions with the Soviet Ambassador in Bangkok concerning trade and cultural exchanges, and there was increasing talk of an "independent" Thai foreign policy and even of neutralism . . .[10]

Then on March 6, 1962, the United States gave an explicit statement pledging U.S. aid to Thailand "in resisting Communist aggression and subversion." "The reaction in Thailand to this agreement was an emotional outpouring of praise and renewed confidence in the United States."[11] In 1967, when the United States was persistently and successfully blocking the communist attempt in South Vietnam, Thailand drew closer yet to the United States, even sending sizable numbers of its troops to fight in Vietnam.

One condition which gives Southeast Asia its weather-vane quality is the large number of overseas Chinese in many countries, particularly Burma, Thailand, Cambodia and Indonesia. These Chinese populations serve as excellent centers for Chinese communist penetration. Their fifth column activities of subversion, propaganda, and agitation can create oppressive burdens for the countries concerned. The intensity of overseas Chinese communist activities and the local reaction to them is greatly affected by the prevailing threats in the area. If China is dominant and the American position weak, then overseas Chinese, believing the communists are advancing and desirous of being on the winning side, may press their agitation with vigor. The local government, fearing the imminent or eventual exercise of Chinese power in retaliation for harsh treatment of local Chinese, hesitates to crush this subversion. Consequently the nation grows more dependent upon Peking. As the American threat grows more real and the belief in eventual Chinese domination consequently diminishes, overseas Chinese grow less inclined to do Peking's bidding and the local governments more bold in repressing those that do.

It seems likely, for example, that Burma's recent independence from Communist China is due, in part, to the strengthened American position in Asia. In 1966 and 1967, the Burmese government dared to accept Western aid, dared to ban "Mao-think" from the schools, and refused to apologize for the anti-Chinese riots provoked by the Maoists who had publicly trampled the Burmese flag. The Chinese were, predictably, angry and withdrew their technicians from Burma while voicing ominous threats to "counterattack."[12] It is doubtful that four or five years earlier, when the American threat was weaker, that the Burmese would have found the courage to stand up to China.[13]

Cambodia's independence from Chinese pressures was demonstrated more quietly. In September, 1967, Prince Norodom Sihanouk of Cambodia ordered the dissolution of the Pro-Peking

Cambodian-Chinese Friendship Association for its subversive activities. When the Chinese protested this move, Sihanouk ordered the resignation of two pro-Chinese ministers and announced the recall of the staff of the Cambodian embassy in Peking. Changing its earlier attitude, China sent an *apology* to Sihanouk, whereupon he reversed his decision to recall his envoys. Chou En-lai's polite words were the first apology sent to a foreign state by the Chinese since the beginning of the Cultural Revolution. Later, in October, when Sihanouk expelled two pro-Chinese agitators, Peking remained politely silent.[14]

Thus tiny, defenseless Cambodia stood up for its integrity and independence. And China was at last brought to recognize standards of decent international conduct. Of course this was not Cambodia's victory alone. The United States, by its defense of Vietnam, had strengthened its deterrent threat in the area and thereby bolstered the courage of the nations in China's shadow. China, aware that its ability to intimidate its neighbors had lessened, was obliged to practice peaceful coexistence.

A war to maintain a deterrent threat, therefore, by no means "turns everyone against us." The contrary is often the case. Nations, seeking their own security, grow friendly toward that nation which demonstrates a willingness to guarantee that security. They grow unfriendly toward those nations which appear unwilling to defend them, and, in the hope of being spared, curry the favor of potential aggressors.

It should also be noted that a nation which fails to live up to its security commitments will, thereby, earn the scorn of those who have trusted in it. It is doubtful, for example, if France was ever more despised in Czechoslovakia than in October, 1938, when the French, pledged to defend this faithful ally, deserted her in her hour of need by allowing Hitler to acquire the Czech Sudetenland unopposed. An American withdrawal from South Vietnam would have left bitter memories, not only among South Vietnamese, but among Thais, South Koreans and Australians, who joined the effort, assuming we would not let them down.

A second fallacious theme in world opinion arguments against American involvement in Vietnam runs this way: If Vietnam were really as critical as we say it is, why aren't other nations, particularly Asian nations, doing more to help? If Vietnam were really a testing ground against communist aggression and if a communist victory would greatly endanger the future peace and security of the area, surely other nations would be there in force. Since they are not, we must be chasing spooks and should get out.

Underlying this position is an unfounded assumption: that nations are sufficiently farsighted to know when, in the interest of future peace, aggressors must be confronted and that they have sufficient courage and capability to confront them. History is strewn with the bones of nations which did not meet these qualifications.* One need only point to the shortsightedness and cowardice of Great Britain and France—and the United States, to some extent—in the 1930s. The Korean episode is another illustration of what *will not* happen if the United States attempts to leave the deterrence of aggression to others. In 1948-1950, when we deliberately and dramatically cut back our defense posture in the Far East, Korea in particular, did other nations band together in an effective collective security arrangement? Or even an ineffective one? South Korea was certainly in danger. Where were Australia, New Zealand, Thailand, India and Pakistan? Where was France or Great Britain or Peru or Chile? For a variety of reasons, these nations had no desire to project a threat of war to defend South Korea.

Aside from shortsightedness and cowardice, nations may avoid collective security arrangements out of a selfish desire for momentary gain. This tendency was exhibited recently by France when Egypt blockaded the Gulf of Aqaba in May, 1967. Nasser's action was a violation of the status quo. A war-provoking act. Aggression. The United States and Great Britain immediately condemned it. But France refused to join the effort. The lure of possible oil rights and preferential Suez Canal use was apparently more important to her than collective security, opposing aggression, or preventing war.·

National selfishness accounts for the failure of other nations to assist us in another way. The existing disparity between American capabilities and responsibilities and those of other nations makes possible a certain amount of freeloading. A nation may enjoy the general protection and stability our deterrent threat affords without contributing significantly to its maintenance, secure in the

---

*Carthage stands as one of the earliest illustrations, see: Donald Armstrong, "Prologue: Unilateral Disarmament: A Case History" in Frank R. Barnett, William C. Mott, and John C. Neff, eds., *Peace and War in the Modern Age* (Garden City, Doubleday, 1965), pp. 5-13.

knowledge that we cannot afford to let it collapse. On occasion, such freeloading can be particularly annoying. India has adopted a supercilious attitude toward most American defense efforts, yet it is our threat which plays an important role in restraining her unfriendly neighbor, China. Cambodia's "neutrality" is manifestly sustained by the American threat in Southeast Asia, yet Prince Sihanouk shows little desire to assist the Vietnam effort on which that threat rests. Other countries—Japan, Singapore, Malaysia, Indonesia, and, for that matter, Switzerland and Sweden—rely to varying degrees on our threat. The tepid position of these countries toward our Vietnam effort reflects not necessarily a judgment about the importance of that effort in stabilizing peace, but the application of a simple principle: when you can get something for nothing, do not pay for it.*

In any given case of communist aggression, the United States has more to lose than these other countries. We have a threat to sustain; other nations do not. The immediate consequence to us of weakening that threat is a greater probability of confrontations and wars which we, in the first instance, will have to fight. If South Vietnam is attacked and overrun, France, Japan, Sweden and India lose nothing directly. It is our deterrent threat which is challenged and weakened. Indirectly, eventually, these other nations will probably suffer if we allow our threat to collapse, but we shall suffer first and most.

The farmer who builds a flood-control dam on the river to protect his crop is supplying a public good, for he is also protecting the lands of many other farmers further down the river. If these other farmers were fair-minded, they would contribute to the maintenance of the dam. But if they are selfish, they can refuse to help. They know that if the dam breaks, the farmer who built it will suffer first and most. He, therefore, can be depended upon to keep it in repair himself. The builder can compel others to help only by refusing to maintain the dam; but, of course, that endangers him more than the others.

---

*Compounding the lack of appreciation people in many other nations have for our deterrence efforts is the relationship between theoretical understanding and practical responsibility: the two go together. In nations which have minimal security problems and no threat there is likely to be little understanding of deterrence theory and the practical responsibilities of a great power. The ignorance born of unfamiliarity feeds a supercilious, critical attitude toward great power behavior.

There appears to be no simple solution to this vexing aspect of our defense policy. We cannot convince other nations that they must do more for regional defense unless we demonstrate to them that we shall not defend the region. But we cannot convince these nations without, at the same time, convincing our opponents of the same thing. That is, we would have to weaken our threat and see a great deal of aggression—which is precisely what we seek to avoid. Encouraging and then allowing our opponents to overrun South Korea, for example, might stimulate Japan to make a greater contribution to Asian security. But the price of such stimulation is exhorbitant: a tragic war in Korea; the loss of South Korea; a weaker American threat to defend other countries; an increase in the probability of aggression and therefore an increase in the probability of our fighting a war elsewhere.

Even if we allow aggression to gather momentum in a certain area to terrorize others into making greater efforts for regional defense, it is unlikely that the threatened countries will have the capability and will to check this aggression on their own. They would almost certainly require assistance from the United States, so we would not escape the deterrent role after all. And since no other country has, or is likely to have in the near future, the economy, technology and nuclear force adequate to counterbalance the major communist powers, the job of deterrence cannot, ultimately, be done by any nation except the United States.

For these reasons, it is possible for many nations to rely on our threat without making a fair contribution to its maintenance; it should not surprise us to discover some of them taking advantage of the opportunity.

We must be careful, then, not to allow other nations to do our thinking for us. To point out that other nations do not unstintingly support our defense efforts, such as our involvement in Vietnam, says little about the wisdom or justice of our action. Instead, it could simply be another demonstration of a well-known feature of international life: most nations most of the time are shortsighted and selfish.

Chapter 9

MANAGING PEACE

Oppose alterations of the status quo made without your consent. The central task of this essay has been to give meaning to this injunction and defend it as a cardinal principle of great power diplomacy. Like all such principles, of course, it affords only a starting point and not a complete solution to any particular problem. As a way of drawing this principle closer to its practical applications, it is helpful to examine some exceptions or limitations which might be placed upon it.

When One Need Not Respond: Leeway

Powers oppose alterations of the status quo because, by so doing, they preserve their threat to defend their values and interests around the world. It follows, therefore, that the importance of responding to a particular status quo violation is partly determined by the general state of a nation's reputation. If firm action has recently been taken elsewhere, then a failure to respond is less damaging; if the nation's threat has been undermined by several successive failures to react, then a response becomes all the more imperative to avoid confirming and emphasizing its lack of will.

This observation can be expressed in the notion of "leeway": the amount of status quo alteration which may go unchallenged without seriously weakening the national threat. Of course, to allow one's interests to be adversely affected will always communicate some lack of will. But that loss may be kept small or even negligible if recently—or ideally, concurrently—one has shown determination elsewhere. It is the succession or combination of retreats which, by *confirming* the opponents' hypothesis of one's timidity, produces the dangerous loss of reputation. When a nation which has recently allowed other challenges to go unanswered faces yet another status quo violation, it has no leeway: a response is imperative.

An awareness of the leeway problem leads statesmen to conceive of patterns and combinations of actions rather than isolated events. Sometimes, the explicit argument for pressing harder in one area is to create leeway for a withdrawal one wishes to make elsewhere. Austrian foreign minister Aehrenthal advanced this principle in defending the proposed annexation of Bosnia-Herzegovina in 1908. The Austrians had wanted to withdraw their troops from the Sanjak of Novi Bazar but there was fear that this movement would create an impression of a declining, retreating power: "The garrisons must be withdrawn from the Sanjak," Aehrenthal argued, "but this could only be done without damage to the prestige of the Monarchy if it were preceded by the annexation of Bosnia-Herzegovina."[1] And thus it was made with the withdrawal of the garrisons from the Sanjak being announced along with the annexation.[2]

The notion of leeway enables us to understand why certain questions of policy cannot be definitively answered beforehand. For example: what is our policy toward a purely internal communist attempt to seize power through guerrilla war in a Latin American country? If they are on the point of succeeding should we oppose or tolerate them? On the one hand, such a communist victory, being an internally produced change, would represent a less grievous challenge to us than a successful invasion of the country by an opponent such as the Soviet Union or Cuba. Nevertheless, it would constitute an alteration of the status quo to our manifest disadvantage. A type of regime which we oppose, which will orient itself toward our major opponents has emerged, and in an area where we are perceived to have a special and traditional concern.

Whether or not we can safely accept such an intermediate loss of reputation depends upon the leeway we have at the moment. If we have suffered several recent reverses, it is unlikely that we can afford another; if we have just successfully resisted a status quo violation elsewhere, then we may have leeway to accept an internal communist victory in the country in question.

Protesters against American reactions to challenges to the status quo—as in Vietnam—are therefore correct in pointing out that deterrence theory does not require that the defender make a forceful response to every single challenge. But this observation is true only to the extent that we have created leeway for ourselves by reacting firmly elsewhere—and generally the protesters would oppose that action too. Somewhere along the way, one must grasp the nettle.

When One Should Not Respond: Proportionality

The reader has already been introduced to the concept of proportionality; it is raised again here as an important constraint in responding to status quo alterations. A whole series of status quo violations or infractions—occasional shots across a border, the shooting down of a plane, espionage overflights—are of such small magnitude that no meaningful and proportional re-violation exists. This is not to say that one makes no reaction, but that it will not be in terms of the status quo. As a way of protesting such infractions, one may take measures from issuing a formal protest to severing commercial or diplomatic relations.

It can be argued that the notion of proportionality is vague. It is quite true that proportionality only defines á range of actions and not any specific action. It does not clearly tell us *which* response to make, but identifies which responses are *not* advisable. Its function in this analysis is, at a minimum, to plug an intellectual loophole in the status quo framework. If we did not introduce the notion of proportionality, we would have no way of accounting for the fact that infractions of the status quo—which are constantly occuring—do not lead to major war. Nor would we have a meaning for the word "pretext" (for aggression), e.g. a disproportionate re-violation.

Proportionality, however, is more than an intellectual construction. People, even people in high places, occasionally ignore it in practical situations. When Castro shut off the Guantanamo water supply on February 5, 1964, some argued that we should have used a "military escort" to restore the water supply.[3] But to do so our forces would have had to leave the confines of Guantanamo and, in effect, invade Cuba—a clearly disproportionate response.

The disregard of the proportionality principle often takes the form: "let's settle this once and for all." Instead of continuing to manage the hostile relationship with his eye constantly upon the range of alternatives proportionality would permit, the national leader seeks to cut the Gordian knot of conflict with a bold, definitive act. This was the view of Count Berchtold, Austrian Foreign Minister in 1914, toward Serbia following the assassination of the Austrian Archduke on June 28, 1914. Serbia was somewhat implicated in the assassination, and we may therefore concede the Austrians a certain right of response. But Berchtold went beyond considering a proportional response, wishing "to make Serbia harmless once for all through the use of force:"

> . . . Austria should get ahead of her enemies, and, by a timely final reckoning with Serbia, put an end to the movement which was already in full swing, a thing which might be impossible later. [4]

Count Stephan Tisza, Minister President of Hungary, opposed this view, raising, implicitly, the notion of proportionality:

> Unquestionably demands must be made on Serbia, but no ultimatum must be sent until Serbia had failed to comply with these demands. . . . If the demands were not complied with, he [Tisza] too would favor military action, but must still emphasize that we aim at the diminution, but not the complete annihilation of Serbia . . . because this would never be permitted by Russia without a life-and-death struggle . . . [5]

Unfortunately, Berchtold won out—the result being that anticipated by Tisza: general war.

When One Should Not Respond But Must: Graduated Response and the Stability of Deterrence

It is easy to lecture national leaders about forgoing a response if a proportional act is not available, but we must not overlook that in order to take our advice, they pay a price—often a price they find intolerable. In not "doing something" about the Berlin wall, in not "turning the water back on," the United States paid a price in suggesting an image of a nation unwilling to defend its interests. One of the strongest arguments for preserving some leeway in one's reputation is precisely this: one needs it to absorb the losses incurred in response failures owing to proportionality problems.

What happens when national leaders feel, for whatever reason, that a response is imperative, yet they have no proportional re-

sponse? Clearly, this is a situation fraught with danger. It can
come about in two ways. First, one does not have the military technology and resources to make a proportional response; second, the
proportional response is, owing to a highly unstable deterrent
posture, intolerably dangerous.

As an illustration of the first, we might consider what our
problems would be if, in the face of opponents widely using
guerrilla infiltration to alter the status quo, we had no significant
limited war capabilities and only atomic weapons and delivery
systems. In response to an infiltration attack on South Vietnam
or Thailand, we would lack a proportional response. Even to accept
the loss of one country in this manner would gravely damage our
prestige; we would quickly feel we would *have* to act—and with
whatever instruments were available. The general solution to
technological graduated-response gaps is, obviously, to acquire the
capability to fill such gaps.

The second condition, instability, which militates against
proportionality is often more difficult to remedy. A deterrent posture is stable to the degree that after an enemy has initiated a
major attack, one still has a substantial military capability to
inflict damage upon him.[6] If, for example, a surprise nuclear attack
by the Soviet Union would virtually destroy our nuclear retaliatory
capability, our deterrent posture would be unstable. When one has
an unstable posture there is the temptation to make the major blow
first, because if you hesitate, the opponent may strike first and
gravely damage or eliminate you. Consequently, if a limited proportional response might trigger the opponent's general first strike,
one is particularly reluctant to adopt such a response when one's
position is unstable.

We saw this principle at work in the Arab-Israeli conflict of
June 1967. Nassar announced the blockade of the Gulf of Aqaba:
a violation of the status quo. Many proportional responses existed
for Israel: attempting to run the blockade; bombing the Sharm
el Sheik fortress; even landing paratroopers to capture Sharm el
Sheik. But if one looks at the map of Israel and the pre-war count
of military hardware, it is clear that an Arab first strike would do
great damage to Israel. By acting proportionally against the
Egyptians at the blockade, the Israelis would probably trigger
such a first strike. Hence, in responding to the blockade the
Israelis were prompted to ignore proportionality (and propinquity)

and make a general surprise attack. By the same logic, Israel's new borders greatly increase the stability of her deterrent posture and thereby reduce the probability of *general war* in the area. (Stability, however, makes harassment and limited actions less risky and, hence, more probable.)

The statesman must strive, therefore, to achieve safe and viable proportional responses to his opponents' potential challenges both by developing appropriate military capabilities and by working to increase the stability of his country's deterrent posture.

Why Statesmen Are Conservative-I

Of all the charges leveled at the managers of American foreign policy perhaps the most frequently voiced is "conservatism." The State Department, we hear, is hidebound and rigid. Policy-making personnel are unimaginative and backward-looking. Hence, our policy becomes one of drift and reaction, rather than one of dynamism and innovation.

One could, of course, meet these charges specifically by compelling each critic to offer his alternative policy and then showing, in ninty-nine cases out of a hundred, good reasons not to adopt it. But since the charge is general, it is more productive to attempt a general response. We may begin by conceding that, yes, statesmen are conservative. But they have good reason to be.

It must be made clear that we are speaking of conservatism about existing international arrangements and foreign policy orientations. We are not speaking of domestic socio-economic conservatism. As a matter of fact, most State Department personnel seem to be liberals; it seems, for example, to be standing policy for U.S. officials to urge liberal reform measures—such as agrarian reform —upon underdeveloped host countries. When we say here that the statesman is conservative, we mean he is hesitant about altering the foreign policies of his nation.

Underlying this attitude is the statesman's realization that whenever a change occurs, national leaders all around the world will attempt to read meaning into the change. One does not simply do this or that because it is convenient or desirable in itself; one always communicates something about one's intentions. It follows, then, that any change is bad either because it might communicate the wrong thing to some allies or opponents, or because one does not know how other nations will perceive it. And if there is anything worse than communicating the wrong thing, it is not knowing if you are.

Shortly after the North Koreans seized the *Pueblo,* many asked: "Why don't *we* adopt a twelve-mile limit?" Quite apart from the specifics that might be involved, there was a more general reason for taking a dim view of such a change. When one suddenly changes from a three-mile limit one has had for centuries to a twelve-mile one, people wonder *why?*: Russians, Cubans, Frenchmen, Peruvians, East Germans, Chinese. They gather together in their foreign office lounges and war ministry cafeterias and ask: What does this mean? What does it mean in terms of the ideas U.S. policy-makers may now have, or be getting into, their heads— ideas which will form the basis for their future decisions, that is, future policy?

Thus, the Russians might think: "This is a challenge to *us.* They are attempting to scare off our fishing trawlers or intelligence ships. We must show them that two can play this game by: 1) increasing our limit to 20 miles as we have been considering for some time doing; or 2) penetrating that limit to show them the danger of such reckless challenges so they don't get the idea they can do such things with impunity."

This is but one, perhaps far-fetched illustration. Scores of nations are looking on; each can place several different interpretations on the act; and the consequences of their adopting certain of these interpretations may be to produce a reaction which, in turn, creates new problems for us. It is for this reason that the statesman resists taking new actions—unless they are clearly appropriate responses to something else that has happened. Notice, incidentally, that to adopt a twelve-mile limit in response to the seizure of the *Pueblo* violates propinquity.

It is change which sets people to thinking, to wondering, "What are they up to?" That is the way we are. A man may come home day after day at 6:37 sharp and then one day arrive at 6:04 and his wife will ask: "Why are you early?" Perhaps she should have asked on every other day, "Why are you late?" But she doesn't. Somehow the presumption is—and it is not really irrational—that continuity is safe and reassuring while change is something to study and worry about.

Vis-à-vis opponents, unilateral action ("initiative") may produce one of two unintended and undesirable communications: that one intends to challenge the status quo, or that one intends not to defend the status quo against the challenge of an opponent. Clearly, either communication can bring unwanted and unnecessary complications. If one's initiative looks aggressive or threatening, then opponents may take counter-measures designed to discourage your possible advance; if the initiative suggests a weakening of one's position in either a specific or general way, then opponents may be prompted to press accordingly.

The relationships between West Berlin and West Germany, for example, are "unnatural." Among other things, West Berlin has representatives in the West German Parliament, but they may not vote. The proponent of innovation in foreign policy might suggest that in a decisive, unilateral stroke the United States and its allies "normalize" the relation between West Berlin and West Germany by giving the Berlin delegates the right to vote. Our reason for this measure could be that we merely wished to give Berliners their rightful democratic representation. However innocent our motives may be, opponents must consider other implications. The Russians and East Germans might interpret this as a first move in a provocative policy of giving West Germans greater influence in NATO affairs, a policy which might end by leaving atomic weapons in German control. In order to deter us from this (supposed) course of action, they might undertake harrassments in Berlin to which we, in turn, might have to respond.

One of the most frequently demanded "innovations" in our foreign policy is approval of Red China's entry into the United Nations. Many Americans cannot understand why we oppose even offering a seat to a nation which obviously "exists." It is not our purpose here to raise the specific pros and cons of the issue, but to illustrate an additional objection to altering our position. Since we have consistently opposed the admission of China, failing to do so becomes symbolic. Why, others must ask, this sudden change? Has China altered its posture? Apparently not. Then the U.S. must have made a fundamental change in its own posture toward China and Chinese policy. What other implications does this change have? That the U.S. shall not defend Quemoy, or Formosa, or resist pressure against Burma? This is not to say that our UN China policy cannot or should not be changed, but only that aside from the specifics, one runs dangers of miscommunication in changing it unilaterally.

We would be exaggerating the dangers of making unintended

communications were it not for the already unstable and delicate structure of international relationships. The unintended signal does not fall upon an inattentive and disinterested audience. The other actors have already formed impressions, plans and hopes. Many are on the verge of acting; some are already making tentative moves. The impression of a world system securely locked into its present pattern is erroneous. The East Germans and Russians nibble and thrust in Berlin. The North Koreans probe our position in South Korea sending infiltrators. The Red Chinese and North Vietnamese promote preliminary action again against Thailand. Burma and Cambodia confront fluctuating pressures from outside communist states and hostile forces on their own soil. The North Vietnamese are constantly challenging the vague truce line in Laos. Cuba periodically sends agents and guerillas into various Latin American countries.

In this sensitive structure, unintended communications need not be the basic cause for the actions of others but merely the triggers which set in motion actions already contemplated. They are the straws which break the proverbial camel's back. They are important because there are many, many camels and all are already heavily burdened.

Anyone who has struggled with the plumbing of a summer cottage can appreciate how the statesman acquires his generalized conservative stance. The plumbing of such a cottage is, for reasons curiously beyond the control of the owner, a jerry-rigged affair in which chewing gum, solder and friction tape play an important role. The home handyman learns—through most painful experiences— that an attempt to repair one part almost always leads to complications. One tightens a joint to stop leakage and at the other end the rusty connector snaps. In replacing that other connector, one jars a sink trap loose. In order to rebuild the sink trap, the sink must be moved and to do that, water connections must be unsoldered. Very quickly one comes to appreciate the delicate, interrelated character of the plumbing system. One becomes a conservative.

An ugly pipe in the living room is left untouched. One's wife and one's city visitors remark that it ought to be removed. And the frustrating part is that you cannot convincingly explain to them the meaning and power of your maxim: leave well enough alone. They think you are lazy and unimaginative.

The point of this discussion is not to argue that unilateral departures in one's foreign policy are necessarily undesirable, but rather that they entail costs which the layman often fails to apprehend. The layman operates with the idea that the desirability of an action—let us say that of "reorganizing the SEATO alliance,"—is determined by the balance of specific gains (G) and specific costs (C) and that action should be taken when these gains outweigh the specific costs:

$$\text{Desirability} = G - C$$

The statesman has a different formula which includes the risk (R) that his unilateral action may entail a communication about our foreign policy posture which will trigger another nation into acting in a way which creates further problems for him:

$$\text{Desirability} = G - C - R$$

And, like the home plumber, the statesman has great difficulty explaining to outsiders the full weight and power of R.

Although the statesman is inclined to view proposed unilateral changes with suspicion, it does not follow that his policy never changes. First, he constantly reacts to changes produced by other actors. And, second, he modifies the existing policy, usually by small increments, to meet changing conditions. Actually, the distinction between a modification of an existing policy and a new policy is largely one of appearance, and it is the stateman's task to make any change appear to be the former, not the latter. In convincing other nations that "nothing has changed," and thereby avoiding the risks of miscommunication, he will convince local academics and journalists of the same thing. Hence, the widespread criticism that our foreign policy is one of stagnation is fully consistent with the proposition that we have brilliant statesmen at the helm.

Why Statesmen Are Conservative-II

The statesman is conservative about specific policies and methods; he is also conservative about the values and interests which underlie his nation's foreign policy. When popular feeling is swinging in one direction, he is not likely to swing with it, but rather base his policy upon the values of the past.

Public opinion—and here we mean public opinion in a democratic state—is astonishingly fickle. In the course of months or years it may oscillate from one extreme to the other. Its most damning feature is its animalistic quality. Its response to events is direct and emotional, not calculating, not future-oriented.

Former Presidential Press Secretary, Bill D. Moyers, gives some provocative illustrations:

> Public opinion, as every President has learned, is a highly variable quantity.
> President Truman discovered this during the Korean War. Two months after the commitment of American troops, 65 percent of the people interviewed in a Gallup poll said the United States had not made a mistake. Six months later, only 38 percent said we had not erred. By July 1951, not quite a year later, a majority of Americans wanted a truce under any circumstances. The undulating nature of public opinion was not lost on Lyndon Johnson. In December 1965, when Lou Harris reported that the "overwhelming majority of the American people—71 percent—are prepared to continue the fighting in Viet Nam until the United States can negotiate a settlement on its own terms," the President remarked to his associates: "An overwhelming majority . . . for an underwhelming period of time . . . wait and see." The wait was relatively brief. In March 1968, 49 percent of the people interviewed in a Gallup poll would say the United States had made a mistake in sending troops to fight in Viet Nam—a percentage that had steadily risen from 25 percent in March 1966. Seven in ten doves thought we were wrong to have become involved in Viet Nam, a Gallup poll reported, but, perhaps more surprisingly, four in ten hawks did so as well. [7]

Clearly a deterrence policy which had its roots in public opinion would be wildly inconsistent and therefore deadly dangerous. The statesman would be ill-advised to follow it. What then should he follow? His own judgement? No, not really, for if he did he would be nearly as fickle as the public.

Public opinion on foreign affairs is schizophrenic and animalistic because people are grappling with abstract and complex matters. Consider what is involved. First, in these matters of war and defense one is dealing with the gravest of human deprivations: violent deaths, torture, atrocities, starvation; destruction of families, of homes, of means of livelihood, of culture, of oppression and repression of the human spirit. These deprivations are happening in many places at the same time: Vietnam, Laos, Nigeria, Tibet, Colombia, Venezuela, Czechoslovakia. And they might potentially happen in many, many other places. Furthermore, there exist relationships between these different deprivations, between the actual ones, between the potential ones, and between actual and potential. Theories are available to account for these relationships— the threat theory advanced here is one—but they are often difficult to comprehend and, in any case, are difficult to prove and have ambiguities. *And every theory worthy of consideration recognizes that the attempt to prevent one deprivation involves perpetrating another.* To prevent Biafrans from starving, one would have to land troops and kill Nigerians to get the food to them. To stop a civil war in the Dominican Republic, one must shoot at those who refuse to cease fighting. To deter aggression in the future, one must wage war against an aggressor today. In addition to all the values involved and all the theories and their implications, there are facts, mountains of them, which would be necessary to intelligently relate one's theories and one's values to policy alternatives.

It is presumptuous for anyone to believe that, all by himself, he can devise a foreign policy for America which is best calculated to fulfill all American values in the world in the long run. But many try. The result is a spasmodic, inconsistent clutching at first one straw and then the other, at one principle and then its opposite. We should reduce our foreign involvements (Vietnam); we should increase our involvements (Biafra). We should not keep our commitments to allies (Thailand); we should keep our commitments to allies (Israel). We should not involve ourselves in internal political affairs of other countries (Guatemala); we should involve ourselves in internal politics (Greece). We should deplore the imposition of a harsh communist dictatorship (Czechoslovakia); we should join demonstrations to ensure the successful imposition of a harsh communist dictatorship (Vietnam). This patchwork of inconsistent positions is the result of momentary emotions and perceptions; it is not grounded on a stable orientation. The statesman, should he attempt to devise his own private foreign policy, would do little better than the citizen.

What is the alternative? For the statesman it is primarily tradition, precedent, and received knowledge. This source of guidance is not as arbitrary as it might first appear. Traditions and precedents are, after all, the net result of choices which scores of policymakers have made in attempting to match national values to theories in policies. The statesman himself will add incrementally to this body of tradition and thus leave it slightly altered for his successor. But he does not begin anew and devise a total foreign policy posture out of his own brain.

The result is, it seems, to strike a mean position for the gyrations of public feeling. Thus, although the statesman may be momentarily in an undemocratic posture, he is, by relying upon tradition, actually providing a policy more closely in accord with the values of his nation and his culture. And, most important, he is providing opponents with a consistent position.

Typically, the action of public opinion in a democratic power produces serious miscalculations on the part of aggressors. In its first phase, public feeling runs against war, aggression is tolerated and encouraged. The reaction of outrage sets in but the aggressor does not realize it, and a direct clash is produced. The statesman, by basing his policy on the traditional national interests, will attempt to ride through this cycle with a constant policy and thus avoid misleading his opponent. An excellent illustration of this phenomenon is provided by Disraeli's handling of British policy on the Turkish question in 1875-78.

In 1875-76, revolts occurred in several of the Balkan possessions of Turkey. In some places, particularly Bulgaria, the Turkish government was unable to suppress these revolts and, in attempting to do so, committed atrocities against the Christian population. British Prime Minister Disraeli faced a policy decision: whether to encourage Russia to invade Turkish possessions to "protect" the Christian population, or to urge the non-involvement of other Powers, including Russia, in Turkish affairs.

Traditionally, Britain had a long-standing policy of protecting the integrity of the Turkish empire, particularly against Russian encroachments. The Crimean War, fought against Russia on just that issue in 1854-56, marked this interest, as did the treaties of Paris (1856) and of London (1871)—both ratified by England among other countries—which undertook to guarantee the integrity of Turkey. Britain's interests in keeping Turkey out of Russian control were long-standing: protection of the route to the Far East; protection of Mid-East interests; a general need to maintain a deterrent posture against Russian expansion which could threaten British interests as far away as Afghanistan; and finally, an interest in avoiding the grave confrontations which would be produced between European powers struggling to fill the vacuum that the rapid and uncontrolled dissolution of the Turkish empire would leave.

Disraeli chose the traditional policy. But for several years, he had difficulty maintaining it in the face of a popular demand, arising on the atrocity issue, that Britain should encourage Russia to drive the Turks from the Balkans—if not join such an effort herself:

> Public meetings were held all over the country, of which the keynote was that grave wrong had been done, and that the wrongdoers must be punished and the wrong righted, regardless of British interests or even of British treaty obligations. It was further claimed that the issue of true religion was at stake, that the followers of Christ must be rescued from the domination of the followers of Mahomet . . . 8

The pro-Russian, anti-Turkish position was taken by many English leaders, including Gladstone who came out of retirement to wage a fierce battle against Disraeli's policy of non-interference. It was a highly moralistic movement, as this statement by E. A. Freeman, one of its leaders, indicates: "Perish the interests of England, perish our dominion in India, sooner than we should strike one blow or speak one word on behalf of the wrong against the right." 9

The implication of this sentiment would have been a British policy of encouraging Russian action against Turkey and, naturally, pledging no British interference on Turkey's behalf. Disraeli held against the tide as much as possible, arguing for continuity in British policy:

> [The guarantees of Turkish integrity contained in the Treaty of London] are our engagements, and they are the engagements that we endeavour to fulfil. And if these engagements, renovated and repeated only four years ago by the wisdom of Europe, are to be treated by the honourable and learned gentleman as idle wind and chaff, and if we are to be told that our political duty is by force to expel the Turks to the other side of the Bosphorus, then politics ceases to be an art, statesmanship becomes a mere mockery . . .10

In managing the government, he strove to give Russia a picture of a Britain steadfast in its concern for Turkish territorial integrity. He privately told members of the Cabinet not to indicate any change in British policy:

> The first and cardinal point, at the present moment,

> is, that no member of the Government should countenance
> the idea that we are hysterically 'modifying' our policy,
> in consequence of the excited state of the public mind. If
> such an idea gets about, we shall become contemptible.[11]

In a speech delivered at Guildhall on November 9, 1876, Disraeli warned an unnamed Russia that Britain was ready and able to go to war should the defense of her interests require it. The leaders of the pro-Russian movement were indignant at the speech.[12]

Although Disraeli pressed for a negotiated settlement between Russia and Turkey at the Constantinople conference, no arrangement was made and Russia invaded Turkey on April 21, 1877. The English reaction was inhibited by the domestic pro-Russian agitation: "To the . . . supporters of Gladstone's agitation, Russia's invasion of Turkey appeared to be a righteous and unselfish crusade . . . "[13]

Within the range permitted by domestic opinion, Disraeli took the firmest anti-Russian position. On May 5, 1877, the British Government sent a note to Russia warning that its present neutrality was watchful and conditional.[14] On July 23, 1877, the British garrison at Malta was ordered strengthened.[15] During the summer, it became clear that Russia would not succeed in overpowering Turkey in that campaign, but would have to pursue the effort in the following spring. In mid-August, Disraeli sent a secret message to Russian Emperor Alexander explicitly announcing that "should . . . the war be prolonged and a second campaign undertaken, the neutrality of England could not be maintained and she would take her part as a belligerent."[16]

This message was not made known to the Cabinet, or even to British Foreign Secretary, Lord Derby, who, along with other Cabinet members, was reluctant to contemplate British military action against Russia. Thus, in sending this message, Disraeli was misrepresenting the true state of British opinion. But he had to misrepresent it in order to prevent the Tsar from miscalculating: " . . . Gladstone's agitation was still powerful in the country, encouraging Russia to believe that in her invasion of Turkey she would always have the sympathy, and never the resistance, of the British people."[17]

By about September, 1877, British sentiment began to shift away from the pro-Russian position. The excesses of Gladstone's supporters; the growing awareness of the Russian advance and the concomitant realization of the British interests threatened; the discovery that the Bulgarians were, in the wake of the Russian advance, committing atrocities against the Turks; the heroic resistance of the Turks at Plevna: these all contributed to a growing popular demand for British resistance to a Russian advance upon Constantinople. During December, 1877, the British Cabinet steadily grew more favorable toward using British forces to defend Constantinople. Some of the earlier objectors, such as Lord Salisbury, came around to the support of Disraeli. By January, 1878, the British public was jingoistic; indeed, the "by Jingo" ditty was made popular at that time. On February 7, 1878—the day the Russians began their second Turkish campaign—Disraeli was mobbed by patriotic crowds now supporting an anti-Russian position. [18]

The British Parliament approved a Vote of Credit of six million pounds for national armaments, and then came the decisive move: on February 9, 1878, the Cabinet ordered part of the British fleet to Constantinople. Would the Russians halt in the face of this signal? There was some doubt. "From many quarters there came warnings that, in spite of all assurances, it was the Russian intention to occupy Constantinople . . . "[19] The Russians might have thought the British action was simply a bluff, that Britain was divided, uncertain, and reluctant to support Turkey. But the British were ready to go to war if Russia occupied Constantinople. Peace depended, therefore, upon the Russian perception of real British intentions. Fortunately for everyone, the Russians did hold back and finally assented to a European conference (the Congress of Berlin) where the complicated Turkish issue was bargained without war—and to the satisfaction of England.

Disraeli, then, by adhering to traditional English policy was ultimately vindicated as public opinion, which had swung away from that policy, swung back to supporting it. Most importantly, Disraeli projected a consistent policy posture to opponents and thereby reduced the risk of war by miscalculation. If he had faithfully tracked public opinion, encouraging Russia to conquer Turkey, during 1876 and 1877, and assuring her of British non-involvement, it is unlikely that, when public opinion reversed in January-February, 1878, the Russians would have fully apprehended the change. Their thought processes, their calculations and expectations would have been geared to the assumption that Britain had given them a free hand in Turkey. When, at the last moment, the British fleet appeared in the Dardanelles the Russians would have been far more likely to consider the move a bluff. Thus, by presenting a British policy which was firmer than public opinion, Disraeli prepared the Russians for the British move toward war in February, 1878. The threat was credible.

American statesmen face an analogous tension between the occasional surges of public opinion and our traditional values and policies. Our traditional values have been, in most general terms, that we prefer not to see Marxist-totalitarian dictatorships established in the world and that we particularly oppose the establishment of such regimes through the aggression of our major opponents and their allies. And, it seems, an overwhelming majority of Americans supports these values. Difficulty arises, however, when, in a given case of aggression, the special circumstances or the public perceptions of special circumstances cause a vocal segment of the public to ignore these traditional values. But one cannot found a safe deterrence policy on changeable specifics. An attempt to do so leads to inconsistency, miscalculation, and much war.

The opponents of the American effort in Vietnam, for example, have many specific reasons for their position: their dislike of Saigon regimes, disapproval of Lyndon Johnson, dismay at the refugees the war has created, and so on. But what they would be saying to opponents, should their policy of withdrawal be adopted, is that, in general, the United States is unconcerned about the rise of totalitarian Marxist dictatorships (however oppressive) and the establishment of such regimes through aggression (however brutal). It does not seem that most of the Vietnam protestors really are —or will continue to be—unconcerned about these values. They have temporarily forgotten these values in this case because their attention has been distracted by other facets of the issue. The statesman, less inclined to think for himself, accepts his nation's traditions and precedents. Whether public opinion or history eventually vindicate him is secondary; at least he has given opponents a consistent position on which they can base their expectations.

In Praise of Bureaucratic Inertia

Frequently when the charge of "conservatism" is made, it is leveled not at specific decision-makers but at the administrative apparatus in general, particularly the Department of State bureaucracy. In the opinion of many senators, scholars, and often State Department officials themselves, what stands in the way of a dynamic and imaginative foreign policy is a bulwark of faceless administrators who resist all change. In a certain sense, these critics are correct. But instead of condemning the bureaucratic inertia they identify, they should praise it, for it performs useful functions.

First, we should remember that thousands of proposals for foreign policy changes flow into the State Department every year. Everyone has new ideas: senators, staff assistants, Defense Department officials, ambassadors, and newspaper editors. Most of these ideas have to be, in the very nature of things, ill-considered and inadvisable. Someone has to turn them down. There is not time to explain to each promoter the defects of his plan; even if there were time, his emotional attachment to *his* view would make it difficult to satisfy him about the rejection of it. If the Secretary of State did the rejecting, he would merely earn much personal antipathy. So "bureaucratic inertia" blocks these proposals. The promoter's ego is protected and so is the esteem of the Secretary.

But running proposals through an obstacle course of middle-level administrators serves an even more important function. It injects that bias of conservatism which a wise and safe foreign policy must have. On the specific level, administrators are familiar with a communication's history and will therefore consider the costs of miscommunication which the proposal contains. The Senate aide who dashes off a proposal for publicly announcing our desire to re-establish diplomatic relations with Cambodia is unlikely to consider what this act might signal to the South and North Vietnamese about our intentions in Vietnam; but by the time this proposal has passed the Cambodia desk, the Saigon desk, the SEATO desk, and the military affairs desk, someone will have considered it.

At the more general level, we can trust middle-echelon bureaucrats to check proposals to see that they are consistent with that great bundle of tradition and value which forms the only secure locus for a safe and, ultimately, a moral foreign policy. The administrators themselves may not understand the virtue of conservatism. Their reason for rejecting a new departure may come from mere habit: "it's never been done before," or "things just aren't done that way." But in the deterrence policy of a great power, where underlying and enduring national values must be consistently pursued, the reason "that's what we've always done" contains much wisdom.

False Parallels: Which Side Are We On?

The evaluation of foreign policy—our own and that of our opponents—is a treacherous undertaking. On one hand, one runs the danger of failing to develop a sufficiently elaborate intellectual framework and thereby overlooking important but subtle issues. But, on the other, one can become so engrossed in intellectual arguments that obvious and common-sense realities are ignored. In attempting to avoid these dangers, it is useful to remember the different perspectives from which an evaluation of foreign policy should be made.

There are, it seems, three distinct levels to a foreign policy: first, the immediate, circumstantial issues; second, the threat or deterrence level; and third, the basic long-term values which define the hostile relationship and shape the deterrence framework.

We need not dwell on the first of these levels, for it is the one at which popular discussion takes place: How much is it costing us? Should we bomb? Use napalm? Do their atrocities justify our use of force? Is the South Vietnamese government worth defending? Would the Viet Cong have won an election in 1956? Although arguments at the circumstantial level are most common, they seem also to be the least conclusive. There are so many facets to be considered; our emotions and preconceptions heavily determine the facts we select and how we perceive them. If there is disagreement on policy, it will be most acute at this level.

The second level is that of deterrence. The concern here is with the long-run probability of aggression and war. The framework which underlies both an analysis of interaction and the criterion of proper behavior at this level is the status quo. The status quo framework makes symmetrical demands upon both sides; it is blind to the inherent morality or justice of the systems or aspirations of either side. The aspects of policy relevant at this level are those which bear upon a nation's threat or reputation and its adherence to the status quo rules.

Notice how, when these two levels are combined, contradictions may arise. What may be "moral" at one level can be "immoral" at the other. It may be proper in an immediate moral sense to send troops to assist Hungarians throw off Soviet oppression; but such action violates the status quo and is therefore improper at the deterrence level. It may be specifically immoral to use violence against the Viet Cong-North Vietnamese forces in Vietnam; but proper to do so in the status quo framework.

The third level of analysis is rarely made explicit because it is so obvious. In most foreign policy discussions, it enters as an unspoken assumption, which, for most practical purposes, takes care of itself. But the obvious has a way of being forgotten just when it is most important. And when an evaluation of a nation's foreign policy is undertaken, the basic goals which underlie the hostile relationship must be explicitly recognized. Otherwise much foolishness will result.

One must ask: Why the hostility? Why the need for a status quo framework at all? There are basic, long-term values underlying the deterrence level. These values determine which other nations one's own country will be in conflict with, and therefore hostile toward; they determine what one's own country values and therefore what it will be perceived to value, and hence, what it "threatens" to defend. Thus, these basic values affect the definition of the status quo. It is not easy to specify these values in detail, but the main issue underlying the Cold War hostility may be summarized thus: our major opponents believe that communist dictatorships are the preferred form of government, to be established and maintained by force if necessary; we believe that such regimes are definitely not preferable, and particularly not when force is employed across national boundaries to establish them.

The failure to recognize that these three distinct levels bear upon the evaluation of foreign policy readily gives rise to plausible but false parallels. One of the most common is to mistake parallels on the immediate circumstantial level for parallels on the deterrence level: "The North Vietnamese are helping the Viet Cong; we are helping Saigon: we are both equally guilty." Or, "The Cubans are training and sending guerrillas to Latin American countries; we are sending military advisors to the same countries; what's the difference?" At the deterrence level, the difference is between attempting to change the great-power status quo and defending it.

When a parallel exists both at the immediate level and at the status quo level, it takes great resources of common sense to resist the conclusion "We're as bad as they are." To illustrate this problem, I have selected the Russian invasion of Czechoslovakia in August, 1968, and the American intervention in the Dominican Republic in April, 1965.

The descriptions of each power's action suggest considerable similarity concerning the immediate circumstances. Each used force in the territory of another country to prevent certain political changes. In each case, overwhelming force was employed and casualties inflicted were—largely for this reason—quite light. Both nations had token assistance from allies.

At the deterrence level, the action of each power was symmetrical. In each case, they did not challenge the status quo but acted to prevent it from changing. The Dominican Republic as a non-communist nation, member of the Rio Pact, stood, in status quo language, in the same position with respect to the United States as Czechoslovakia, a communist nation and member of the Warsaw Pact, did to Russia.

Moreover, the reasons for each power's action, in deterrence analysis, were similar. Each had a reputation to protect, a reputation vitally important to it for the successful management of other actual and potential conflicts. The Soviet Union's reputation was being eroded by: the blatant refusal of various communist states and parties to accept its leadership; its unwillingness to support Castro's aggressive designs in Latin America; its failure to prevent its aggressive ally, North Vietnam, from being badly hammered by American bombers; and its failure to assist its Arab allies from being crushed by Israel in the June, 1967, war. That in many of these cases, the Soviet failure to act more strongly was a failure to support aggressors illustrates the danger of having such allies. If an ally engages in aggression and the power does not repudiate that ally, then when that ally is punished or humiliated, the great power will share that humiliation.

Moreover, the Russian reputation was being challenged in Eastern Europe; the status quo seemed to be melting there. Most noticeable was the independence shown by Rumania in establishing diplomatic relations with West Germany. Consequently, when changes began to take place in Czechoslovakia to the obvious delight of the West—and to the presumed disadvantage of "communism"—an already tarnished Russian reputation was being gravely challenged. Already it appeared that the Soviets were unwilling to use force to defend what was perceived to be their interests; a failure to act in Czechoslovakia would mark a further decline in the Russian reputation and encourage, among other things, the disintegration of the Eastern Europe satellite bloc. Other countries, discovering the Soviet Union was a toothless tiger, would increasingly ignore her.

The United States also had reputation problems. We might single out two specific arenas where our threat was important. In many Latin American countries, a debate was going on among Marxist extremists about the advisability of adopting the guerrilla-terrorism route to power. Those arguing against this path had to appeal to the low probability for success such ventures would have. One important consideration in making estimates for success would be their perception of American willingness to oppose their efforts. A communist victory in the Dominican Republic would all but destroy the position of marxist moderates arguing against the violent route; a defeat there owing to American action would strengthen their position. Thus, if the Cuban revolution encouraged Marxist extremists to believe that guerrilla warfare and terrorism would work, and therefore should be adopted, the Dominican Republic episode was an important step in discouraging this trend.

In Southeast Asia, particularly Vietnam, a strong threat was precious. The situation in South Vietnam had deteriorated. American bombing of North Vietnam had begun, the hope being that this signal of our intentions would produce restraint on the part of North Vietnam. The chances of avoiding a long and costly struggle rested heavily upon the North Vietnamese perception of our willingness to defend South Vietnam. As it looked at the time, the chances of deterring the North Vietnamese were perhaps low; but with a failure to act in the Dominican Republic they would have been nil. Lyndon Johnson understood this when, in a private discussion, he observed that he did not intend "to sit here with my hands tied and let Castro take that island. What can we do in Vietnam if we can't clean up the Dominican Republic?"[20] Or translated into threat terms: What will opponents and allies perceive about our intentions in Vietnam if we fail to react right on our own doorstep?

So, in Czechoslovakia and the Dominican Republic each power, the Soviet Union and the United States, played by the status quo rules and acted from a desire to maintain their general

threat to defend their interests. What should be the conclusion?
"We're as bad as they are; I'm deserting to Sweden"? Many
would conclude thus.

To do so would be to ignore the values which underlie the
hostile relationship. In the deterrence perspective, when we employ
the phrase "status quo" and point out a nation's "interests" which
shape the status quo, we take those interests for granted. If a nation acts within the status quo framework to defend its interests
then, from the deterrence point of view, it is acting "properly."
Hence, in this perspective, the Russians acted "properly" in
Czechoslovakia. But if we seek to evaluate foreign policy behavior
and decide which side, if any, we ought to support, we must ask
what these "interests" are and evaluate them. We must examine
the underlying goals of the two powers which bring them into conflict.

The Soviet "interest" in Czechoslovakia was that of maintaining a narrowly defined Communist dictatorship. That is to say,
when a communist state "liberalizes," the Soviet Union feels
itself being threatened, and is perceived to be "losing." Hence,
such a liberalization represents a melting of the status quo. The
Soviet values can be seen in both the verbal demands made upon
Czechoslovakia and the counter-reforms imposed upon her after
the invasion. The Soviet Union reimposed press censorship,
abrogated freedom of assembly, strengthened the secret police,
opposed the democratization of the communist party, and put an
end to all consideration of allowing parties other than the communist to exist. The Soviet Union also had economic demands. It
seriously crippled the introduction of profit incentives and arrested
the further development of Workers' Councils which were designed
to give workers participation in supervising factories (an ironic
negation of one of the most fundamental communist promises).

The American interest in the Dominican Republic was, in a
minimal sense, the negation of the Soviet goal: should a communist dictatorship have been established in the Dominican Republic, we would have felt dismayed and would have been perceived to be "losing." One must, at this juncture, form an opinion
about the desirability of communist dictatorships in order to evaluate the foreign policy of each power. If one disapproves of them,
either because of their domestic practices or their typically aggressive posture toward neighboring non-communist states, then
he is on the American side.

Preventing the emergence of a communist dictatorship was

our minimal goal; our positive values also found expression to the degree that circumstances permitted. In the Dominican Republic we were able to pursue a number of our ideals with some success. One of the most important of these is our desire to see regimes chosen by the will of their people. This is indeed an ambitious goal, and in this complex and imperfect world it is difficult even to approach. In the Dominican Republic, we did surprisingly well.

The truce which was finally arranged between the two sides in the civil war (the pro- and anti-Bosch factions) was genuine with both sides represented in the government. If anything, the provisional government favored the pro-Bosch rebel side. The provisional president was Héctor García Godoy, who had been foreign minister under Juan Bosch in 1963. Many non-Bosch public officials lost their posts to be replaced by members of Bosch's PRD. The elections which were then held on June 1, 1966, for a constitutional government were quite fair.* Joaquín Balaguer, who won the election, did surprisingly well in stimulating economic activity and preserving democratic freedoms. While in the Dominican Republic in 1968, I purchased seven books and pamphlets intensely critical of the American intervention. All were published in the Dominican Republic. We count such freedom of the press a positive value; to the Russians it is a negative one.

Our position on the Dominican economy is also worth noting. As a consequence of Trujillo's acquisition of industrial and commercial establishments, the Dominican government had (and still has) wide control of the Dominican economy. Tobacco, cement, paper, glass, sugar, automobile dealerships, and aviation: it becomes difficult to find important firms which the government does *not* own. The Dominican economy is undoubtedly the most socialized in the free world. According to Marxist demonology, then, one of the central objects of our intervention should have been to force "capitalism" on the country. Instead, the issue never came up. We were quite content with whatever economic arrangements the Dominicans wanted to make for themselves.

Finally, the distinction between an invasion and an intervention ought to be examined. While in terms of the Cold War status quo

---

*Most observers, even hostile ones, agreed on this point. One PRD Deputy I interviewed on July 17, 1968 told me that he had been requested by the PRD to issue a statement alleging fraud (the standard practice for losing parties in this latitude). He said, "I refused to do it because I didn't believe there had been any fraud—not that I knew of anyway."

the Soviet action in Czechoslovakia was not aggression, with respect to the Czech-Russian status quo it certainly was. Military
forces entered the country against the will of the established
government.

In the Dominican Republic the situation was significantly
different. A civil war had broken out. The de facto president,
Donald Reid, had resigned and so had the next possible president,
José Rafael Molina, President of the Senate. One could not look
to the commander-in-chief of the armed forces as a de facto chief
executive: the armed forces were divided, fighting among themselves. The arrival of American troops in the Dominican Republic
did not take place against the will of an established government:
there was no established government. Hence, while the American
action represented some type of violation of the Dominican-
American status quo, it was qualitatively less than an "invasion."

The distinction between an intervention and an invasion is an
important one, for it reflects an important American value: that of
avoiding outright violations of specific (non-Cold War) status
quo's. It has been a principle of our policy not to invade countries
even when, in Cold War status quo terms, such an invasion is both
permissible and desirable—or even when compelling moral arguments might be raised in favor of the destruction of an existing
regime (as in the case of Haiti, for example). The Bay of Pigs
fiasco was, in fact, the result of our trying to compromise this
value of not invading against established regimes with the need to
defend the great-power status quo. As is evident from the behavior
of the Russians in Czechoslovakia, they do not consider outright
invasion an illegitimate means to maintain the status quo.

It can be said, then, that our reluctance to violate local status
quo's—while it may make us a "good neighbor"—puts us at a
disadvantage *vis-à-vis* our opponents. When the status quo melts
in Cuba against us, we do not invade; when it melts against the
Russians in Czechoslovakia, they do invade.

An inspection of the Soviet action in Czechoslovakia reveals
that our opponents played within the status quo rules of the Cold
War. But an examination of the values they pursued in that action,
which are profoundly contrary to our own, clearly illustrate why
we are hostile to the Soviet Union, why there is a Cold War, and
why status quo rules are necessary.

with certain challenges to the status quo opens up
 new problems. Avoidance of one challenge does not
her dangers and possibilities to disappear; it is likely
 them. An American withdrawal from Vietnam would
led our problems in Southeast Asia. There still would
n Laos, Thailand, Cambodia, Burma, and Malaysia.
ifficulties, which a Vietnam withdrawal would likely
would raise grave and agonizing dilemmas similar to
might hope to escape by withdrawing from Vietnam.
wer to the incredulous citizen who asked above, "Do
o say?" is "No, not exactly. Our failure to confront
 will result in a *worsening situation*. If we continue
enges with the lack of determination implied in your
withdrawal in this case, we are likely to get into more
ble where dreadful events, perhaps even the one you
ome possible."
words of a practitioner, Dean Rusk (referring to
ncern about Laos in 1961): "If you don't pay attention
hery, the periphery changes. And the first thing you
riphery is the center." 1   Because he is not aware of
s types of actual and potential challenges and the con-
lations between them, the citizen conceives of the
 a distinct entity which will somehow take care of itself.
, action at the "periphery" is, necessarily, peripheral.
zen in his ignorance is overconfident; the statesman is
zen believes that events which look improbable, are
The statesman knows that the improbable sometimes
, therefore, no possibilities can be dismissed. Would
uclear weapons against Japan? The citizen feels that
obable and the possibility should be dismissed. The
ows that it *seems* improbable, but it could still happen
 act accordingly. It seemed improbable that the Rus-
lace missiles in Cuba. But they did. One could imagine
 in January 1962:

an: We must maintain a highly credible threat.
 What for?
an: Well, to give one of a score of possibilities, if
 Russians come to doubt our firmness they might,
example, put missiles in Cuba.
 Now, really, aren't you being fanciful? They'll
er do that.

Chapter 10

CONCLUSION

One purpose of this essay is to show why the American involvement
in Vietnam was a reasonable policy. One need not conclude—as
many did conclude—that our public officials must have been incom-
petents to have led us into Vietnam. Wise and humane decision-
makers, carefully considering the consequences of different
alternatives—in 1954, 1961, 1964, or 1965—could have adopted the
policy we have followed.

It is not possible, however, to prove by steps of infallible logic
that a particular military involvement, such as the one in Vietnam,
is the best policy. A question of judgment is ultimately involved.
This essay has attempted to isolate that question from the many
other secondary or inappropriate issues which customarily arise in
foreign policy debates.

The central question for determining the desirable scope of
American military action abroad is this:

> How coercive does our threat to resist our opponents'
> aggression have to be to prevent more and larger wars in
> the future?

The more coercive our threat, of course, the better. Aggression is correspondingly less likely. But this proposition expresses
only one side of the problem. The other is, simply, that a coercive
threat is not free. We must make sacrifices and take risks to maintain our reputation. Threats have a price: the more you pay, the
more you buy. How much should we buy at any given time? How
much should we be willing to pay in risks and sacrifices to maintain
our threat?

The answer, clearly, reflects a judgment about how badly we

need a coercive threat. If one believes that our threat is a precious national asset which shields us from uncountable dangers and disasters, then it is worth paying a high price for. If one feels our threat is relatively unimportant or will do a satisfactory job for us even if not particularly coercive, then we do not need to make so many sacrifices in its defense.

Why the Statesman Values a Credible Threat More Than the Citizen Does

Americans generally place a lower value on having a credible threat than do their statesmen. When Americans have supported military action abroad it has rarely been because they thought maintaining a threat was worth these sacrifices. Motives of patriotism, anticommunism or humanitarianism account for most of the popular support of, or acquiescence to, foreign involvement. When presented with the theory of deterrence most citizens would find, it seems, "a credible threat" a flimsy reason for sacrificing American boys or risking American society. When, for example, opponents of the war in Vietnam argued within the deterrence framework, they regularly concluded that the reputation we would have lost by withdrawing from Vietnam would not have been worth the sacrifices we were making. In this judgment these citizens disagree with four Presidents, their Secretaries of State, and virtually all their diplomatic advisors who approved the policy of involvement in Vietnam. Apparently the statesmen have felt the sacrifices are worth it.

The statesman seems to feel that having a coercive threat is a desperately important matter; the citizen finds that, while probably necessary, it is secondary or peripheral to the issues of the day. Which view is more likely to be correct? An answer may be approached by examining how this difference in perspectives arises.

The citizen can believe in a basically benign world; the statesman cannot. The citizen can believe that aggression and war are highly unusual phenomena; he can believe that most international disputes "take care of themselves," that "negotiations" and "diplomacy" are substitutes for war and the threat of war. The citizen can believe that "negotiations," not bullets and a threat of atomic war, brought the Korean conflict to an end, that "diplomacy" settled the situation in Laos in 1961-62. He can believe that aggres-

sion does not take place in B[...] Pakistan, Quemoy or Turkey si[...] uncivilized enterprise which no[...]

The statesman's full-time j[...] war. He cannot consider aggre[...] remembers, in his own lifetime, [...] only the crises which citizens [...] confrontations which were re[...] Crossing his desk are daily i[...] movements, political plots, con[...] diplomatic maneuvers. His file[...] for military contingencies. Fo[...] the threat of war are not far-o[...] daily life. The statesman know[...] settle themselves; the statesm[...] great sacrifices to manage a s[...] are not substitutes for violenc[...] violence, actual or potential. [...]

The citizen can believe in [...] danger points. He imagines [...] which threats might be useful. [...] Vietnam involvement as neces[...] discourage aggression elsewhe[...] lous response: "Do you mean [...] Vietnam the Russians would i[...] What the citizen has not assi[...] dangerous contingencies arou[...] has in mind are among the lea[...] attaches little importance to l[...]

The statesman is watchi[...] this long list in the forefront [...] a war of liberation against l[...] push for the communist conq[...] Quemoy; the Russians could [...] communist African nation [...] could give atomic weapons to [...] guerrillas in Haiti. A few co[...] moment, improbable. But tog[...] maintaining a secure deterre[...]

Furthermore, the states[...]

successfully[...] sequences[...] cause the c[...] to aggravat[...] not have e[...] be dangers[...] And these[...] exacerbate[...] the ones we[...]

The an[...] you mean[...] this proble[...] to face cha[...] demand for[...] serious tro[...] mention, b[...]

In the[...] American c[...] to the peri[...] know the p[...] the numero[...] tinuous gr[...] "center" as[...] In this view[...]

The cit[...] not. The ci[...] improbable[...] happens an[...] China use[...] that is imp[...] statesman k[...] and he mus[...] sians would[...] this dialogu[...]

Statesr[...]
Citizen[...]
Statesr[...]
    th[...]
    fo[...]
Citizen[...]
    ne[...]

Finally, the citizen disregards the unforeseen; the statesman constantly prepares for it. The citizen is content to imagine that the future will resemble the past—or be an improvement over the past. Therefore one need not make special preparations. But history is full of unexpected events. And, sometimes, these events produce confrontations in which one desperately needs a credible threat. One would not have supposed, early in 1967, that the American threat would come in handy in the Mid-East later that year. Unexpected developments made it so. Egypt violated the status quo by blockading the Gulf of Aqaba; Israel reacted with a stunning re-violation. And the Russians stood timidly by while Israel gobbled up tons of Russian arms and miles of Arab territory. Why did they remain aloof? And why, following the victory, was Israel able to ignore the Russian demands for a withdrawal? Surely in the face of a Russian threat to intervene, during the war or after, Israel would have immediately retreated. But there was a countervailing American threat. The Russians assumed that if they went in, we might go in. The Israelis understood this. And why did the Russians seem to believe that if they went in, we would? Because the President of the United States was the kind of person who will take risks and make sacrifices to counter the advances of his opponents. What gave them that impression? Did the Russians believe the same thing about Harold Wilson or Indira Ghandi?

The statesman wants to maintain a highly credible threat not only to guard against all the existing dangers, but to have a margin of safety for the unexpected. China may now be relatively prudent in her foreign affairs. But an adventurous leadership could suddenly come to power. These leaders might, for example, be tempted to invade India before India could acquire nuclear weapons. The justification for a preemptive or preventive war might appear quite compelling to them. Whether or not they do invade would depend heavily upon what they believe the American response will be.

Or, suppose the Chinese do invade India and we wish to stop them. The President of the United States may tell the Chinese that we shall come in with everything we have, including nuclear weapons, unless they withdraw. If the Chinese believe him a great disaster will be averted. If, however, they believe that the United States is timid, not willing to make sacrifices to protect faraway lands, overwhelmed by a fear of using nuclear weapons . . . When the President has to voice that ultimatum it will be too late to do anything about the Chinese belief in our determination. The job of teaching them that we mean what we say had to be done, if at all, in earlier Koreas and Vietnams.

For these reasons, then, the statesman values a coercive threat more highly than the citizen. He is willing to pay more to keep that threat credible.

There is one other point which should be noted concerning the differing attitudes of the statesman and the citizen. The statesman, in his thinking about threats, is consistent and disciplined; the citizen's thinking on the same subject is inconsistent and superficial.

Few people reject the basic logic of deterrence. One has to search long to find someone who does not believe that the threat of war is ultimately the only effective instrument to counter an opponent willing to use force to further his international goals. But although citizens easily make "Then we'll threaten them with. . . ." statements, they are not at all consistent when it comes to the implications of such positions. They do not consider the grave and complicated issues involved in making any threat credible, but simply assume that to "say" is to threaten. And they do not consider the consequences of actually carrying out the threat that they voice —consequences so awesome that, in practice, they would probably be unwilling to carry out their own threat.

Some time ago, I witnessed a conversation which took place between a colleague of mine and a campus visitor. The visitor, it quickly turned out, was strongly opposed to the American involvement in Vietnam. My colleague questioned him about his proposal for dealing with the problem and the following dialogue ensued:

Q. What would you do?
A. All right. Here's my solution. We tell Ho that he can have South Vietnam, only he's got to give us two years to get out, before we turn it over to him. In this time, we relocate all the South Vietnamese who want to leave before the communists take over—in other Asian nations or even the United States. If we accept Hungarian or Cuban refugees, why not from South Vietnam?
Q. And what do we get in return?
A. I'm getting to that. In return, Ho agrees to get his troops out of Laos and Thailand and to stay out.
Q. But what if he doesn't agree? Or what if, after we get out of South Vietnam, he starts attacking Laos and Thailand again?
A. Then we'll tell the North Vietnamese we will bomb them.

Q. What?! We're already bombing and it isn't changing
   their minds! It's already being tried. Or do you mean—?
A. No, not nuclear. Conventional.
Q. Then you mean more . . . ?
A. Yes, more.
Q. Like what?
A. The cities.
Q. You mean bomb the cities, the civilian population?
A. (He nodded).
Q. But that's "genocide"! That's something that even the
   administration hawks don't want to do!
A. (Somewhat flustered).

Here we have a threat theorist, certainly. But not a thoughtful
one. He has, as my colleague pointed out, voiced a threat which
U.S. policymakers—and probably he himself if it came to that—
would be unwilling to carry out. But even more importantly, he has
not considered how he is going to make this threat credible. Indeed,
his plan contains a step which practically ensures that his threat
will not be believed: the withdrawal from South Vietnam. Such a
step demonstrates, in fact, that he is not willing to make sacrifices
to defend Southeast Asian countries from North Vietnamese
conquest. If he really were willing to make such sacrifices, then
why should he want to give up South Vietnam in the first place?

Furthermore, he assumed that all Americans—senators, students, college professors—would join together to carry out *his*
threat. Surely this was an unreasonable expectation—particularly
in light of the fact that he himself was working to undermine someone else's threat (to defend South Vietnam).

This illustration points up one of the general shortcomings of
the many arguments for "redrawing our defense perimeters:"
how can we make these new lines *real?* A child with a crayon and a
map can draw lines of containment, but what will they mean? What
will they mean to us and to our opponents? If these new lines are—
as has been the case in recent proposals—merely a device to avoid
the difficult defense of old lines, then line-drawing is a sophistic
technique for appeasement. Our opponents can trust us—or our
sons—to draw more new lines every time they challenge old ones.

Moreover, the lines as they have come to exist are real. They
reflect the axis of great power conflict; they represent the inter-
face of the value conflicts between the hostile camps. While we may
not be united and enthusiastic about making a particular defense
of the existing status quo, we are definitely disunited when it comes

to selecting alternatives. The line-drawers are unable to agree upon a new line. Some want us to defend Thailand, others do not. Some say to include Malaysia, others say to leave it out. Some are for Taiwan, others against defending it. Such confusion arises because people are attempting to draw linès without regard to the under-lying national values, traditions, and world expectations which would make such lines meaningful. They believe in deterrence. They agree that lines must be drawn and war threatened if they are crossed or undermined. But they have paid insufficient attention to the problems of making their threats real.

The citizen, then, seldom rejects deterrence theory outright. What brings him into conflict with the statesman is his superficial application of the theory. The citizen picks and chooses, almost absent-mindedly, the elements of threat policy which seem obvious, emotionally satisfying, or reasonable on an abstract level. The statesman cannot be inconsistent; he has to seek out and accept the practical, the difficult and the subtle implications of deterrence.

Ultimately, as I said, deciding how credible our threat ought to be is a matter of judgment. But the citizen should understand this threat, its vast application, and its many implications before he decides.

Sacrifices or Risks?

Sacrifices are men killed, cities destroyed, and moralities trampled. Risks are probabilities of sacrifices, probabilities of losing men, having cities demolished, and acting counter to moral principles. For the statesman, risks and sacrifices are roughly commensurable. To sacrifice 10,000 men is about as bad as taking a moderate risk of sacrificing 100,000 and clearly preferable to accepting a high risk of losing 500,000.

The American public does not treat sacrifices and risks as commensurable. When a President takes a grave risk and things come out well, the only major consequence is a jump in his Gallup rating. Perhaps academics will, for a few months, quietly reflect on past dangers. When the President makes sacrifices, even modest ones, a steady and corrosive wave of opposition builds. Public criticism is vigorous, persistent, and widespread. Let the President risk war in Iran, in a Berlin airlift, or in a Cuban missile crisis, and his action is unnoticed or, if noticed, "heroic." Let him make sacrifices in a Korea or a Vietnam and he is scorned, battered, and driven from office.

Did it not proceed from ignorance, the illogical public attitude toward risks and sacrifices would be seriously hypocritical. Sacrifices are, after all, the result of taking risks which turn out badly. If one is to oppose the sacrifices, then he should oppose taking the risk which may lead to those sacrifices. It makes no sense to remain silent while the gambler places his bets, cheer when he wins but release a storm of abuse when he loses.

In March-April of 1961, the United States moved to the brink of war in Laos to induce the communists to halt their conquest of that country. Had they not halted, Kennedy was apparently prepared to commit American Marines to the defense of Laos. There is no reason to suppose that one Marine regiment would have been enough. Probably the Pathet Lao would intensify recruitment; probably North Vietnam would increase infiltration of troops and supplies; probably more American troops would have to be committed. It might have become necessary to bomb North Vietnam to hold down infiltration. Thus, a war in Laos could have resulted which would have resembled the Vietnam war in almost every particular: a far-off country, "on the Asian mainland," "of no strategic value," undergoing civil war, with incompetent local troops, its "undemocratic local regime," and "civilian casualties."

Surely, anyone who opposed the war in Vietnam should have implored Kennedy not to take the risk. Yet, where were the publicists, the demonstrators, the draft-card burners, the Mothers, Psychiatrists, and Salesmen for Peace? Where was the National Council of Churches, the British Labor Party and the Center for the Study of Democratic Institutions? Most people never knew what was happening—let alone why it was happening. Of the few that realized war was being risked, many could not realistically grasp the blood and destruction of war and therefore did not really fear it.

The willingness of the American public to accept risks while at the same time rejecting any policy of sustained sacrifice may have profound and potentially disastrous consequences. To a certain extent, it is possible for the statesman to substitute risks for sacrifices. Eisenhower chose to risk a serious escalation of the Korean war by threatening to use atomic weapons against China. The risk paid off and the sacrifices of a protracted ground struggle were avoided. Had the threat of escalation failed, a larger war would probably have resulted.

But a deterrence policy based entirely on risks would be neither viable nor safe. A risk is accepting the probability of a sacrifice. If one has a standing policy of making no sacrifices, then one cannot take any risks. In effect, then, one cannot project a threat. If it is well-known that the United States will not accept the sacrifices of fighting a war, then we simply shall be unable to threaten war. Ultimately, the only way we can prove that we will make sacrifices is to make some.

In practice, a serious attempt to substitute risks for sacrifices would deprive us of the option of limited war, which involves sustained sacrifice, and place full reliance on a nuclear threat. When violations of the status quo occurred, we would either have to accept them or threaten to use nuclear weapons. Although this nuclear threat might work sometimes, it is unlikely to work in every case. In many cases the threat of a nuclear response will be incredible because such a response would dramatically violate the rule of proportionality. If two hundred guerrillas infiltrate Thailand from North Vietnam, would we use atomic bombs on Hanoi and Haiphong? Moreover, if we did carry out such a disproportional response, our opponents would rightly treat our action as aggression and feel compelled to take equivalent counteraction. If Red China dropped atomic bombs on Formosa in reaction to a Nationalist commando raid on the mainland, could we idly stand by?

The option of limited war provides us with a proportional and, therefore, credible and coercive response to marginal violations of the status quo. Eliminating this option will not prevent aggression and it will not end the bargaining or threatening process between hostile states. If all we have to threaten is a general conflagration, then that is the threat we will use. In this imperfect world full of miscalculations and accidents, such a threat will, on occasion, fail. And then we shall have the conflagration.

The genesis of World War I illustrates the great dangers of an all-or-nothing deterrence system. In those days (indeed, until the 1950's), limited war was often technologically impossible. Aggression in one theater could not be successfully resisted in the specific locality alone because the defender could not get enough forces and supplies to the area. Nations bargained with the threat of general war—avoiding war for many years. But one miscalculation was enough. Austria sought to invade Serbia. Russia was determined to prevent this aggression. But she could not successfully resist Austria in Serbia. Russia could not get troops and supplies there. If she was not to retreat again, Russia had to mobilize to attack Austria directly. Had the C-47 transport existed in those days, a limited war in Serbia might have been substituted for a World War.

We would be ill-advised, then, to substitute a purely atomic deterrence system for the option of limited war. Limited war gives us a margin of safety. It enables us to say to a reckless actor—such as the North Koreans or North Vietnamese—"See, you have miscalculated," and still live through it.

The American public must learn to accept the sacrifices of limited war. If the war-protesters ever succeed in depriving our statesmen of the option of limited war—and that is, in effect, what they are attempting to do—they shall have placed us still closer to the cataclysm we all dread.

It would not be the first time in history that an honest but naive search for peace has led further down the road toward war.

The Past and the Future

A complete inventory of all the resources which the United States has to work its will abroad would fill an entire volume. This brief study has explored only one: the American threat of war. This resource has been a central instrument of American foreign policy since the Second World War. All our President have used it, knowingly and perhaps unknowingly too. The threat of American military action, that is, war, lurks behind the frowns of our Ambassadors, hides between the lines of our diplomatic messages, and darts in and about Presidential press conferences.

What have we accomplished with American power in the world over the past 25 years? What beneficial effects does our threat have today?

First, we have not had total war, or even a major war. That is something no other 20th century generation can say for itself. To point out that total war would be a miscalculation does not diminish the magnitude of the achievement. Both the First and Second World Wars were also miscalculations, as winners and losers would readily admit. They happened nevertheless. The opportunity for miscalculation still exists today. We have had many miscalculations: the Berlin blockade was one; there were two in Korea, one theirs, one ours; the Cuban missile crisis. The war in Vietnam is probably another; one doubts that Hanoi and its supporters would have acted as they did had they foreseen the consequences.

These and other postwar miscalculations have not led to major war because they took place in marginal confrontations and to marginal degrees. The United States, by exerting pressure at the margins of the struggle against the aggression of its opponents, by correcting the miscalculations that take place there, has made it difficult for its enemies to make major miscalculations. Because they *see* us fighting at the periphery they *know* we will fight elsewhere. A Russian invasion of West Germany or a Chinese invasion of India—events which would lead to major war—are today most improbable. And so not only have we not had major war, but such war seems less likely today than before.

To withdraw from marginal areas under communist guns would seem to be the road to a major miscalculation. Our opponents would learn that we definitely will not fight at the margins and come to guess that we might not fight at more "central" areas. Or, to put it another way, they would be unable to recognize what was marginal and what was not. It has been suggested that Kennedy's policy of "non-provocation" during 1961-62 led to the serious Russian miscalculation in the Cuban missile crisis. And, after all, Kennedy retreated very little. But the Russians came to believe we would tolerate something we, in fact, considered intolerable. This same pattern would be repeated on a grander, more dangerous scale by larger, more dramatic American retreats.

American power has also made at least two major tactics of aggression impractical. The first is nuclear blackmail. It would be possible for either Russia or China to dangle nuclear weapons over the heads of neighboring countries and thereby terrify them into submission. But because everyone believes that the United States might respond in kind, aggressive nuclear threats have little coercive value. The way to bring nuclear blackmail on the world stage is to convince everyone that we are panicked at the thought of nuclear war, and are unwilling to risk war or make sacrifices to protect the free world.

The massive land invasion has gone out of style. Since 1950 the communists have attempted no major land invasion. Korea was, clearly, some sort of turning point—but it remains a turning point only because everyone continues to suppose that the United States, with or without the United Nations, is unlikely to tolerate the open communist invasion of a free-world country. It is not unreasonably optimistic to hope that American success in Vietnam would bring us a similar lull in the use of the so-called "peoples' war" strategy of aggression.

Back in the 1950's, there was much talk about the spread of nuclear weapons, and dire predictions were voiced about the "nth" nation possibility. At that time the letter "n" stood for a large and indeterminate number of nations with nuclear arsenals. Today, a decade later, "n" is not large nor highly indeterminate. It seems to equal five. What has happened?

Although many do not realize it, we live in an unusually peaceful world. Nations do not live in mortal fear of annihilation by their neighbors. Aggression does not flourish. Few small nations tremble in the shadow of larger ones. This stabilized world scene contrasts markedly with the ominous, menacing atmosphere that prevailed in periods such as 1933-1939. The peaceful world situation is, in large measure, the result of the American deterrent threat. Russia, East Germany, China, North Korea, North Vietnam, and Cuba: American power has blocked these aggressive states and caused them to moderate their expansionist orientations.

The only thing about the future we can say with certainty is that the threat of war will continue to play a central role in international affairs. Even in our own country, after almost two centuries of nationhood, the threat of force is necessary to discipline political sub-units. When, in 1957, the governor of Arkansas defied the federal court order to integrate Central High School of Little Rock, the President of the United States sent federal troops to ensure compliance. And the basic problem of threatening to use force—that of credibility—also remains. If President Eisenhower had shown himself unwilling to use force to have a federal court order obeyed in Little Rock, then other state governments would have doubted his determination to use force against them in similar circumstances.

If we cannot eliminate the threat of force from our own intergovernmental relations, how could it be eliminated between nations divided by more profound conflicts and where no unit has a monopoly of force? Even should we succeed in eliminating war in the distant future, it will be eliminated only because, and as long as, the threat of war compels nations to accept non-violent processes for the resolution of conflict.

The United States will be in the business of deterrence when our grandchildren grow old. The job may become easier—as we hope—or more difficult. The Cold War axis may disappear only to be replaced by another alliance and perception system. We may find ourselves attempting to deter a reckless and aggressive Brazil or Japan or France. But we will still be manipulating our threat of war.

Unfortunately, the American tradition of debate on foreign policy practically ignores the role of threats and their beneficial consequences. About the evil effects of power, we are well-informed. The tragedy of war is repeatedly emphasized. We question and criticize our motives with energy. Our moralistic, critical tradition of free debate on foreign policy focuses upon the dangers of using force for evil purposes.

We do not have, however, a tradition of debate which protects us against the evil consequences of a failure to use force. If a war appears moral or necessary in an immediate, compelling way, we support it. But we have not grasped the inextricable link between war and the threat of war. And we have not understood that our threat of war, properly managed, reduces the occurrence of war. As a consequence, the public debate on foreign policy is unbalanced, taking place over the immediate pros and cons of a particular American involvement with little attention given to the indirect and future effects.

This situation is in no way surprising or unusual. It is, unfortunately, characteristic of public opinion that it fixes upon the direct and immediate perception of issues and ignores the indirect and future aspects. Machiavelli pointed this out some time ago:

> If we consider now what is easy and what difficult to persuade a people to, we may make this distinction: either what you wish to persuade them to represents at first sight gain or loss, or it seems brave or cowardly. And if you propose to them anything that upon its face seems profitable and courageous, though there be really a loss concealed under it which may involve the ruin of the republic, the multitude will ever be most easily persuaded

to it. But if the measure proposed seems doubtful and likely to cause loss, then it will be difficult to persuade the people to it, even though the benefit and welfare of the republic were concealed under it.2

In the management of foreign policy, the inability of the public to weigh concealed gains and losses is profoundly dangerous. Being unable to grasp the connection between a present war which involves obvious loss and future wars which cannot be seen, the desire is to avoid the present loss. Distracted by the circumstantial issues it happens to perceive in a particular conflict, the public fails to apprehend the connection between that particular challenge and the enduring national values. These values will not be dead; they would merely be dormant. We would eventually return to defending them—and probably with a vengeance. Then military action will seem courageous. And our enemies, misled by our failure to defend our values consistently, will have miscalculated.

The public, with its gaze fixed upon the immediate and obvious, wants, in effect, to fight only those wars which are morally compelling or necessary for national survival. But wars which are morally compelling or necessary for survival are the ones which should never have to be fought. They are the catastrophes.

If we are to avoid such tragedy, we must grasp the relationships between American action—or inaction—in the present and the indirect and future consequences of that action. The focus for understanding these relationships is our nation's most powerful foreign policy instrument: the American threat of war.

FOOTNOTES

Chapter 1

THREATS AND THE APPEASEMENT THEORY OF WAR

[1] Frederic II, *The History of My Own Times* (Part I, London, G. J. and J. Robinson, 1789), pp. 87-90.

[2] In John Bigelow, *The Life of Benjamin Franklin* (3 vols., Philadelphia, J. B. Lippincott, 1874), Vol. III, p. 123 (italics in the original).

[3] Sidney Bradshaw Fay, *The Origins of the World War* (2 vols., revised edition, New York, Macmillan Co., 1930), Vol. II, p. 204.

[4] *Ibid.,* p. 240.

[5] *Ibid.,* Vol. I, pp. 368-406.

[6] *Ibid.,* Vol. I, pp. 474-75.

[7] *Ibid.,* Vol. II, p. 276.

[8] Niccolo Machiavelli, *The Prince and The Discourses* (New York, Random House, 1950), pp. 321-22.

[9] Oleg Penkovskiy, *The Penkovskiy Papers* (Garden City, N.Y., Doubleday, 1965), p. 213.

[10] Statement of Secretary of State Dean Acheson, in David Rees, *Korea: the Limited- War* (New York, St. Martin's Press, 1964), p. 101.

[11] See: Christopher Thorne, *The Approach of War, 1938-39* (New York, St. Martin's Press, 1967), p. 13.

Chapter 2

THE APPLICATION OF THREAT: THREE CASES

[1] Harry S. Truman, *Memoirs,* Vol. I: *Year of Decisions* (Garden City, New York, Doubleday, 1955), p. 380.

[2] James F. Byrnes, *Speaking Frankly* (New York, Harper, 1947), p. 120.

[3] *Ibid.,* p. 119.

[4] Reproduced in *The New York Times,* March 1, 1946, p. 10.

[5] James F. Byrnes, *All In One Lifetime* (New York, Harper, 1958), p. 350.

[6] Reproduced in *The New York Times,* March 17, 1946, p. 12.

[7] *The New York Times,* March 6, 1946, p. 4.

[8] Truman, *op. cit.,* pp. 551-2.

[9] *The New York Times,* March 12, 1946, p. 4.

10 *The New York Times,* March 14, 1946, p. 4.

11 *The New York Times,* March 13, 1946, p. 2.

12 *The New York Times,* March 31, 1946, p. 1.

13 *Ibid.,* April 2, 1946, p. 9.

14 *Ibid.,* April 1, 1946, p. 1.

15 D. F. Fleming, *The Cold War and its Origins, 1917-1960* (2 vols., Garden City, New York, Doubleday, 1961), Vol. I, pp. 345, 350.

16 Stanley Karnow, "Dean Rusk's Debut," *The Reporter,* April 27, 1961, p. 38.

17 Hugh Sidey, *John F. Kennedy, President* (New York, Atheneum, 1963), p. 81.

18 Arthur M. Schlesinger, Jr., *A Thousand Days* (Boston, Houghton Mifflin, 1965), p. 336.

19 Denis Warner, "Unfinished Business," *New Republic,* December 7, 1963, p. 18.

20 See: Denis Warner, "The Loss of Laos," *The Reporter,* July 6, 1961, pp. 21-24; Eric Pace, "Laos: Continuing Crisis," *Foreign Affairs,* October 1964, pp. 64-74; Sidey, *op. cit.,* pp. 74-85; Schlesinger, *op. cit.,* pp. 329-340; Theodore C. Sorensen, *Kennedy* (New York, Harper and Row, 1965), pp. 639-648; Pierre Salinger, *With Kennedy* (Garden City, Doubleday, 1966), pp. 214, 237; Donald E. Nuechterlein, *Thailand and the Struggle for Southeast Asia* (Ithaca, Cornell University Press, 1965), pp. 138-220.

21 On January 2, 1961, Khrushchev at a reception in Moscow; Khrushchev in a note to Kennedy in April, 1961; Dobrynin's statement to Robert Kennedy on September 4, 1962; Russian statement of September 11, 1962: see Elie Abel, *The Missile Crisis* (New York, J. B. Lippincott, 1966), pp. 15-20. For another general account of the missile crisis see: Henry M. Pachter, *Collision Course; The Cuban Missile Crisis and Coexistence* (New York, Frederick A. Praeger, 1963).

Chapter 3

HOW A THREAT FAILS

1 *The New York Times,* July 10, 1960, p. 2.

2 Schlesinger, *A Thousand Days,* pp. 367-8; Sorensen also reports Kennedy telling Khrushchev that he wanted to decrease commitments made by prior administrations, *Kennedy,* p. 548.

3 *Peking Review,* July 20, 1962, p. 22. (From *Renmin Ribao* editorial, July 12, 1962).

4 "A Major Victory for the Laotian People and the Peace Forces of the World," *Peking Review,* July 27, 1962, p. 5. (From *Renmin Ribao* editorial of July 24, 1962).

5 Schlesinger, p. 332.

6 D. C. Watt, *Survey of International Affairs 1961* (London, Oxford University Press, 1965), p. 232; *The New York Times,* June 9, 1961, p. 3 and June 12, 1961, p. 13; Hans Speier, *Divided Berlin* (New York, Frederick A. Praeger, 1961), pp. 115-117, 151.

7 George Bailey, "The Gentle Erosion of Berlin," *The Reporter,* April 26, 1962, p. 19 (Copyright 1962 by The Reporter Magazine Company); also see: David

Binder, "Are We Really Standing Firm in Berlin?," *The Reporter*, March 15, 1962, pp. 20-22; D. C. Watt, *Survey of International Affairs 1961*, pp. 211-281; Jack M. Schick, "The Berlin Crisis of 1961 and U.S. Military Strategy," *Orbis*, Vol. 8, No. 4 (Winter 1965), pp. 816-831.

8 *The Penkovskiy Papers*, p. 216.

9 Sorensen, pp. 652, 653.

10 "Afterthoughts on the Cuban Blockade," *New Republic*, November 10, 1962, p. 19.

Chapter 4

THE EXCITATION THEORY OF WAR AND THE STATUS QUO

1 The reader will find many of the ideas appearing in the following pages advanced in a different framework in Thomas C. Schelling, *The Strategy of Conflict* (Cambridge, Harvard University Press, 1960) and *Arms and Influence* (New Haven, Yale University Press, 1965).

2 See: David Rees, *Korea: The Limited War*, p. 419.

3 Sidney B. Fay, *The Origins of the World War* (2 vols., New York, Macmillan, 1930), Vol. II, pp. 263-64.

4 *The New York Times*, May 28, 1966, p. 1; May 30, 1966, p. 3.

5 Arthur M. Schlesinger, Jr., *The Bitter Heritage* (Boston, Houghton Mifflin, 1967), p. 71.

6 Christopher Thorne, *The Approach of War, 1938-1939* (New York, St. Martin's Press, 1967), p. 71.

7 From an interview in Bernard B. Fall, *Ho Chi Minh On Revolution* (New York, Frederick A. Praeger, 1967), pp. 353-4.

8 *The New York Times*, May 22, 1967, p. 14.

9 Quoted in Winston S. Churchill, *The Gathering Storm*, Book I (Bantam Books, New York, 1961), p. 282.

10 Schlesinger, *The Bitter Heritage*, p. 72.

11 John W. Wheeler-Bennett, *The Nemesis of Power: The German Army in Politics 1918-1945* (London, Macmillan & Co., 1953), pp. 349-350.

12 Quoted in William L. Shirer, *The Rise and Fall of the Third Reich* (New York, Simon and Schuster, 1960), p. 293. Other observers concur in Germany's weakness at this time, see: Churchill, *op. cit.*, p. 175; Ian Colvin, *None So Blind* (New York, Harcourt, Brace, 1965), p. 99; A. L. Rowse, *Appeasement: A Study in Political Decline* (Norton, New York, 1961), p. 40; Alan Bullock, *Hitler: A Study in Tyranny* (Revised edition, New York, Harper and Row, 1964), p. 346.

13 Wheeler-Bennett, p. 352.

14 Recorded by former German Foreign Office Interpreter, Paul Schmidt, cited in Shirer, p. 293, also in Bullock, p. 345.

15 Shirer, pp. 291, 292; Wheeler-Bennett, p. 352.

16 See for example Churchill, pp. 278-281.

17 Schlesinger, *The Bitter Heritage*, p. 72.

18 "It must not be thought that Adolf Hitler operated to a carefully prepared time-table," Wheeler-Bennett, p. 345.

19 Lord Lothian quoted in Shirer, p. 293.

Chapter 5

THE DEMONSTRATION OF WILL

1 *Newsweek,* April 22, 1968, p. 48.

2 Arthur M. Schlesinger, Jr., *A Thousand Days,* pp. 251-258, 394; Theodore C. Sorensen, *Kennedy,* p. 307; Hugh Sidey, *John F. Kennedy, President,* pp. 127, 129.

3 Schlesinger, p. 812; Elie Abel, *The Missile Crisis,* p. 119. Fulbright had given his policy of "tolerating" Cuba a proviso: "That the Soviet Union uses Cuba only as a political and not as a military base." The problem we would have as Soviet strategists, however, would be in picking out and assigning great significance to this single hypothetical statement suggesting a hard line, from the enormous volume of speeches, comment and positions taken suggesting a more accommodating posture. Schlesinger reports that Kennedy was surprised to hear Fulbright's invasion position. If Kennedy and his advisors had not selected the above quotation as the indicative one, it seems improbable that the Russians would have.

4 Viscount Grey, *Twenty-Five Years 1892-1916* (2 vols., London, Hodder and Stoughton, 1925), Vol. II, p. 273. Winston S. Churchill made the same point: "This sincere, wrongheaded, purblind old Prussian [Von Tirpitz] firmly believed that the growth of his beloved navy was inducing in British minds an increasing fear of war, whereas it simply produced naval rejoinders and diplomatic reactions which strengthened the forces and closed the ranks of the Entente." *The World Crisis 1911-1914* (New York, Charles Scribner's Sons, 1923), p. 117.

5 George McT. Kahin, "Excerpts from National Teach-In on Viet-Nam Policy" in Marcus G. Raskin and Bernard B. Fall, *The Viet-Nam Reader* (New York, Knopf-Random House, 1965), p. 289.

6 Arthur M. Schlesinger, Jr., *The Bitter Heritage,* p. 68.

7 Luigi Albertini, *The Origins of the War of 1914,* translated and edited by Isabella M. Massey (3 vols., London, Oxford Univerity Press, 1952), Vol. I, p. 257.

8 *Ibid.,* pp. 21, 27.

9 *Ibid.,* p. 294.

Chapter 6

THE DIMENSIONS OF COMMITMENT

1 United States Senate, Committee on Foreign Relations, *Supplemental Foreign Assistance Fiscal Year 1966—Vietnam,* 89th Congress, 2nd session, pp. 595-96.

2 *Ibid.,* p. 610.

3 *Ibid.,* p. 8.

4 United States Senate, Preparedness Investigating Subcommittee of the Committee on Armed Services, *Worldwide Military Commitments,* 89th Congress, 2nd session, part 1, p. 9.

5 United States Senate, Committee on Foreign Relations, *Supplemental Foreign Assistance Fiscal Year 1966—Vietnam,* 89th Congress, 2nd session, p. 336.

6 *Ibid.,* p. 331 (italics added).

7 See Chalmers M. Roberts, "The Day We Didn't Go to War," *The Reporter,* September 14, 1954, pp. 31-35.

8 U. S. Senate, Committee on Foreign Relations, *Foreign Assistance, 1966,* 89th Congress, 2nd session, p. 638.

9 *Ibid.,* p. 640.

10 Philip Ben, "Everything Comes Back to—'But What about Vietnam?' " *New Republic,* October 29, 1966, p. 9.

11 Clark M. Clifford, "A Viet Nam Reappraisal," *Foreign Affairs,* July 1969, p. 613.

12 *The New York Times,* July 6, 1967, p. 1; July 7, 1967, p. 1.

13 *The New York Times,* July 11, 1967, p. 1.

14 Declaration of Marshal Lin Piao reproduced in *The New York Times,* September 4, 1965, p. 2.

15 Stefan T. Possony, "Mao's Strategic Initiative of 1965 and the U.S. Response," *Orbis,* Vol. 9, No. 1 (Spring 1967), p. 171. These paragraphs are drawn from this penetrating and strangely neglected article.

16 *Ibid.,* p. 181.

Chapter 7

THE UTILITY OF COURAGE

1 Friedrich II der Grosse, *Military Instructions Written by the King of Prussia for the Generals of his Army* (trans., London, 1777), pp. 95-6, italics added.

2 Arthur M. Schlesinger, Jr., *A Thousand Days,* p. 397.

3 United States Senate, Committee on Foreign Relations, *Supplemental Foreign Assistance Fiscal Year 1966—Vietnam,* 89th Congress, 2nd Session, p. 671.

4 *Ibid.,* p. 501.

5 *Ibid.,* p. 526.

6 *Ibid.,* p. 597.

Chapter 8

PRESTIGE AND WORLD OPINION

1 Hans J. Morgenthau, "To Intervene or Not to Intervene," *Foreign Affairs,* April 1967, p. 431.

2 United States Senate, Committee on Foreign Relations, *Supplemental Foreign Assistance Fiscal Year 1966—Vietnam,* p. 332.

3 *Ibid.,* p. 335.

4 *Ibid.,* p. 424 (italics added).

5 George F. Kennan, *Memoirs 1925-1950* (Boston, Little, Brown, 1967), p. 359.

6 *Ibid.,* p. 486.

7 Hans J. Morgenthau quoted in *Newsweek,* July 10, 1967, p. 30.

8 Anatole G. Mazour, *Finland Between East and West* (Princeton, D. Van Nostrand Co., 1956), p. 175.

9 Donald E. Nuechterlein, *Thailand and The Struggle for Southeast Asia* (Ithaca, Cornell University Press, 1965), p. 201.

10 *Ibid.*, pp. 221-22.

11 *Ibid.*, p. 231.

12 See *Newsweek,* November 27, 1967, p. 60; *The Christian Science Monitor,* November 15, 1967, p. 1.

13 For a discussion of Burma's dependence on Communist China prior to 1963, see William C. Johnstone, *Burma's Foreign Policy* (Cambridge, Harvard University Press, 1963) especially pp. 158-200.

14 *The New York Times,* September 12, 1967, p. 1; September 14, 1967, p. 20; September 19, 1967, p. 12; October 6, 1967, p. 2; *Keesing's Contemporary Archives,* Vol. XVI (1967-68), pp. 22283-84.

Chapter 9

MANAGING PEACE

1 Albertini, *The Origins of the War of 1914,* Vol. I, p. 198.

2 *Ibid.*, p. 219.

3 For example, Senator Goldwater: *The New York Times,* February 7, 1964, p. 16.

4 From the minutes of the Ministerial Council, quoted in Sidney B. Fay, *The Origins of The World War,* Vol. II, pp. 228-29.

5 *Ibid,* pp. 229-30.

6 See Thomas C. Schelling and Morton H. Halperin, *Strategy and Arms Control* (New York, The Twentieth Century Fund, 1961), pp. 9-61.

7 Bill D. Moyers, "One Thing We Learned," *Foreign Affairs,* July 1968, p. 659.

8 George Earle Buckle and W. F. Monypenny, *The Life of Benjamin Disraeli* (6 vols., New York, The Macmillan Co., 1920), Vol. VI, p. 50.

9 *Ibid.*, p. 107.

10 *Ibid.*, p. 47, (speech in Commons, August 11, 1876).

11 Letter to Sir Stafford Northcote, September 11, 1876 in *Ibid,* p. 61.

12 *Ibid.*, p. 92.

13 *Ibid.*, p. 131.

14 *Ibid.*, p. 134.

15 *Ibid.*, p. 155.

16 *Ibid.*, p. 174.

17 *Ibid.*, pp. 176-77.

18 *Ibid.*, p. 242.

19 *Ibid.*, p. 250.

20 John Bartlow Martin, *Overtaken by Events* (New York, Doubleday, 1966), p. 661.

Chapter 10

CONCLUSION

[1] Quoted in Max Ascoli, "Foreign Policy after Cuba," *The Reporter,* May 25, 1961, p. 19.

[2] Niccolo Machiavelli, *The Prince and The Discourses* (New York, Modern Library, 1950), p. 248.

INDEX

Berlin, 52
Bosnia-Herzegovina, 115
China, 105
Cuba, 37, 46
Czechoslovakia, 204
Hungary, 167
Iran, 23
Turkey, 196
World War I, 15

Sacrifice, 216
SEATO, 32
Serbia
 proportionality, 187
 World War I, 15
Selfishness, national, 181
Sihanouk, Prince, 179
Southeast Asia
 China, 179
 U.S. commitment, 133
Southeast Asia Treaty Organization, 32
Soviet Union. *See* Russia
Stability of deterrence, 187
Stalin, Joseph, 25
State Department, U.S.
 communism, 111
 inertia, 201
Statesmanship
 conservatism, 189
 consistency, 195
 credibility, 210
 hostility, 2
 lying, 83
 prevention of war, 2
 as profession, xii
 status quo, 66, 102
 use of threat, xiii
 world opinion, 176
Status quo
 alterations of, 184
 coercive alterations of, 12